VOICES

VOICES

How a Great Singer
Can Change Your Life

NICK COLEMAN

COUNTERPOINT
Berkeley, California

Voices

First published in 2018 by Jonathan Cape, an imprint of Vintage. Vintage is part of the
Penguin Random House group of companies.
First Counterpoint hardcover edition: 2018

Library of Congress Cataloging-in-Publication Data
Names: Coleman, Nick, 1960– author.
Title: Voices : how a great singer can change your life / Nick Coleman.
Description: First Counterpoint hardcover edition. | Berkeley, CA : Counterpoint Press,
    2018. | Includes index.
Identifiers: LCCN 2018002256 | ISBN 9781640091153
Subjects: LCSH: Popular music—History and criticism.
Classification: LCC ML3470 .C6236 2018 | DDC 782.42164/117—dc23
LC record available at https://lccn.loc.gov/2018002256

Jacket design by Donna Cheng
Book design by Jordan Koluch

COUNTERPOINT
2560 Ninth Street, Suite 318
Berkeley, CA 94710
www.counterpointpress.com

Printed in the United States of America
Distributed by Publishers Group West

10 9 8 7 6 5 4 3 2 1

FOR TOM AND BERRY

"Whooooooooooooooooooo!"

— LITTLE RICHARD, 1956

"Love . . . is a losing game."

— AMY WINEHOUSE, 2006

Contents

Preface

Patti Smith is crammed on to a balcony in a stately ballroom in Stockholm with a small orchestra.

She's up there on behalf of Bob Dylan to accept his Nobel Prize for Literature, and she is going to sing his famous song "A Hard Rain's A-Gonna Fall" to the accompaniment of small guitar, lap steel, and strings. She is dressed in a black tuxedo and planted like an Easter Island statue.

The audience is composed of the great and the good of Swedish culture and the Swedish royal family, who are all done up in formal fig, bibs and tuckers, gowns and jewelry, stoles and tiaras. And medals. They are arrayed formally, as for a state portrait. Smith has no medals though her white shirt beneath the oversized tuxedo is nicely ironed. Her steel-colored hair is long and heavy and parted severely in the middle. She is like Albrecht Dürer, who did not do state portraiture. She is also faintly reminiscent of Buster Keaton.

The introduction is strummed artlessly on two chords. Smith sings. The sound she and the guitarist make is as severe as her hairstyle and so is the intent of the words she sings. Yet she is singing beautifully with total involvement, her rich, twangy contralto, with its flattened vowels and its inclination to yodel, driving hard and straight into the language, as if the song had been written this year, the year of all hateful years, 2016.

All is suspense.

But then, after a couple of minutes, Smith appears for a moment to be overwhelmed. She stops singing. She gulps. "I'm so sorry," she says, blanching. She tries to carry on. . . "Unh. . ." But it won't come. She apologizes again and looks up in appeal to the conductor standing above her left shoulder. "I'm sorry. Could we start that section . . . ? I apologize." She looks out into the audience. They are frozen in their places. "I'm so nervous." She forces an agonized smile.

There is sustained, kindly applause from the audience. You can almost hear the jewelry rattling.

And soon enough she goes again with renewed resolve until, a minute or two later, she dries once more, and again looks up at the conductor with the mute appeal of a frightened child. The conductor, out of shot, presumably makes encouraging faces because Smith, suddenly somehow heartened, hooks quickly back into the song and then seems to grow, to expand in her place and to move her hands a little and then her shoulders and then to pace, striding on the spot, no longer an Easter Island statue but a living, breathing, marching embodiment of the hipster-symbolist song lyric she is singing, all about the doom of the world and the love that may save it. She reaches the end of the song in a sea of strings.

It is impossible to watch without tears.

It is also as great a passage of singing as you are ever likely to hear, if singing is to you not about the observance of musical correctitude and extravagant display and signaled passion and technical virtuosity, but about the inhabitation of the moment up to and including the moment when the moment bursts.

VOICES

Introduction

Hearing Voices

The human voice is the very first medium that we take for a message. At the time, being babies, we do not understand that what we are hearing is a medium and are unable fully to interpret the message. But that's what happens. We hear a sound; we listen; we intuit that the sound means good; we learn quickly to draw comfort from it and to enjoy feelings of expectation and curiosity . . . and then we learn to shape identity from it. It's possible of course that we do the identity thing first—our mother's voice, our father's voice: the first intimations in life that rowdy, meaningless chaos does in fact submit to meaning, the message "I love you" boring like a drill through the big-bang debris of not knowing anything at all.

But the message is not encoded in words. There are no words yet. There is only sound, as there was only sound in the womb. It is the *sound* of the voice that makes the feeling happen—the tone and timbre of the voice, its comforting rhythm and, of course, its sheer familiarity in its association with touch, proximity, warmth, comfort. And our capacity for feeling these things develops as we develop, keeping an even pace, side by side, as if going somewhere. From the very start of our lives we know that voices carry information, yes. But much more than that, they also express emotion—they *confer* emotion. They stimulate it. We know, even without the involvement of clearly articulated and comprehended language, that voices are vessels brimming with stuff: that a voice can itself be a message. We learn that we don't actually need to hear the words of an altercation to know that anger is being expressed, even at low amplitude, even in a whisper. Equally, we can hear love through gibberish. A voice is a ship, and sometimes it is enough to know that it is a ship and that it is coming, whether or not we can picture in our minds precisely what it carries in darkness below the waterline.

It's fair to say, then, that before words are distinguishable, voices make some sort of case for our close attention. We learn from the start to read voices and to engage with them, as if the voice itself and not the language is the primary agent of meaning. Voices *invite* inference. They switch us on. Even before we have words with which to encode and decode meaning, voices are an event.

And then we learn that voices have other modes. They can sing, too.

* * *

I have no idea when singing first became noticeable to me. In our house, when I was growing up, singing was just what happened. It was part of the everyday fabric of life, not in any particularly attractive or impressive way but in a comfortable, pleasing, homely way; because it was quite a nice thing to do and because singing constituted a significant feature of the family's social breathing. There was nothing fancy going on here—there was no "agenda." I'm afraid we just sang. We sang neither cutely nor Von-Trappishly, and certainly not with any zeal—in fact we sang in rather a methodical way, without any great consideration of how we might sound to others or even what the point of singing was. We sang in church as we sang in school assembly, because it was required. We sang at home because it appeared to give my parents pleasure and because it was normal. None of us sang particularly well. We sang either solo or in harmony, sometimes contrapuntally, never in unison (what's the point of that?), sometimes accompanied, sometimes not. Victorian parlor songs, church music, carols, arias, lieder, A. A. Milne—the middle-to-highbrow middle-class repertoire of the mid-twentieth century . . .

Why? Well, I suppose my dad—the instigator—thought it was a good way to engage responsibly with his children without having to be overtly educative, or run around or dress up or build things or compete; plus it was a creative and enjoyable activity for himself. We children went along with it because it was quite fun to do and because . . . well, because it was normal.

After all, doesn't everyone do this?

When I discovered as a moderately small boy that not everyone did it, I came to know the sting of embarrassment possibly for the first time. To my friend Nigel over the road, singing was wholly disturbing. It signified not only weirdness but also girliness, and he disapproved of both of those things. My dad once asked us in passing (Nigel and I were doubtless on our way upstairs from the kitchen to play Subbuteo) whether Nigel and I fancied joining the rest of the family in the living room to try out a four-part Christmas carol he'd reharmonized—"just belt out the tune, Nigel!"—and Nigel reacted as if he'd been invited to participate in group sex. He appeared for a moment to have had a seizure, while standing upright next to the cupboard under the stairs. He then backed into the cupboard door with a thump. Then he came to and shuddered and was quite unable to speak for a period, which was unlike him. In the end he managed a choked "No, thank you," but was obviously shaken and left the house soon after.

Singing, then, was evidently both normal and not normal, and obviously much less normal in the world beyond the front gate than it was within. What was a boy to make of this?

I quickly learned to swallow the embarrassment along with the niceness, and without too much chewing or gagging. If singing was now associated in my mind with prissy gentility and the dangers of effeminacy, then that uneasiness was always redeemed by the uncomplicated pleasure it gave me when the gaze of society was turned elsewhere and I might sing unselfconsciously—especially in church, where there were echoes and candles after dark, and sustaining, cloaking, caressing harmony, which was like being held. Singing was two things to me: both shame and the sensation of being held. I still feel that way, a little.

But that was only my singing. What about other people's?

There is of course a considerable difference between the act of singing and the act of listening to other people sing. One is active, the other less so; one is a pushing out, the other a taking in; one is fraught with the potential for embarrassment, the other can be an unselfconscious, even selfless, pleasure that can take you out of the quotidian and into another place and time altogether. Yet—and this is a very important thing to me—it can also make the quotidian vivid and beautiful.

Singing and listening to singing are conjoined but non-identical twins, profoundly linked but really quite different from each other in actuality, and it feels somehow like an act against nature to separate them. But separate them I must, for the good of all. Although it may sound grossly insensitive, I know which twin I prefer and which one I can happily live without. I always want to separate them.

Discounting sex, I love listening to singing above all other activities that are common to all cultures. Other people's singing is to my mind the highest and deepest human attainment. To me it represents not only the glide of evolutionary progress—the transformation of primordial throaty gurgling into an exquisite, expressive, life-sustaining, tuneable communication system—but also authentic transcendence, through the transmutation of melodized language into something that really does go beyond its functional self, both literally and metaphorically. Singing is, to me, where human life flowers most brilliantly, most subtly and most diffusely.

But that's enough about flowers. I also like singing as I like food—for its nourishment, its sensory stimulus and for its abiding quality of uncontingent necessity. I really cannot think of anything other than food, warmth, shelter, and love more needful in life than the sound of other people singing. I've got to have some, every day. And on those rare days when I don't manage to get some, I find myself going cold turkey and then relishing the feeling of deprivation because it means that the next time I do get some, the hit will be a rush.

But actually, even that isn't the whole story, not if I'm honest. I think I like listening to singing most of all because it allows me to be *unselfconscious*. Singing—other people's singing—actively encourages unselfconsciousness,

facilitates it, ensures that it happens, supports it. I hope that you will indulge this thought on the grounds that you also feel that way—or, if you
don't, that what I'm saying at least rings true and not like the ravings of a
solipsist who has spent too much of his life shut up in the box of his own
head—and may even have serious attachment issues to resolve. I am afraid
it is true, though. Singing throws a switch in me, turns the flux around. It's
as if the sound of singing gives me permission to phase down the arc lamps
of self-scrutiny and to focus on a compelling exterior phenomenon to the
exclusion of all else. (Although of course what I mean by this really is that
singing makes selfhood palatable: I *like* myself more when I'm listening to
singing.) My father was a bit that way inclined too—although, strangely
enough, not when his methodical children were doing it. But plonk him
down in front of properly good singing done by people who can really sing
and he'd go all funny. He'd switch off, as if unplugged at the mains, only to
flip over in the same instant to another private circuit, one that was deeply
enlivening to his senses and compelling of his attention but just happened
to exclude everything else going on in the shared world. And then we would
all laugh at him because his mouth would fall open and his eyeballs would
bloom over like plum skins.

For me, then, singing is not necessarily cathartic, but it does always
compel, provided it fulfills two criteria. One requirement is that it be *good*
singing and the other that it is *true* singing. True singing does not necessarily have to be "good," but good singing really does have to be true—
otherwise it is not useful.

What do I mean by that? Well, this whole book is an attempt to explore
what I mean—what, for me, makes good, true, useful singing.

This is not a technical exercise, nor an academic one, nor a talent competition in prose form. It isn't a beauty pageant. It is not my intention to
isolate "the best voices," nor to model an ideal voice or way of singing, but
to explore the voices that count, that have done something for me, that connect with me, that thrill me, that make me wonder, that fill me with quanti-
fiable emotion or weird thoughts or feelings that just can't be accounted for.
These are the voices that have shaped—and continue to shape—my world.

It is a subjective study, as it has to be. There is no such thing as the Platonically perfect voice or way of singing; a voice is not a thing, after all, and it cannot be fixed with tools. There is only transaction: transaction between the voice and you, you and the voice. That's all there is. The push and pull, the give and take. The loom of interaction.

Is this fair to the singers in question? Is it useful? Is it even sensible? I don't really know. Possibly not. But it seems to be something I have to do, for my own edification, to explain my voices back to myself. Because nobody else is going to do it for me, and there are plenty of people out there who are more than happy to show me how voices *should* be, and what they're worth.

Yes, we would all probably trust an *X Factor* winner to deliver the prevailing sentiment of "The Wind Beneath My Wings" in more marketable terms than, say, Winston Rodney would, especially in the context of a TV talent show filmed in front of a partisan audience under flashing lights accompanied by a crashing, hyperventilatory arrangement pre-recorded elsewhere and then processed into a sequence of cadential cues specifically designed to frame the drama of the act of singing for judgment. (It's exhausting, isn't it, just reading about it? But then exhaustion is central to the *X Factor* experience, which defines singing as the sinew-straining, health-threatening, competition-shredding, life-changing exercise of supreme *effort*.) But *X Factor* vocalization is to true singing what keepy-uppies are to football. It is the exhibition of decontextualized skill, a measurement of the ability to show off. Where's the *use*? What does singing like that *mean*, beyond the advocacy of exhibition and the solicitation of admiration? We might admire what we hear for its technical accomplishment and even feel moved by the singer's effort and commitment to the moment (without which no one ever "nailed" anything). We might even think that the singer has a nice voice. But we will also be experiencing lots of other things. We will certainly be aware that what we are doing is sharing in a ritual, a ritual that requires participants to consume an elephantine product on an enormous scale as part of a multidimensional entertainment cascade, which, inter alia, entails social jousting at home with fellow sofa-sitters, all of us bantering and passing judgment both on the singing and on the judgments made about the singing, as well as boggling at the spectacle, marveling at the costumes, choking over the plastic surgery, the social semiotics, the desperation, the agony, the expense, the cruelty . . . *The X Factor* is by definition a self-conscious mass experience, as the Roman Colosseum was a self-conscious mass experience—it literally depends on mass consumption to warrant its existence, while the mass is incentivized to rejoice in its own mass-ness as it does so—with the result that we are unlikely to be haunted by it on any personal level at all.

I can't argue with the *X Factor* definition of singing. It is what it is. It makes money. It titillates. It reminds us, feverishly, of our mass-ness. It offers the suggestion that the only real and worthwhile object of singing is personal celebrity. But what I am interested in with this book has little to do with showing off, nor with mass consumption, nor lights and costumes and cruelty and, least of all, competition. I'm interested in what makes a good haunting.

I am pretty certain that we are only haunted by singing when we experience it not as an act of showing off but as an act of authorship, and then as a personal invasion; an invasion conducted privately, discreetly, loudly or quietly, at home or abroad, upright or lying down, tearfully or dry—it doesn't really matter where you experience it, or how, so long as the context is felt to be your own and that you listen to the singing not as a constituent of a mass consciousness but as the sole occupant of a single one. Psychologically alone. For what *is* singing, if not the creative assertion of individuality? And what is a voice, if not the most inimitable, indelible mark of an individual's individuality—the vessel, the ship sent out bravely over the horizon to export the fruits of our consciousness to places unknown.

I am not entirely comfortable with admitting this, but I am quite sure that a disproportionate amount of my own socialization was accomplished through the agency of other people's singing. I have never told my mother this.

* * *

Does it matter how old you are?

Of course it matters. It matters enormously. It matters as much as it matters that you engage with the world beyond the compass of your family in terms that may, at the time, be defined as your own. Otherwise we'd all be excited only by those officially approved things we are given to know in our early upbringing. (I, for instance, would be turned on more by Alfred Deller and Janet Baker than I am by Al Green and Mary Margaret O'Hara.) The evolution of personal taste is always a small act of rebellion, and when we make it, we begin to separate ourselves from all that we are given to know. The constellation of moments in which you accomplish this separation are among the most important moments of your life, and so the context in which this transition takes place matters tremendously.

So I didn't choose Mick Jagger; he just happened to be passing at the time.

I first encountered his voice at pretty much the same moment, in broad historical terms, as everyone else heard it for the first time, in 1964, shortly after hearing Lennon's and McCartney's. "You Better Move On" was the first Rolling Stones song I ever heard, and it is not insignificant that I not only heard it, but saw it, on television. And I have no doubt that, had I been a teenager then, I would have been struck by the underpinning authenticity of Jagger's voice. I would not have couched it in such terms, but some part of me, at some unknowable depth, would have recognized his slightly self-conscious English suburban sneer as the real thing, a vessel of an unaccommodating new articulacy demanded by a brand-new social mobility—unattractive on the surface, yes, hopelessly *in*authentic in R&B terms, but irresistibly compelling in other, less-anticipated ways. I would have been excited by it, plain and simple. Turned on.

On the other hand, if I had been an adult in 1964—perhaps one who had endured the war and the long passage of economic austerity and social conservatism that followed it—it seems likely that Mick's hipster insolence would have struck a different chord.

As it was, I was four—and I was scared.

A decade later I was trying to sing like that with my own band, because it seemed like the only way for semi-knowing white English middle-class boys to sound authentic to themselves—even as the real thirty-year-old Mick was himself essaying a series of knowing parodies of "black" voices as part of his enjoyment of his new status as a leading light in a new kind of sophisticated jet-setting global elite. His desire for upward social mobility had by then been slaked, pretty much. He'd reached an acceptable ceiling. Of course it matters how old you are when you hear a voice.

Of course it does. It's because I was born in 1960 into a churchy middle-class East Anglian family that my formative voices were not those of Sinatra and Bennett and Streisand and Nat "King" Cole, but Jagger and Lennon and Hendrix and Dusty and Otis and Orbison and Bobbie Gentry. It's because I was a teenager in the 1970s that I am still moved by the utterances of Marvin Gaye and Peter Gabriel and Gladys Knight and Joey Ramone and David Bowie; much more so than by those of Morrissey and Lennox and Prince and Whitney, or Cobain and Gallagher and Adele and Sam Smith. The complexities of human neurology and biochemistry see to that, as well as the wearying effects of fashion and time. Whether we like it or not, it is a neurological fact that the developing brain disposes us to soak up experiences most vividly and adhesively during our teenage years. If you must blame something for my taste, blame dopamine.

But that doesn't mean I dislike Morrissey and Whitney and Prince and Frank Sinatra and Adele. On the contrary, I have plenty of time for all of them, one way or another—as voices, if not necessarily as "icons" or as movers of my heart. The point is that even though none of them connected with me on first, second or—in one case—even thirteenth contact, I have *learned* to at least "get" them, as a direct consequence of the listening habits formed in my childhood by my terror of Mick Jagger and, a little later, my horny bewilderment in the face of Marvin Gaye, the weird disturbance wrought by Suzi Quatro and the utter conviction, arrived at rather later in life, that even if I didn't like his voice much when I was younger, then Bob Dylan's best singing is as true and good as singing has ever been. There you go: the habit of paying attention to voices breeds tolerance, patience, and curiosity, as well as horror, distaste, and contempt.

The bottom line is that voices ask questions, and some of the questions are very hard to understand, let alone answer. Which is one reason why we have to keep on listening.

1

The Horsemen in the Box

first heard of the Cuban Missile Crisis ten or eleven years after the event, by which time I was twelve or thirteen years old. The story unfolded on a grave Sunday evening in 1972 or 1973 and my parents seemed slightly alien for a moment. I'd never heard them talk like this about anything before. They told me what it had been like to live through the experience. "It felt as if the whole world was holding its breath," my mother said, ladling soup. "We really didn't know what we were going to wake up to—or even if we were going to wake up at all."

My twelve-year-old self thought about what it would be like to be caught in a nuclear holocaust at the age of two. It was a hard picture to hold in my mind. I thought of my fat baby cheeks melting like butter and then, as the nuclear wind pursued the heatflash across the Home Counties, saw my high chair, with me in it, shooting across the kitchen floor to disintegrate against the wall by the door as everything turned to carbon dust. I imagined a sort of *PLUFF!* sound. I thought it likely that I would at least feel no pain.

The world was young in 1962. I was even younger; so young in fact that I have no memory of the Crisis. Memory starts for me in 1963, around the time of the first Beatles album. But for those old enough to actually remember it, the Khrushchev/Kennedy face-off in the Caribbean seems to have constituted one of those harshly indelible memories, the sort you feel as a charge in the body every bit as vividly as you experience it in the mind as a story. Probably more so. They felt it like disease. People really did think the world might end.

It would have been a dreadful shame if it had. Think what such a catastrophe would have meant. No Beatles, no Stones, no Animals or Yardbirds or Kinks or Small Faces or Led Zeppelin. In America, no Hendrix or Dylan or Aretha. No Otis, no Sly or Marvin Gaye and Tammi Terrell. And that's just the sixties. Ultimately, it would have also meant no Taylor Swift.

It's not an easy thought.

Eventually, of course, at some inconceivably remote future date, armored ants would have emerged from the subsoil to build a new kind of civilization, one based on carrying and heaping. I think we may presume that. But what would they have made of the relics of 1962, the archaeological remains of *our* time?

Let us suppose then that some worthwhile things did survive the blast: an old Dansette record player, for instance, heat-stripped of its leatherette skin but otherwise intact, having been shielded for the passing centuries of radioactive nothingness in the angle of a pair of crumbling suburban walls. There'd be nowhere to plug the thing in, obviously, but it would surely not be beyond the wit of highly evolved armored ants to figure out how to get the juice on in due course. Then it would be a matter of a few millennia spent pondering the significance of the shiny black discs in paper sheaths found not far from the Dansette, handily insulated from the blast in a metal box beneath a drift of carbon dust behind what appears once to have been a living-room door. And then the ants would have music.

I'm going to ask you to make another imaginative leap here, I'm afraid, an even bigger one than the first. This time I want you to believe that the box found by the ants only has good records in it.

It is a simple mathematical improbability that a real box of records from 1962 would *not* contain a minimum of 70 percent crapola (especially a box recovered from the suburbs of what was once the UK), and this is perhaps the point at which my scenario does become a little implausible, perhaps even crumbles to yet more dust. But I am asking you nevertheless to make that leap. *This* box, sifted from the wreckage of a Home Counties semi, does not have any Wally Whyton in it, nor indeed Harry Secombe, nor Perry Como, nor Dean Martin, nor Elton Hayes. Not even Mantovani or Pat Boone. There is nothing in it from the brief recording career of Florence Foster Jenkins. "The Nativity Story," declaimed by Dame Flora Robson at 45 rpm, is nowhere to be found.

But the box does contain a handful of discs stylishly roundeled with the liveries of a quartet of old American recording firms: Specialty, Sun, Chess, RCA Victor—records by people called Chuck, Jerry Lee, Elvis, and Richard. Nothing too extensive. Just the good stuff they did before 1962, in due proportion. You might call it a nuclear collection.

So, assuming that the ants realize that the black vinyl discs are meant to go on the turntable in the Dansette, and they figure out that Chuck, Jerry Lee, Elvis, and Richard sound better at 45 than they do at 16, 33 or 78— what then? Would they dance? Would they clack their mandibles? Or would they simply turn away without curiosity, on the grounds that what they're hearing is "an infernal racket"?

Let's be specific here. Specifically, what have we got? This is a hypothetical situation, remember, so we can speculate wildly. We'll offer the ants a round dozen tunes. These are, with one exception, A-sides which have somehow suffered neither heat damage nor, in their sealed, airless metal record box, the natural chemical decay to which 10,000-year-old vinyl is sadly prone. Some songs just survive, as they always do. "Mystery Train," "Heartbreak Hotel," "That's All Right," "Tutti Frutti," "Slippin' and Slidin'," "Ready Teddy," "Whole Lotta Shakin' Goin' On," "Great Balls of Fire," "Mean Woman Blues," "Johnny B. Goode," "Memphis, Tennessee," "Let It Rock." A round three songs each by four artists—once again, the Apocalypse has been even-handed in a way that music consumers, historically, have never been. Twelve cuts by four artists defining . . . what, precisely?

To an armored ant, of course, such names represent nothing at all. The words "Elvis Presley," "Chuck Berry," "Jerry Lee Lewis," and "Little Richard" are not freighted with legend. Not even myth. Not yet, anyway. The words on the record labels are mere squiggles. Glyphs. Meaningful, no doubt, to someone once—but meaning what now? You see, the armored ants of the future do not read English. They just don't have the brains for it. Remember, the ants' civilization is almost entirely organized around an evolved social imperative to carry and heap. They don't do culture. Reading is unnecessary in a world governed by obedience to the nest mind. "Individualism" for them is an alien and frankly unappetizing concept. The ants are not given to reflection, even in their rare moments of repose. To ants, life is a dance already. Well, a dance routine.

And yet something stirs them. Through the ragged membrane of the now-functional Dansette speaker, flapping and pulsating in its exposed chipboard frame like a thorax struggling to breathe poisoned air, something connects with the ants. Despite all the rigmarole of getting the electricity to work and then figuring out how to get the vinyl onto the turntable and then the tone-arm onto the revolving disc and then, after all that, evolving the brains with which to hear the music as music, which is no mean feat in itself . . . Despite all that palaver, which would have daunted lesser species at a much earlier stage, there is something in the music of Elvis, Jerry Lee, Richard, and Chuck that speaks to them.

What can it be?

An obvious answer would be rhythm. The early work of all four rock 'n' roll captains is characterized by what we might call rhythmic assertiveness. Rhythm is the first thing you feel in the music, whether you're listening or just hearing, never mind dancing. The records rock. (And we know now, because the balloon did not actually go up in 1962, that in its strictly musical application, the verb "to rock" has a very specific meaning.)

"Awop-bop alu-bop alop-bam-boom," yells Little Richard at the top of "Tutti Frutti," and it is clear that he is not inviting you to meditate earnestly upon the meaning of what he is saying, nor to consider what he might be thinking, nor even to try to understand what tremulous emotion skulks blushing beneath the veil of his utterance—no: he wants you to get his rhythm. He wants you to get it as skiers get an avalanche. Here it is, all of a sudden, with horns: *boom!* You feel the sound as a charge in the body every bit as much as you grasp it as an idea in your mind. In fact, more even than that, it's as if the charge in the body exists primarily as a means of *overpowering* the idea in your mind. It is the negation of thought.

But that's Little Richard.

"That's All Right, Mama" by Elvis Presley isn't like that at all. But it's still all rhythm. A sort of bobbing 2/4—*BONG-bong BONG-bong*—inviting the listening body to go up and down like a plastic duck on a choppy river. It's irresistible. Furthermore, the conceptual material Elvis offers is fractionally less obtuse than Little Richard's, and much less screamy. He starts with a shrugging, wailed "well"—"We-e-ell, that's all right, Mama"—but the bridging "well" is of course merely the lift to a larger sentiment. Not a deeply considered one, it's true, but at least a passionate, possibly sardonic, certainly irresistible assertion of something the singer feels in his gut: his commitment to his own path. "Mum, fuck off!" is what he is saying. But what he's *doing* is rhythm. Of course the ants don't care about what Elvis is saying to his mum, because they don't speak English. But they get the rhythm.

Jerry Lee, too. Rhythm, rhythm, rhythm: pound, pound, pound. Let's imagine the ants' first encounter with Jerry Lee Lewis is "Mean Woman Blues." What will the ants get? They'll get rhythm. Locomoting, thrusting rhythm. Mandibles will surely clack along to this one, if no other. This is a different kind of pulse: not the pompadoured avalanche of "Tutti Frutti" and certainly not the ingratiating, house-trained, even feminine wriggle 'n' bob of "That's All Right." Certainly not. Right from the off, from its dark declarative rooting in the slightly-out-of-tune piano arpeggio which constitutes both the first notes of the song and also Jerry Lee's first assertion of his hungry potency, "Mean Woman Blues" describes a muscular arc of rhythm, a growing, extending, straightening, protuberant, hardening, thick-veined blood-thump of irresistible momentum, which eases momentarily—"E-e-e-asy now!"—to allow Jerry Lee to admire himself for a stretch before heading off north again into the antechamber to ecstasy . . . and then sudden collapse into nullity.

The climax never comes. This rhythm is all about the hair-raising excitement of getting there. And when it no longer has any use for getting there, it just stops. Flump. You can see the ants turning to one another after the flump and intuiting a collective understanding of what has just passed. "So *this* is what it is to have flexible tissue networked renewably with a fine mesh of nerves and capillaries!"

Chuck.

What can be said about Chuck in this context? The very thought of Chuck Berry feels like a category error next to the thought of Jerry Lee Lewis. An anomaly. An intellectual proposition next to a punch in the face. His rhythm is a semi-detached rolling thing, a track-bound, wheeled conveyance heading for any destination you might choose to nominate—and of course ants have no time nor use for rolling stock. It is nothing like a biological command, this rhythm. Its horizon is limitless but its feel for the present is chiefly philosophical. Not a now rhythm but a forever groove: drums, guitar, and piano, interlocking for all eternity.

The ants will not of course appreciate that the narrative of "Let It Rock" features a steel-driving hammer; and they will certainly not infer as much from the sound of the rhythm section—for this is not the sound of steel being beaten but of it locking a multiplicity of subtly articulated parts into a functional mechanism that, for all its smoothness, relies on friction to generate meter. Something much less atavistic is going on here. Something less gravitational than Little Richard, less ingratiating than Elvis, less animal than Jerry Lee. Chuck's rhythm is all about words. Language. The rhythm that counts in Chuck's mind is the same one that counted in Shakespeare's.

So it is really very likely that the armored ants will have no time for Chuck Berry.

However, being an intuitive species with an insatiable sense of curiosity, they will be less troubled anyway by the literal meaning of the words being sung on these dozen sides (the decoding of verbal language can await the consideration of boffin ants in the future) than by the curious feeling generated by the assortment of voices riding the rhythms. The rhythm the ants can get without thinking, without feeling. They can do it together, almost by reflex, *clickety-clack,* as a sort of group activity. Life is, after all, a dance routine. Rhythm is, as each and every armored ant will attest, a stimulus, an organizing principle, a matrix, a vehicle, a notation of flow, a repetitious scratchmark on the hull of time's great vessel . . .

But rhythm does not speak. It has nothing in particular to *say*. It does not articulate anything other than its own pattern and the excitement that a good pattern vigorously expressed can impart to a nervous system, however primitive its wiring. A rhythm is a mark of activity, not a nomination of ideas. It gets you going—but that's all it does. Ant brains, like human ones, are always compelled by patterns, but they are not necessarily stretched by them: stretching comes only with the recognition and enjoyment of difference.

So what *of* voices? What is the meaning of all this uttering? For the one other thing upon which the armored ants clacking in front of the Dansette will surely all agree is that, even if they have no comprehension of what is being expressed through the agency of indecipherable linguistic gibberish, Elvis, Jerry Lee, Chuck, and Richard are all expressing something *individual*—not because of the language they are speaking in but because of the voices they are singing with. Where words convey no meaning, voices still speak . . . And that's what gets the ants.

Jerry Lee's voice, his butch-antic holler, will at the very least convey menace. The ants will shudder within their shiny black armor at the furious sound of the uncontrollable boor, at the threatening, sneering, electrified self-loathing hunger of a creature who sees a boundary in life and interprets it as an invitation to crash on. They will find nothing in Jerry Lee's voice that speaks of heaping or carrying, but they will hear his appetite and they will hear his disgust. And they may even understand that his disgust is not merely self-directed but is in fact universally directed, arising not only from the lack of perfection in the world but from the very idea that perfection might conceivably be said to exist in a world that is altogether made out of imperfections. Brrrrrrr. How the ants will shudder. That is not how they see the world at all.

Little Richard on the other hand is on a hiding to nothing—and he's taking the hiding because it's better than nothing. Richard screams because that's what Richard has in him. He is beyond thought or consideration; he is all body and sensation and that is what he has to say: screaming, unappeasable appetite, the unholy "wooooooooo-oooooo-ooooo" that really is the most exciting sound in the world. The ants will get that, even if they don't see it as an appropriate way to behave.

On the other hand—on the other claw—there is Chuck . . .

"Long-distance information, get me Memphis, Tennessee," he enunciates through his fine teeth, as if addressing himself quite matter-of-factly to a telephone exchange operator up the road—some respectable Republican granny in tortoiseshell specs, jabbing jacks into a socket-board. "Help me find the party tryin' to get in touch with me," he goes on, while the instrumental rhythm burbles and lurches beneath him like a lairy old V8 engine. The "hurry-home drops on her cheek that trickled from her eye" will mean nothing to the ants. Nothing. Ants don't do sentiment, and they don't conceptualize the world through the agency of language. They hear Chuck's voice and they hear the wiry slyness of a trouper, a creature who has been around the block a time or two and, in doing so, has sensed poetry in the block—and then extrapolated from it. The ants will sense that this voice has form, that it embodies knowledge almost amounting to wisdom, and that perhaps not all forms of wisdom are to be trusted. They will meet Chuck's voice with compelled suspicion. But they will love the *clickety-clack* of the words. They will conclude that perhaps Chuck Berry had mandibles for sound evolutionary reasons.

They will not understand Elvis Presley, though, not at any level. Why, this sound is like burnished gold! It *shines*. Carapaces are shiny; and eyes are too, and mucus. Shiny and bright in a veiled and sunless world. As is metal, if you buff away the scorchmarks and rust. But how can a voice be shiny? How can a sound reflect light, even radiate it, yet be soft and strong at the same time, and pliable and expressive and giant? How can a mere vibration in the air stand for the actuality of anything, let alone permeable tissue networked renewably with a fine mesh of nerves and capillaries?

If it isn't an ant, what *is* an Elvis Presley?

In Elvis the ants will have to confront the awful possibility that they, the armored ants, do not represent the highest peak of evolutionary development, nor are their remarkable achievements all that there is, was or will ever be. The group mind will have to unhitch itself to grasp this one; it will need to rethink. Because here, manifestly, on the knackered Dansette in a blasted landscape in the time after Time, in which nothing lives but ants and life is a dance routine, something new has stirred. Something from beyond the compass of knowledge. In Elvis's voice the ants will hear manifest destiny.

Somebody else's.

And they will shudder yet again, not this time in prurient excitement but in naked fear. The ants will share intuitions. They will click and clack. Perhaps, after all this time, *this* is the clue they've been searching for, the key to unlock the Great Whatnot. The mystery. The mystery of What Went Before. They will be compelled to speculate that perhaps this is how the world once was . . . Or perhaps—and at this intuition the ants will literally cower—Elvis, along with Chuck and Jerry Lee and Richard, is the very *reason* that everything is the way it is: bleak and inhospitable and devoid of meaning—a sub-rhythmic howling emptiness that goes on forever.

Yes. Elvis, Chuck, Richard and Jerry Lee . . . Perhaps they were the warning, these bodiless creatures who ride rhythm like ants ride one another. Perhaps, then, these ghastly yelling ghosts were the prophets of the Apocalypse, the ones carrying the message. There were four of them. Chuck and Jerry Lee and Richard and Elvis—the quartet of voices heralding the end of all things (apart from ants).

And they will stand in awe.

GRACE NOTES

LED ZEPPELIN: "IMMIGRANT SONG"
Atlantic Records, 1970
One of rock's nagging compulsions down the decades was to stay in touch with its very first instincts—first instincts that were of course purer than its more evolved ones, by definition; purer and somehow more youthful, less contaminated by . . . well, what have you got?

And so *soi-disant* rock 'n' roll revivals of one sort or another dogged postwar popular music all the way into its latter days. Some of them were puritanical, others really quite cavalier. But hardly a half-decade has passed since 1962 without some gang of arbitrary youths ditching the civvies for drainpipes, creepers, and a drapecoat to tattoo the 'billy beat for a new generation of retro-reprobates.

Some of these gangs have been so confident in their own contiguity with their source material that there has been no need for dressing it up. They just do it—wallop, just like that, out of boredom or preciousness or even out of earnest conviction. Led Zeppelin did it in 1970 dressed in cheesecloth and flared denim, and they repeated the procedure throughout the duration of their twelve-year career, as if a periodic rereading of the Ur-text were a sacrament necessary to the group's continued existence. Bashing out old rock 'n' roll numbers also gave them something to do during sound checks.

The song "Rock and Roll" on their fourth album is probably the most literal-minded of all their authored rock 'n' roll retreads. John "Bonzo" Bonham's intro brings loutish new life to the drum figure that launched Little Richard's "Keep A-Knockin'" and then the rest of them hammer through a powerful (if foggily mixed) litany of the form's most knockabout clichés. They do it as if gabbling in the dark from a scroll recently discovered in a jar in a cave in Syria: the song iterates the quartet's undiluted reverence for the form and expresses their abiding desire always to be identified with the garden of rock's origins, as well as its mystic power.

"Rock and Roll" is great, but it isn't that interesting. This is possibly because it actually expresses nothing much more than postwar English youth's inclination to make the Mississippi Delta feel more like home than Kidderminster. Rather more interesting, and a lot more open to counterinterpretation, is "Immigrant Song" which kicks off *Led Zeppelin III*. This obtuse yet marvelous piece was recorded earlier in the same year, the chief by-product of a Zeppelin diplomatic mission to Reykjavik.

"Immigrant Song" is rock 'n' roll not reverenced from a jar but taken apart, then reassembled with gleaming new parts and rebranded as a weapon in service of a new mythology; very much, it should be said, in the spirit of the music engendered by the original rockers, who did much the same in the 1950s with the constituent parts of blues, country, and R&B.

What defines the song as "rock 'n' roll," as distinct from the mordantly heavy blues with which the group was identified at that stage in their career, is its pace, the impression it gives of unrelenting, barely controlled momentum, its streamlined sleekness. "Immigrant Song" is not a draggy, bludgeoning 12- or 32-bar edifice constructed out of huge girders, pentatonic intervals, and the molten lava of adolescent sexual angst. It is a hurtling stem, steel-tipped and penetrative. In fact it barely assumes song form at all, except incidentally, as an aid to its main purpose, which is to get where it's going hard and fast. Harmony is certainly implied but not really developed (the chord structure modulates narrowly from an F#-minor riff to an uneasy E-major verse) and more or less the same is true of the melody, in so far as you can call it a melody: it's a torque of incantations and howls which wrap themselves closely around the shaft of the rhythm like twists of silver wire. Robert Plant, who does the howling, is drenched in wind-tunnel reverb to further emphasize the general effect of unstoppable propulsiveness. The thing comes at you like a javelin.

In other words, the sound of the music supports the basis of the diplomatic mission to Iceland. This is Led Zeppelin indulging Plant's interest in Dark Ages history—specifically, the Viking colonizations of northern Europe in the eighth, ninth, and tenth centuries—and extruding from that interest a metaphor for what loud rock bands were about to do to settlements everywhere in the mid-twentieth century: the rock band as war party, arrowing in from distant lands to smite, ravish, take, and lay waste. And then assimilate with the smoking ruins.

I am not convinced that this one song gave rise to the entire subgenre of Viking metal which swarmed all over the provinces for the next three decades or so, but it certainly served as the junction point—the twisted bottleneck—through which the immortal spirit of Little Richard had to pass to arrive at Manowar and Megadeth. And to ten-, eleven- and twelve-year-old boys at the time—boys with no prior context for it and therefore no possible conception of the song's potential consequences—"Immigrant Song" was as excitingly threatening as music could ever get.

And no, for once it wasn't the guitars that so stirred the berserker in the teenage breast. Page's overdriven Marshalls and Bonham's battery play their part in getting the raiding party ashore, but it is Plant's voice which drives the longship high on to the beach, lays waste to the hinterland, and then executes a punitive blood-eagle on survivors. "Immigrant Song" is "Good Golly Miss Molly" redeployed in fuller force and with a new kind of edge—and once again it would be Anglo-Saxon settlements everywhere that copped the sharp end.

SUZI QUATRO: "CAN THE CAN"
RAK Records, 1973

It is not insignificant that the Four Horsemen of the Rock 'n' Roll Apocalypse did not include a woman in their number. It being the 1950s, women just didn't register as a significant factor in rock's earliest stirrings, unless they happened to be passing at the time and were equipped with the sort of lusty chops that might sit atop a bucking pell-mell rhythm without falling off—women such as the blues's Etta James or Brenda Lee, a country juvenile, both of whom were capable of melting chrome at a distance just by singing. But these were co-optees enjoying walk-on parts. Sideshows. Accommodations with the Other. They were not agents of progress; none of them was going to conduct rock 'n' roll into a more equitable future—not least perhaps because they had other things to do. Even "the Queen of Rockabilly," rasping Wanda Jackson, flipflopped back and forth between country music and its younger, rowdier, hopped-up junior relative, as if unsure whether she had a berth in rock. To the gaping populace, it was almost as if a woman getting frisky at high tempo with a flattened melody and at maximum amplitude were a spectacle only to be giggled at from behind hands, like Bearded Ladies at traveling carnivals. Women were just not *idiomatic*.

Clearly, this did not mean that women could not be idiomatic; merely that a woman acting that way ought to be taken as exceptional, the point being that it just ain't nat'ral for distaff-bearers to respond so gracelessly and, let's be biological about it, hormonally to their environment. After all, why would any mindful woman *want to do that*? It is not as if women don't have their own ways to get what they want ... And so on. It's an age-old argument and a tired one.

And so men rocked and rolled in modulated, "progressive" form throughout the 1960s while women thought of better things to do with themselves (many of them involving very big beats indeed: just not thrusting, jet-heeled, maxed-out, testosteronal ones—think Motown, think Spector, think Dusty and Lulu . . .). In fact it is hard to think of a single successful female proponent of the rock 'n' roll impulse who came on stream between Wanda Jackson in the early 1960s and Suzi Quatro more than a decade later. Rock 'n' roll, in the decade of the expanded mind, was viewed as conservative, Neanderthal, retrograde, unthinking, boorish, and short. And there's nothing quite so out of time as last decade's boorishness. Even Grace Slick didn't fancy it. Janis Joplin took a different route.

Then, in 1973, "Can the Can" blitzed the radio and Suzi Quatro went on television to mime it, clad in tight-fitting leather and surrounded by thugs. The 6/8 rhythm chugged, and the thugs and Suzi bounced up and down in time to a slappy beat further augmented by many handclaps, as if enacting a collective voodoo ritual of . . . well, it was hard to tell precisely what. In fact, as a close reading of the lyric reveals, "Can the Can" is composed mostly of animal metaphors describing a brace of scenarios in which eyes are scratched out and "your man" gets "put in the can." It is a Grand Guignol of violently stereotyped female sexual jealousy, ending not in reconciliation but with the gleeful restraint and incarceration of male prey.

On telly, Quatro did her yelling from a crouching position, bracing her tiny frame against the weight of her bass guitar with no resources other than the naked energy of her will and the serrations in her voice, which seemed to tear the very ether into spittable shreds. She threw out her lines like a boxer throws out punches—jab, jab, hook, jab—crouching, ducking, coiling, bobbing, her sweat-thickened feather-cut lashing about her face in ropes. Her pubertal boy's shriek was absolutely electrifying to the thirteen year old wearing my trousers. Electrifying and arousing. She made me wonder if I might not be gay.

PATTI SMITH: "GLORIA"
Arista Records, 1975

By the time Patti Smith came along I was certain that I was not gay. Nevertheless, I continued to be aroused by women who dressed like men and asserted their feelings vigorously and at high tempo.

"Gloria" is a pivotal song for me, and I suspect not only for me but for a significant proportion of my precise generation of sketchy males—that demographic of adolescents born between the very late fifties and very early sixties, who by the middle seventies were middle teenagers and had become accustomed to reading their inchoate social and sexual sensibilities back to themselves through the lens of rock music.

If rock 'n' roll expresses a self-contradicting chaos of rebellion and desire through the domineering assertion of hormonal angst—which I think it does—then a handsome, hook-nosed woman making free poetry out of it in the voice of a self-denying God, while dressed as a gentleman of the road who's been dragged backward through a hedge, is going to bring down the house.

She brought my house down to rubble.

"Gloria" was written by Van Morrison for his mid-sixties Belfast R&B mob, Them. The song had then been taken up by suburban garage bands across the American continent as repertory stock, along with "Louie Louie," "Dirty Water," "96 Tears," and other classics of the mystic-dumbass genre: three chords, not many words, lots of scope for shifting resentfully from foot to foot while everything hurtles on around you in a vortex . . . But Patti's mystic-dumbass "Gloria" unfolded like a real poem, a poem interwoven with scratchy guitars and piano, a slow, tortured, dripping poem of religious disavowal, which develops gradually, step by unsteady step, speeding up unevenly as if lurching toward some longed-for objective of relief, hard against a gusting headwind, until arrival is secured in that state of full-tilt all-out affirmative grace that always makes questioning of any kind so very worthwhile, once you get there.

"G-L-O-R-I-EH-EEEE!"

The voice of the self-denying God which intones the blasphemous opening stanza of this mutant "Gloria" is by the end a primal squeal-yodel, not singing but choking out its rapture, as if being alive is excitement enough without having to worry about what is poetry and what God.

It really doesn't matter what sex it is.

2

Boys and Girls and Girl Groups

Voice-over . . .

"You don't make up for your sins in church. You do it in the streets. You do it at home . . . The rest is bullshit, and you know it."

A young man wakes up in bed as if from a bad dream, the sheets and blankets rucked up under his chin. Light is filtering through drawn blinds. His bedroom is in a city somewhere. The sound of traffic can be heard. A police siren.

The young man hauls himself upright, and he shuffles to the bedroom mirror where he fingers his face—to ensure that it is real? To confirm that he is the man he thinks he is?—and then, apparently unresolved, slumps back into bed. As his head makes its slow descent to the pillow, the image cuts and jumps back, as if to make time stop and snatch as it passes.

Big drums beat: *blat-blat blat-BLAM!* Guitars, pianos, and other nameless instruments begin to thrum like rain on the roof. The thrumming becomes a song, one you know as well as you know your own knuckles: the Ronettes' "Be My Baby."

"Be My Baby" is a slight but shapely composition by Jeff Barry and Ellie Greenwich produced and arranged into grandiloquence by Phil Spector in the summer of 1963 and then released into the world like a herd of elephants. But the man in the bed is not thinking about elephants. His mind is on other things. He tugs the blankets up round his ears and closes his eyes, as if to shut out the world. The screen is instantly dark and then illuminated by a glimmer of unsteady light, an emanation from the lens of a film projector. The mind of the man in bed is playing home movies.

Meanwhile, the Ronettes thrum on. But it is not clear whether they are thrumming inside the man's head or only in our heads, as we watch. Or whether the song in fact "belongs" to a third intervening head, that of the film's director, who wants the music to leave something of himself all over the images on the screen, as a sort of commentary.

It is just possible of course that the Ronettes are serving different purposes in everyone's head.

* * *

Thus begins Martin Scorsese's 1973 film, *Mean Streets*, with a dynamic paradox: a high-energy pop record sending a weary soul back to bed. It was a great film to see when you were a teenager in the 1970s, and it is just as great a film to watch now, especially if you've ever wearied of the hollowed-out contrivances of twenty-first-century American cinema. However, I am not sure whether I shouldn't just think of it as a great opening sequence with an excellent movie attached, because that's how it feels in memory. That twisty waking scene has hummed in my recesses ever since I first saw it four decades ago, partly because of its beautiful image/soundtrack cutting rhythm but also because, for me, it stands as a perfect expression of the metaphysical question unwittingly asked by pop music every time it plays: the one concerning ownership. Who owns it? To whom, during the brief period of its activation, does a pop song actually belong? We're speaking the language of the psyche here, of course, not copyright.

So, who?

Them? You? Me? Us? The guy rucked up in bed over there? Come on, who has the most convincing claim? The boys and girls in the studio who produced the music decades ago and thousands of miles away? The men and women who made money out of it, and still do? Or solely the great abstracted "I"—the solitary ear that activates the magic, by snatching the music from the ether and sending it on a short journey to the ear's controlling brain, which then converts that signal through a process of complex filtration into pleasure, excitement, lust, dismay, empathy, self-consciousness, unease, exultation—all of the emotions that a song can ever stir . . . Whose experience of it is the one that really counts? Who has the right to claim the song as an indivisible part of their selfhood?

Or is pop music, when you boil it down, just a hook on which to hang the politics of identity? *Mean Streets* never asks any of those questions at any stage of its scatty, scratchy, 112-minute duration. That isn't its job. But those questions are implicit in the very structure of the film itself. The *New Yorker's* film critic Pauline Kael wrote this about it at the time:

"The music is the electricity in the air of this movie; the music is like an engine that the characters move to. Johnny Boy, the most susceptible, half dances through the movie, and when he's trying to escape from Michael he does a jerky frug before hopping into the getaway car. He enjoys being out of control—he revels in it—and we can feel the music turning him on."

Johnny Boy (Robert De Niro) is, in other words, interacting with the music soundtrack, which—theoretically at least—he can't hear. But perhaps he can. Is he perhaps not unlike the rest of us and is in fact living out the rhythms of his life to the beat of a well-stocked internal jukebox? Perhaps he "owns" the music in his head so completely that it compels him to frug himself alive?

Scorsese has always loved music immoderately. It's almost as if he wishes, really, that he'd been a musician and he makes movies only out of a hunger to be as close to musical as he can be. Certainly, no single film director of his clout has invested his films with so much music so radiantly, nor made such essentially musical films. Even with the sound turned down, the best Scorsese films shout and shimmy. They reach for the transcending arc of aria. They get on down. The films—the early ones at least—are music in film form.

We should not expect Scorsese's works to be any other way. He was, after all, the kingpin of the "movie brat" generation that emerged snapping its fingers from the film schools of the sixties, as much in thrall to hip-sterism and its soundtrack as it was to European New Wave cinema and Forties American film noir. For Scorsese in particular, the music in a film is not ancillary to what he has to say; it *is*, in part, what he has to say. And to say it properly he requires his music to do its work "internally," actu-ally within the world of his cinematic stories, rather than externally in the soundtracked world of an onlooking audience as a sort of bolted-on emo-tional direction-finder and stirring stick. Scorsese has of course used music "externally" too, throughout his career, even during his purple period: think of Bernard Hermann's overpowering jazz-orchestral compositions for *Taxi Driver*, directing the audience to see the streets of a rotting New York with Travis Bickle's eyes, issuing unmissable clues as to Travis's sense of trans-forming dread. But in *Mean Streets* the music takes form *within* the frame-work of the drama. It is internal; it literally emanates from the fibers of the story, like a smell, like Johnny Boy. Here's Kael again: "[The film] doesn't use music, as *Easy Rider* sometimes did, to do the movie's work for it . . . The music here isn't our music, meant to put us in the mood of the movie, but the characters' music."

So there you have it, in the words of the mighty Kael. The music belongs to those who act upon it.

* * *

I always feel this same sense of perspectival disorder whenever I hear "Be My Baby," as if it belongs in someone else's movie. What a thing it is, a cyclone of a pop single, all whirring torque and no surrender, Ronnie Spector's juve-nile bleat fighting those massive thrums as wishfully as a spring lamb fights the weather. Indeed, "Be My Baby" is a contender for Greatest Pop Record Ever in more than a few hearts, purely on account of the fact that it distils all pop's primary formal virtues into a single two-and-a-half-minute blast. The Beach Boys' resident genius Brian Wilson certainly used to think as much.

But whenever I hear it, alongside the roaring pleasure it gives me, I also register in myself strange notes of anxiety, worry, resentment even, and I always have done. This is because "Be My Baby" can never be one of *my* pop records, not truly. Not really. I can make no existential claim to it, not like I can to "(I Can't Get No) Satisfaction." I can't identify. "Be My Baby" wasn't mine when I first heard it some time in the 1960s and it isn't mine now, not even for nostalgic purposes. It is unpossessable.

Which is a ridiculous thing to feel, of course. Why bother? What does it matter, whom a piece of music "belongs" to psychologically? But there it is: it seems to, to me. It's part of the sense-making labor of music listening. And it's a fact that I have always felt this way: that identification is a key element of the impossible equation that explains the power and grip of music. I could write a list right now of the ten greatest pop records that I don't identify with, and "Be My Baby" would be close to number one. Good pop music always plays games with one's narcissism. I admire all Phil Spector's girl-voiced records in this manner—at one slightly anxious remove—not because I feel that my interest in them isn't justified, or welcome, but because I can't find a place for *myself* in them, however much I adore them and however much I might once have wished that one day I might become Ronnie's baby.

This is not down to stringent self-analysis—I know without thinking that I am not a 1960s girl with a beehive hairdo, as much as I also know that, when she sings those words, Ronnie Spector does not have me in mind. No, this strange sense of non-engagement has to do with the way "Be My Baby" was designed by its producer-creator.

For a juvenile pop song expressing the mad energy of teenage desire, it is a remarkably remote and forbidding thing, as if adolescent desire has a Gothic dimension to it and there is danger implicit in every approach you make, as if the echoing corridors and oubliettes of the Spector sound reverberate with a special warning. Beware trapdoors and sudden falls, doors that slam, chambers that echo. Be terribly aware of the untraversable distance that separates you from your baby. Indeed, here's a worry: Are we actually listening to Ronnie Spector's voice in "Be My Baby" or is that the wild pleading of a caged animal? If it weren't for the generous spirit implicit in Spector's marvelous *A Christmas Gift For You* album, one might be tempted to suspect that Phil Spector himself was an altogether dubious proposition.

Do pop records have psycho-architecture?

Of course they do. And "Be My Baby" is a classic example. It was produced and created—*designed*—by a man who later went on in real life to imprison the woman who sings it behind real gates and barbed-wire fences in the Spector marital home, contriving to kill both her career and her independence of mind in a protracted fiat of possessive jealousy. Ronnie writes about it in her autobiography. She claims that, following their marriage, Spector kept her under lock and key in their mansion for most of the latter part of the 1960s and early 1970s, hiding her shoes to hobble her, keeping the lights off to conceal his baldness (he wore a hat in bed), showing her endless repeats of *Citizen Kane* to remind her of his power over her; even telling her mother about the glass-topped coffin he kept in the basement for Ronnie's final repose . . . Eventually, she did a runner in bare feet.

But before that, back in 1963, he was merely working himself up. Getting in the mood. He made "Be My Baby" sound vast and cavernous and imposing and unapproachable as if it were some edifice immuring beautiful Ronnie's teenage screech forever inside high walls. It was her sonic dungeon, as were all the other Ronettes records. It is only because of the sheer carry of Ronnie's bellow, its serrated, barely musical, desperately reaching edge, that she can be heard at all.

And I knew that I was not wanted there, even as a child. I knew it long before I heard the story of what Phil did to Ronnie, even longer before it became apparent what Phil habitually did to women. *You may look at her,* the record seemed to say. *Just be aware of her existence, briefly, and then go away. Go on. Get outta here. She's mine.*

"Be My Baby" is girl-group pop expressing a man's emotions. And not a very nice man, either.

* * *

But then perhaps my frail psyche needs safer buildings to play in. I have never been one for cruelty and imprisonment. Call me a snowflake if you must.

My actual favorite girl-group record—and therefore, it necessarily follows, a contender for the status of my favorite pop record—was also the first girl-group record ever to make the top of the pop charts, which it did in both the United Kingdom and the United States during the doo-wop afterglow of 1961.

Historically, the Detroit suburb of Inkster has given much to the city's industries. Its secondary school, Inkster High, has given even more. It gave the Marvelettes to the world. They were the first girl group Berry Gordy signed to his fledgling Motown enterprise and their adaptation of a local doo-wop knock-off, "Please Mr. Postman," became the company's first number one hit on the Tamla label. In just about every sense conceivable, "Please Mr. Postman" is the opposite of "Be My Baby."

Let us first consider its sound.

In place of booming thrums, we are met by the hyper-present snap and lollop of tight Motown rhythm: drums (reputedly played by the young Marvin Gaye), bass, and rolling piano. And that's it. Phil Spector had a habit of loosening drum skins and then multitracking them, to create the hollowed-out "distant" percussion effect that underpinned his Wall of Sound. He also layered the rest of the instrumentation over and over again in thick sediments of reverb, as if to demonstrate some sort of puissance: guitars, pianos, percussion, strings piled high . . . The instruments on Motown's "Please Mr. Postman," however—and there appear to be three, possibly four, of them—are recorded relatively "dry" with a minimum of reverb and no multitracking, while the voices sit not in the center-bottom of a towering arrangement, bellowing to be let out, but instead ride the ensemble in touch-proximity, right on top of the rhythm section as if in the same small room, at the same time, rubbing shoulders, exchanging grins and frowns at the improbable but thrilling sweaty hard work of it all. The Marvelettes sound like girls having fun in the room you're in, rather than girls miles away, trying to sing their way out of a missile silo.

But whatever technical postulations might be offered to account for this unusual sense of immediacy and presence, no element of the "Mr. Postman" package is as important to its intimate impact as the voice of the Marvelettes' lead singer, Gladys Horton.

Any day of the working week I would take her "Please Mr. Postman" as one of the all-time great juvenile pop vocal performances, not just because it swings like a lemur and evinces an abundance of freshness and detail, energy, and tone, or because it dignifies a somewhat corny contrivance of a lyric with real-world heart, or because it is sweet and comely and funny and husky—although it is all of those things and more. Not even because Horton slips into a larky Detroit-Caribbean accent halfway through. No, I'd take Horton's "Postman" as a great performance because it has always convinced me that she is knowable; and as a result, *because* she is knowable, the sentiment of the song then becomes real, recognizable, permeable. There are no walls of sound holding you at bay. There is room for you in there too, and welcome.

My fourteen-year-old daughter has school friends who sound like Gladys most of the time—not tonally, necessarily, but certainly attitudinally. They go about their business with exactly the same mixture of sauce, insouciance, cheek, and grave sincerity. And when they're gathered after school in our kitchen, gabbling away among themselves as an accompaniment to the ingestion of too much Nutella, then it is for me, as I sit writing upstairs at my desk, a Motown moment. They're at it right now, in the room beneath my feet. I can hear them. And I love to hear them at it in the same way that I love to hear Gladys.

Depending on whom she's addressing, my daughter refers to her aggregation of mates either as "the Squad" or, more solemnly, as "my friendship group." Me, I just think of them as the Marvelettes.

* * *

However, I sometimes wonder if I they wouldn't prefer it if I thought of them as the Shangri-Las.

When I was twelve years old, in 1972, the big girl-group hit of the year was the Shangri-Las' "Leader of the Pack." This was the record's second coming in the UK: it had first invaded the pop charts seven years previously, in 1965, and it would return there for a third term in 1976. But 1972 happened to be the year in which I first became seriously interested in pop, and "Leader of the Pack" was everywhere.

This was also the year of "I'd Like to Teach the World to Sing," "Telegram Sam," "Without You," "Son of My Father," "Metal Guru," "Vincent," "School's Out," "Puppy Love," "You Wear It Well," "Mama Weer All Crazee Now," "How Can I Be Sure," "Mouldy Old Dough," and "Clair," so it was not a year to be trifled with—the above list is merely a representative sample of the more memorable number ones of 1972, from January to November. "Leader of the Pack" only made it to number three that autumn, held manfully off the top spot first by Lieutenant Pigeon, then Gilbert O'Sullivan. But it was the record that cut all the others to shreds for mystique. It was Betty Weiss who wielded the shears.

No matter that Slade had a chainsaw with ginger mutton chops to do their singing for them (Noddy Holder); or that T. Rex had the fey gurgle of Marc Bolan; or that Rod was in his first pomp. And perish the superior technical accomplishment of Nilsson, whose "Without You" is a true vocal tour de force of the old school. As for the New Seekers, David Cassidy, Donny Osmond, Gilbert O'Sullivan, Alice Cooper . . . ? Come *on*. Betty Weiss of the Shangri-Las chopped the lot of them into confetti.

The song had two qualities which struck me at the time as salient, neither of which my twelve-year-old self was in a position to analyze. One was the archaism of it. In 1972, no one else's voice reached you like that, deadpan but cutting, as if through a loudhailer across a crowded playground. And the strangely muffled kickdrum-and-piano heartbeat of the rhythm track (plus appliquéd motorbike noises) did not belong to the bright new rocking soundworld of glam, where guitars, drums, and saxes interacted with muscular clarity, not mysterious minimalism. George "Shadow" Morton's production of "Leader of the Pack" was transporting, not only because it sounded old and other, but because its mystery presented a challenge: come on, boy—find room for yourself in *this*.

I found myself tiptoeing across the threshold really quite nervously. Boys and cheap motorbikes were everywhere in the East Anglian fens of the 1970s; boys dead in ditches beneath mangled motorbikes weren't that uncommon either. So I understood "Leader of the Pack" not as bubblegum melodrama but as a form of heightened naturalism—a representation of the world as it really is, neither allegorical nor mythical but dotted with real teenagers living out real incidents involving real sex and betrayal and recklessness. What pubertal youth would not register the soulful truth expressed in the couplet, "They told me he was bad / but I knew he was sad"? This was not someone else's movie but my own, as narrated by girls.

And here was the other aspect of the song that made it sing to me in 1972. The Shangri-Las were intimidating. The voices of Betty and Mary Weiss and the blank-faced Ganser twins ("Yes, we see") scissored not only the competition in the pop charts but also the hopeful sense in me that girls were, at bottom, just like boys: that maybe girls were just boys in dresses, boys with higher-pitched voices and softer hair and prettier faces; boys who didn't want to fight you, boys who didn't mock, boys who offered consolation, sense, and sensibility; boys you might actually kiss . . . No, these had been vain pubescent hopes and now they were fluttering in whorls like autumn leaves. The Shangri-Las were not like boys at all.

They were girls without compunction. It was audible in every note of both "Leader of the Pack" and the seething "Remember (Walking in the Sand)," which was even more archaic-sounding than "Leader" and possibly even more darkly compelling in its brevity and simplicity. It was present above all in the peremptory slash of Betty and Mary Weiss's voices—the absence of swing, the apparent lack of concern with anything remotely resembling elegance or maturity or sophistication or empathy. The blankness, the shrugging, the disdain, the flat-out assertive reserve of everything both records had to say.

This was a facer for a twelve year old intent on unveiling not the mystery but the hard-edged reality of girls.

* * *

So I took the Ronettes, the Marvelettes, and the Shangri-Las downstairs to meet the Squad. I thought: This'll be interesting. This'll put the cat among the aerial vermin. There will be plenty to observe and to learn and even the occasional laugh to be had along the way. Whether or not they've heard "Leader of the Pack," "Please Mr. Postman," and "Be My Baby" before—and there exists the shocking possibility that they won't have—the Squad will certainly have a fresher take on them as examples of pop psycho-architecture than I do. Berry, Esme, Ruby, and Rose will take a view for sure and it will trump every one of my own shallow thoughts and will possibly even go some way to giving me an interesting answer to my question about "ownership." They will let me know once and for all whether or not I have any right to my long-standing, passionate but nervous investment in girl-group pop. They might after all, being forthright girls, tell me that I am a perv.

So I carted the laptop down into the kitchen and asked whether they might be interested in taking part in a little experiment involving both their critical faculties and their sense of fun. Would they listen to the three re-cords with me and then allow themselves to be interviewed on the subject?

"Not now, Dad, We're busy," said my daughter. The others laughed.

"But would you, please, at some future date?"

"Yeah, sure," they said, as if they were agreeing to allow fish to swim in the sea.

A week or so later I managed to corner my daughter again.

"When are you and Esme and Ruby and the others next planning to have an after-school session in the kitchen? Could we maybe do the inter-view after that—when you've finished your more important business, of course?"

"Tomorrow, probably."

"Can we do it then?"

"Yeah, sure. If we have to."

Tomorrow duly came, and the Squad convened as usual. I left them to do their thing for an hour or so and then padded down from my room above the kitchen . . .

"Not now, Dad. We're just going out."

"Yeah, sorry, Nick. Another time, eh?"

I was sure I could detect a derisive edge to their laughter as they exited the front door.

And so it would be repeated the following week, and the week after that, and then the week after that. And on and on. Occasionally, I would stand my daughter up on it and ask her, when the Squad wasn't around, whether she had any intention at all of complying, or whether it was, like, y'know, too much to ask—I'd quite understand, though I'd be disappointed and so on. Half-cocked arrangements would be made to collect the Squad in one place on Thursday afternoon with the sole purpose in mind of doing the interview . . . and then, at the last minute—and sometimes not even at the last minute—other arrangements would take precedence or parental authority would intervene or there'd be a match on in Haggerston or Ruby would have a headache and they'd all have to go and attend to her at Ruby's place, all of them, yes, all of them, and slowly it began to dawn on me that it was simply not going to happen. I was never going to find out the secret of girl-group pop and, by extension, the secret of girls.

In fact more than a year has now gone by—fourteen months, to be precise—since I made my initial request for half an hour of their time together and I have now, today, officially given up the hunt. I have to accept reality. I have been strung along.

GRACE NOTES

THE FOUR PENNIES: "WHEN THE BOY'S HAPPY"
Laurie Records, 1963

We're having a party in the basement of a house in town I share with a friend, prior to me trolling off to university. It's 1979 and we think we're pretty hip. The music is a mix of danceable post-punk obscurities, glam rock, disco, power-pop, and girl-group hits from the early 1960s.

I am getting down to the Four Pennies' (a.k.a. the Chiffons) "When The Boy's Happy" and thinking, yes, this is about as bang-up danceable as sixties pop ever got. It is a great swirling vortex of a pop record. It has a massive Spectorish beat. It thrums. It churns. Its methodical harmonic structure resolves exactly the way you want it to. Its voices are real. And if it isn't actually funky at all, not like Motown, that doesn't matter because the dynamic energy of the playing and singing is such that your hips keep swinging anyway.

I am in the middle of this thought and enjoying it no end when, for some reason I cannot articulate, I find myself listening to the catchline of the song: "When the boy's happy, the girl's happy too." And something stirs. Something goes through my body in a fast ripple. "When the boy's happy, the girl's happy too"? Do what? Oh dear. There's something not quite right about that, isn't there?

Or am I being priggish again? It's a pop record, for heaven's sake, and we're dancing, not taking notes for discussion in open forum later . . .

Well, I was dancing. I *was* dancing well and feeling good. But now I'm not dancing any more, not really. Nothing like. I'm moving my body around roughly in time with the music, but it's not what you might call dancing. I am now galumphing self-consciously.

When the boy's happy, the girl's happy too!

Well, haven't we come a long way since 1963? And good, too, sixteen years on in '79, that I've spotted this example of presumptuous sexism—I am right up to speed. In fact, I am probably ahead of the curve, because nobody else dancing in the basement seems to have noticed the text, the actual *words* of what they're dancing to, neither men nor women, boys nor girls: they're bucking and swirling and getting it on like there's no tomorrow. The basement is ablaze. Nobody's taking a blind bit of notice of the words the Four Pennies are actually singing.

But then does it really matter what words they use, when what the record's actually *saying* is contained within the sound of that swirling beat and in the unsubservient rip of those incandescent voices? What "When The Boy's Happy" is saying is: "It's great to be alive! It's great to be a teenage girl! It's just unbelievably great to be so young and independent and doing stuff in the grown-up world that my parents would never have been able to back when they were sixteen . . ."

Suddenly, I feel stupid as well as pleased with myself.

And on I go, shifting inelegantly from foot to foot, thought to thought, from prig to beast and back again, like some dull pendulum in drainpipes and brothel-creepers—and before I know it, "When The Boy's Happy" has ended and I have missed its moment almost completely.

It is not recorded whether the next track up is David Bowie's current hit, "Boys Keep Swinging," though I rather imagine I'd remember if it had been.

BANANARAMA: "ROBERT DE NIRO'S WAITING"
London Records, 1984

There were two golden girl-group eras: the early 1960s and latter two-thirds of the 1990s. But that does not mean that girls didn't bother to form groups at other times. Not at all. And not all of them were singing/dancing troupes as per the classic "girl-group" formulation (see Fanny, the Runaways, the Slits, the Raincoats, the Bangles, etc.). Indeed the very concept of the "girl group," in which cohorts of young pretty women sing, dance, and dress up at the behest of male producer/managers, is intrinsically dodgy—as exemplified by the "greatest girl group of them all," the Ronettes.

But it was entirely in keeping with the spirit of their times that Bananarama should have a string of sizeable hits throughout the 1980s, the decade in which British pop turned itself inside out and upside down in a desperate and self-consciously postmodernist effort to feel relevant and true to an emerging new social and political reality.

Bananarama were scruffy but glamorous; they sang pretty tunes with deadpan insouciance; they took the mick out of the girl-group concept while embracing it enthusiastically; they were never shy of a masculine production team (Jolley & Swain followed by Stock Aitken Waterman), but they asserted their feminist credentials at every turn. They certainly lacked a voice as great as Gladys Horton's and so instead chose to deploy a sort of artless, democratized unison chorusing, expressing very little character of any kind other than that of the droogishly homogeneous girl gang. They were some kind of a hoot, for a while, and you took their point—but they didn't make you shiver with anxiety and desire. This was true of a lot of pop in the 1980s.

TLC: "NO SCRUBS"
Arista Records, 1999

In the early years of the 1990s, when TLC made their first sassy bid to escape their home town of Atlanta, Georgia, the Spice Girls, All Saints, and Girls Aloud were not even close to the drawing board. They had not registered as a twinkle in anyone's eye. So it was possible to tangle with the mouthy, street-smart hip-hop-into-swing sound of TLC and hear it as wonderful genre music and not as the auditory component of a self-aware marketing entity with an attractive secondary line in spin-off merchandise and ancillary business opportunities. In those innocent days it was possible to think of the group as the daughters of the Marvelettes and the Shangri-Las.

Of course the TLC story turned in due course into a god-awful muddle, with group members getting themselves into legal disputes with their management and then bickering endlessly among themselves—and one of their number, the wayward but charismatic Left Eye, winding up dead in a car crash. But at the time, right up until the end of the decade, they sounded not only like girls in the real world but girls who know the real world better than you do.

Tionne "T-Boz" Watkins, Lisa "Left Eye" Lopes, and Rozonda "Chilli" Thomas gave it to you straight: This is what girls do and don't do. This is what they find acceptable and unacceptable. This is how they are, not how you think they ought to be. These are the ropes. Oh, and take this wit-choo on the way to the door, homeboy, 'cause *we* are the ones in charge around here . . .

They were fantastic and very easy to adore. The *CrazySexyCool* album of 1994 remains one of the best-selling girl-group albums of all time. And for that due credit must always be extended to producers/writers L. A. Reid,

Kenneth "Babyface" Edmonds, and Dallas Austin, for that clever elision of hip-hop and cutting-edge pop-R&B: the music had movement in it as well as melody and vivid messaging—TLC were, among other things, artistically satisfying.

And "No Scrubs" is a great pop single. It clicks along like street-corner bantz, po-faced and deadpan, supported by acoustic guitar, artificial string stabs, and tight beats, half sung, half rapped in squeezed little voices, a gang sound, cocked, impermeable, unchallengeable and actually very, very slight, for all the acuteness of its posture. The substance of it is all over in two minutes, effectively, and you're left in no doubt: you've been told. TLC have told you what is not acceptable behavior, and now it is appropriate for you to move along and leave the girls to their business. Nobody is losing their cool here—unless you are.

3

Vulnerable

A hovering cloud of strings.

A voice, half simpering, half singing above the cloud: "You are just too cold. You are cold as ice. You wasn't very *nice* . . ."

The dubious grammar does not help to clarify the singer's sentiment, which is expressed with an ingratiating lilt, as if in the voice of a small girl ticking off her hamster for nipping her finger—sweet-faced, disingenuous, "coming from a loving place": the lilt that fig-leafs a threat. He (for it is actually a grown man's voice, not a little girl's) goes on, not simpering now but singing properly, in a soft, high register.

"Why did I choose you? What did I see in you?"

The voice is high, light, floating, self-harmonized, as if draped. The strings beneath the voice surge like water. A question is being asked: "Were you worth it? Were you *really* good enough for me?" And after a verse or two the voice appears to reach a conclusion: *"And if I had to choose again / I would still . . . choose . . . you."*

The strings sloosh. Above the strings the voice dips and soars like a swallow, sometimes multiplying itself to harmonize in shapely contrapuntal whorls. And at the end of the song, having exulted for more than two minutes in its own beauty, the voice cedes the point that, yes, he'd still choose her—despite her coldness and her not-very-niceness: yeah, go on then, all right, he'd *still* choose her. Despite everything.

The song is "Why Did I Choose You?" by Michael Leonard and Herbert Martin, a ballad originally written as a straightforward testament to the wonder of enduring love, a sweet and guileless croon, full of hope and comfy reflection, composed in the mid-sixties and recorded by such easy-listening titans as Johnny Mathis and Barbra Streisand, among others. But as interpreted in this instance by Marvin Gaye and prefaced with his deathless simper, it is an object lesson in rank, canting smarm.

It is also startlingly beautiful.

Beauty and self-delusion conspire in most Marvin Gaye recordings. They conspire to shroud his other inclinations, toward bitterness or narcissism or anxiety or melancholic pathos, twining thickly like ivy on an overwrought Victorian cenotaph to Departing Incomprehensible Love. One of Gaye's great unfulfilled longings as a musician was to devote a whole album to "the ballads," that artificial canon of sophisticated and fairly upmarket standards which stood then, in the 1960s and '70s, as the stock-in-trade of such international go-anywhere, be-seen-everywhere superstar figures as Streisand and Mathis—not to mention the slightly less superstarry Lou Rawls, the hunky baritone who used to win showbiz gongs as if gongs were going out of style (and, in doing so, invite Gaye's catty derision). Presumably at that time Marvin saw "ballads" as rather classier songs to sing than his own manufactured-by-the-yard Motown soul-pop, and that a well-thought-out "ballads collection" would facilitate his ascension into the Tintoretto glory of universal acclaim: you know, Marvin haloed at the center of a celestial explosion of worshipping mums and grans, in addition to the adoration of the daughters and sons to whom he had already laid claim. Gaye longed for peership with Sinatra and Nat Cole.

And so, at the height of the 1960s—just before "I Heard It Through the Grapevine" and well in advance of his great authorial breakout, *What's Going On*—he instigated a project that would see him enter the studio with the "classy" film-score composer and arranger Bobby Scott, who was duly tasked with the job of arranging a handful of modern ballads for voice and full orchestra, as sophisticatedly and as intimately as might be feasible in 1967. Marvin wanted the full Sinatra treatment.

The songs were duly chosen, the arrangements composed, the orchestra rehearsed and eventually the tape rolled. But what emerged at the end of the process was callow in the extreme. The suite of songs simply didn't work. Cushioned within billowing strings, often suspended on elastic reins in the tempo-less stasis of next-to-no time, Marvin sounded like what he was: a bumptious R&B twentysomething seducer playing grown-up; overween-ing, weightless, thin bordering on shrill, straining for both effect and affect, unsubtle, unswinging; a voice lost in space without the stabilizing forward propulsion imparted by Motown's rhythm turbines. Not even ghastly, just feeble. Artistically, the project was a flop and Marvin knew it—for which insight he should be given due credit.

Being Marvin, however, he could not afford to acknowledge the failure and so he just sat on the tapes and waited for the hurt to subside, even al-lowing it to be thought for a while that his plans to release a ballads album were being actively thwarted by Motown owner (and brother-in-law) Berry Gordy.

The project lay abandoned for years and was only resurrected more than a decade later as the Gaye imperium crumbled in a storm of cocaine and his divorce from Gordy's sister, Anna. Scott's orchestral arrangements were retained but the songs were voiced again from scratch. And this time Gaye had enough in his locker—experience, technique, judgment, not to men-tion a welter of "personal suffering"—to make the performances stick. The violins still slooshed and swirled, and of course many of the arrangements still drifted, untethered, in tempo-less space, neither playing to the singer's rhythm and blues strengths, nor suggesting new ways to be strong—just hanging around sounding attractive. Heftless.

But by this point Gaye had new strings to his own creative bow, to go with the suffering and the technical development—in particular a spec-tacular talent for harmonizing with himself in extravagant yet apparently spontaneous bursts of off-the-cuff vocal rapture.

This was a real gift, doubtless founded in the experience gained as a very young man singing in gospel quintets and doo-wop groups—but with one significant difference. Where gospel and doo-wop harmony tends to be tightly focal, orientated toward the articulation of single, collectively expressed emotions and ideas, Gaye's auto-harmonies were diffusely articulate, polyphonous, polyvalent—as if each and every voice in the cloud of voices were speaking only for itself, and not subordinate to the conventions of the choric bloc (the only function of which is to support and amplify the articulations of a central protagonist-voice). On the contrary, Gaye's shifting voice-clouds served to suggest that at all times a multiplicity of thoughts and feelings are churning away *in addition* to the central one, as if Marvin's soul is indeed as teeming as the universe itself. You might even stretch the point to suggest that the self-harmonizing Marvin Gaye constituted the perfect post-Freudian choir, standing at once for all of his agonies and ecstasies, cubistically offering all the angles into his psyche at any given moment—and of course binding the listener to the idea that he or she is equally subdivisible. Soul music as a representation not of a singular soul but of the fragmented self: a prism, if you'd prefer it put that way, splitting the voice into its constituent sub-voices. But of course, in conscious reality, the high-functioning narcissist Marvin was probably only going for the Tintoretto angel-choir effect to maximize impact. He was all about impact.

Whatever his motivations and strategies, he first tried this autopolyphony out as a method on *What's Going On* and then *Trouble Man*, to grand effect. He developed and disciplined it significantly with *Let's Get It On* and then over-refined the process on *I Want You*, to the point where the multiple voices were so diffuse and frictionless that the listening ear found nothing to hold on to that didn't immediately slip away again in a lotioned slither. *I Want You* is virtually an instrumental album—lush, upholstered, "sophisticated" soul instrumentalism—with Gaye's voices functioning as just another instrumental section, alongside the strings and horns and rhythm unit.

Perhaps it is not surprising then that this was the point at which he chose to revisit his ballads project. And typically, this most painterly of vocal artists does not go *all* the way with it, by committing himself completely and wholeheartedly to the full vocal impasto, but instead, rather gingerly, chooses to dip only the fine point of his brush into the colors of his palette, making do with two voices mostly and occasionally three, dripping the metaphorical canvas with flecks of vocal pigment but not making the bold, even decisive, strokes which such highly conventionalized songwriting cries out for—a hesitancy of which Barbra Streisand might never be accused.

Gaye would argue of course that the material doesn't cry out for boldness or decisiveness, just truth: truth as he sees it. And that the truth of what he's after cannot, by definition, be rendered with either boldness or decision—but only by evasion and suggestion, drip and fleck, softness and fade. What Marvin wants to express is his sense that love is an evanescence, a shading and fading of feeling rather than a firmly dependable thing; that, once you take sex out of the picture (which is what his ballads album seems to be concerned with: the sublimation of sexual feeling in favor of "better" feelings—compare and contrast with his sex opus, *Let's Get It On*), then what you are left with is abstraction and anxiety and fear and vincibility, plus good will and bad faith, slippage and decay, escape and fugue—nothing that actually *stays*. In which case, Marvin expresses his truth with withering accuracy.

"Who isn't vulnerable to love?" he once asked his most reliable biographer, David Ritz. And by funny coincidence, after thirty years, when Marvin Gaye's re-refined ballads album did at last see the light of day, posthumously, it bore the title *Vulnerable*.

* * *

It's funny to think that vulnerability has not always been regarded as a virtue in postwar pop music. But there it is. We are accustomed now, sixty years after Elvis's coming, to encountering "vulnerability" everywhere and finding everywhere that it means good things. It's what we expect of singers: that they can do vulnerability, along with everything else.

But what is meant by "doing vulnerability"?

Well, there's the "vulnerability" that gives us insight into the psyche of the singer, should we be so bothered. It is an *X-Factor*-sponsored orthodoxy that a good singer's personality should at all times be expressed, and that to listen to a singer's voice is to "discover" him or her as an individual (which is a pretty thin way of arguing the case that the point of listening to singing is to consume the singer). But that is mere projection and fantasy—a pseudo-analytical overlay which might attach an attractive narrative to the act of singing but doesn't necessarily help the act of singing to mean anything at all, much less help it to ring true.

Much more telling—and much more ringing—than the viability of the singer's singing personality is the impact his or her singing has on our emotions, as we internalize the sound—irrespective of the singer's own nature. For the real reason we attach importance to "vulnerability" is that it affords us contact with our own sense of what it is to be vulnerable: it is the job of singing not to draw attention to the singer's little peculiarities but to help us turn to face our own most hazardous feelings.

How often have we heard a voice, of whatever size and shape, and thought: Well, I'm not sure whether I'd want this singer next to me in a trench, but I *am* touched by his or her vulnerability? Furthermore, this singer's suscepti-bility to attack makes mine feel so much more justified. That's not wimpiness I'm getting, that's *sensitivity*. And so on. It is a modern virtue to be transpar-ent like this. Yes, the perception of others' vulnerability breeds identification and sympathy, but how about the perception of our own? What are the consequences of inciting vulnerability? What does that do?

Not a lot in 1956. Not when the Four Horsemen started their charge. Rock was then, by definition, a demonstration against vulnerability. It pro-posed that young men and women—but usually young men—had every-thing going for them if only they would learn how to throw off the shackles of impecuniousness, war, obedience, and conformity that had made such ironclad respecters of authority out of their parents. Rock 'n' roll was the great shout out against all that, a rebellious yell in favor of the individ-ual spirit and its urges, against repression and obedience and dependency. Even attachment. Especially attachment. Yet even though it did all that, to begin with rock wasted little thought on human frailty. Rock was about invincibility—or at least the invincible moment.

The importance of Roy Orbison cannot be overestimated, then. He emerged from Wink, Texas, in the 1950s, blinking astigmatically behind heavy-rimmed spectacles, a pudding-faced introvert of limited social adaptability but with a voice like a sad trumpet (among other similitudes, depending on which part of his three-octave range was being deployed).

After a fairly uneventful career as a rockabilly juvenile at Sun, he found work for a period in Nashville as a jobbing songwriter before breaking big in 1960 with his voicing of one of his own compositions, "Only the Lonely," a song that had already been offered to both Elvis Presley and the Everly Brothers and been turned down: reverb; doo-wop harmony; a diffident, slightly prim, tripping tempo executed nimbly (but certainly not rocked) by Nashville's finest; the sad trumpet looping out of the arrangement almost passively, as if subordinate in status to the nominally-background "dum dum dum dummy-doo-wah," then settling, bashfully, into its shiversome place in the downstage spotlight.

Big hit.

It gave Orbison the excuse to spend the next half-decade spreading courtly despondency far and wide with the introversion and attention to detail of a horny Victorian basement scientist. His idea was not to create a gorgeous monster but to sell loads of records and to make the world more beautiful, and of course he achieved both of those things.

The home town of Orbison's adolescence, Wink, was—and would still appear to be—a crossroads in the middle of nowhere, dozens of miles north of the main highway connecting Abilene to the Mexican border. The landscape is flat, arid, acned like the most poisonous locations in *Breaking Bad*. The vegetation, such as it is, hunkers into the dust. Road surfaces are pocked. The horizon gapes. The few buildings that constitute what looks from a distance like a temporary settlement are stunted by an overwhelming bowl of sky, as if physically oppressed. It's a place to pass straight on through. You can see why the people who live there might be ingrained with a sense of dread.

Orbison's expressions of dread were uniquely potent, so much so that they became integrated into rock's stylistic vocabulary almost as soon as he'd articulated them. Dread as vulnerability. In Orbison's hands "dread" was actually a gentle, even genteel thing, something to be offered hesitantly across a gleaming Formica table in a spirit of companionable empathy, like a cup of tea trembling on a saucer. He was polite, stoic, well-meaning. His sense of dread did not, even for a moment, contaminate his impeccable manners.

Of course, "dread" and "vulnerability" did exist already in mainstream pop, after a fashion—think of the theatrical self-abasement of Johnny Ray and the tremulous cadences of all those wet-lipped, quiffy Bobby boys of the period—but they were gestural feelings, expressed histrionically and often rather camply on the presumption that such emotional deviancies ought to be taken by teens as tokens of error, that visitations of "dread" and "vulnerability" constituted at most a tiresome disruption of the glittering diurnal norm, akin to finding the wrong shoes for today's outfit on your feet. There was no suggestion of depth or reach or texture to these feelings. Or scope. Or seriousness. Dread and vulnerability were not, in Bobby's world, the portal to another dimension.

In Orbison's, though, they opened up new possibilities not only for Roy himself but for rock 'n' roll. When Orbison is singing in the room you find yourself deposited, alone, on the threshold of existential space, a resonating void in which there are of course girls—well, *one* girl; *the* girl—but the girl is herself a continuation of the void by other means, her very inaccessibility or prettiness or dreaminess or departedness the measure of the void's emptiness. Roy's loneliness was cavernous like the bowl of the sky. It went on and on. The girl merely served to confirm it. This was not vulnerability as worked-up angst but as manifest reality: the teenager as existential argonaut, stapled for all time to his mast, nervous, bespectacled, helplessly engorged ("Mercy!"), and tilted back and forth on the mighty swells of his romantic anxiety—the teenager not only inhabiting his life in earnest but seriously considering whether he oughtn't to examine it, too.

"Only The Lonely," "Blue Angel," "Running Scared," "Crying," "Dream

Baby," "In Dreams," "Blue Bayou," "It's Over," "Oh, Pretty Woman" . . . these are not frivolous songs. Indeed there was no weightier nor more brilliant succession of hit pop singles during the interregnal years separating the drafting of Elvis from the coming of the Beatles and Bob Dylan. During that period Orbison reeled off the hits, a couple a year, deploying the very best Nashville sessioneers to extract the juice from his peculiar vision of what a rock-derived pop song might aspire to be and do. He was a proper auteur, every bit as much as Chuck Berry. His songs were like strange 3D sonic sculptures you might walk around and poke. You could enter them, as you might enter a ghost ride at a fairground. You might be swallowed up in them. Orbison had a *sound*.

This sound was shaped not only by the formidable ranginess of the voice—Orbison was able to access even the outlying reaches of his three-plus octaves smoothly and without discernible effort—but also by the cool musicianliness of the players and technicians who worked on the songs in well-endowed Nashville studios. In Orbison's case, though, the sound was also intrinsic in the way the songs were structured.

They were, with one or two exceptions, balladic in atmosphere and tempo but also steeply climactic, as if each melody itself constituted a careful reaching for something elusive or rare or transcendent, the point being that whatever precious thing he was reaching for, it was surely out of Roy's reach and would remain there however nobly he strained. (But hell, this is America and the point of life is to reach, isn't it?) Several of the songs were step-shaped, with comely harmonic lifts and twists built into them, while others evinced a torrid, highly tensioned rhythmic stasis, less like Motown's propulsive turbines than ceiling fans in a sweltering room, insistent, pulsating, dynamic but soberly cooling. Some of the rhythms actually give off a sort of rotary swish. The Big O never got hot under the collar, even when reaching for the top notes.

And that's the paradox that makes the Orbison sound shiver. It is rock 'n' roll all right, that sound, rock 'n' roll through and through and through. Everything about the music is sheened with sweat and lustfulness and the desire for proximity to shiny things—yet its surface is cool, as if the drive inward to the void has iced it over en route. Everything about the music is frosted.

It's partly an inherent effect of all that Nashville restraint—Nashville does not incline willingly toward lust. It can contend with excess, for sure, and longing and vulgarity, but it will always organize these things with genteel restraint, and never, ever admit the animal. Take the chorusless "Running Scared," the campest of all Orbison's hits. The bolero-style accompaniment is halt with inhibition right from the start, as if dreading the inevitable caesura that actually stops the song in its tracks, the "runner" in his flight—the steep ramp up to an unresolved, teetering-on-the-brink climax and . . . termination. Compare and contrast with Jerry Lee Lewis. This is the sound of inner choking controlled, then cut off, by the maintenance of surface calm. Which is no kind of rock 'n' roll impulse at all.

But rock 'n' roll it is.

It is often said that Orbison's is an "operatic" interpretation of the idiom. This is because of his range, his drama, his fastidious control, his fierce melodic discipline, his taste for a mountainous climax . . . Fair enough. He is operatic by comparison to Jerry Lee Lewis. But what he does isn't opera, nor is it operatic in intent or outlook, and the word should not be used to mist over the fundamental truth, nor glorify it. Orbison's idiom is rock-'n'-roll-derived pop music, pure and exquisite, with all that this implies to do with the dynamic capture of compressed moments of feeling in real time. He is interested in distillations; in intense doses of ordinary emotion expressed with proportionate physical energy; moments that do not develop, embroider, and expand on those emotions so much as drill into them to hold them steady, keep them where we can see them. Orbison uses big-sounding methods to achieve small-scale but concentrated results.

The "candy-colored clown they call the sandman" of "In Dreams" might be a benign figure in American children's lore, but clowns are frightening, whatever their hue, especially when they visit teenage bedrooms after dark. In "In Dreams," the clown is introduced in offhand, perfunctory style, like a friend of a friend concealing something about his person you might be tempted by . . . and he stands inside the room—perhaps half hidden in the shadow behind the door—inviting the listener into a world of unending sleep: the only place where happiness can be found, or so he seems to be indicating with his clown's moue of exaggerated empathy, half hidden, half visible in the gloom—rock's first encounter with Mephistopheles, the Big O its first Faustus juggling with his offer of eternity . . . This isn't a wrong-shoes-for-my-outfit issue, boys and girls; it's rather bigger than that.

And then Orbison qualifies that offer with his sad trumpet. The bridging passage where he makes his penultimate lift on to a suspension over the circulating chords of C, F and G7—"It's too ba-a-ad that a-a-all these things can only / Ha-a-appen i-i-in my dreams" (not quite the zenith of his arc, but close)—is one of the most thrilling passages in all 1960s pop. It only lasts four bars but in that time the universe seems to gape naked, as the night sky must do over Wink. Roy is taking up the clown's offer and he is in rapture. *Yes. Why don't I?* In that four-bar moment, you know what it is to feel the intimate exhilaration of vulnerability.

I was only two when "In Dreams" made its modest inroad into the UK top ten in 1963, and so I have no memory of it from its own time. But a decade on from that moment, when the record was played occasionally and wholly frivolously on British radio as a rubber-stamped Golden Oldie, I was old enough to get the picture in all its eye-popping wonderment. The scale of the imagery was not unlike one of those Hubble images of a birthing star, exploding into existence so far back in time that no one who has ever lived can remember the day, and yet also minutely fine in its resolution. The voice seemed to extend forever into the infinity of space, both vast and tiny. Big and small, big and small. The stuff of hallucination. And I quite clearly recall thinking as far back in time as 1972 that this man's voice was not like anything I'd ever heard before. It really is both vast and tiny. It's not like an opera singer's, and it's not like a rock 'n' roll crooner's; it's not like an MOR balladeer's, and it's not at all like the singing of the ultra-modern rock singers I like now, such as Dan McCafferty and Mick Jagger. And it's really not like anyone in my family.

It is like itself and none other. And it makes feeling infinitely small and damageable into a really, really big deal—like the biggest deal you can think of.

* * *

The American philosopher Cornel West has described the blues as "personal catastrophe elegantly expressed." He might have been describing the latter stages of the creative career of dear old Marvin Gaye, whose life, according to the biographers, was an intractable mess of narcissism and quasi-Oedipal compulsion from the beginning, later compounded by untimely bereavement, career misjudgment, cocaine, and the sort of rampant professional insecurity that might have daunted a lesser ego terminally. Where Gaye's music is concerned, there is no stoic resolution written into its depths, nor release into animal joy. And certainly no escape. There is only the unending agony of vulnerability and suffering, beautified.

This "agony" should not be confused with the aestheticized suffering beloved of the Gothic imagination, in which uneasy feeling is abstracted, darkened, and weighted by the artist's ability to make gloomy and/or scary things sexy. Nor does it correspond with the cold reporting eye with which the grim realist habitually rakes the world. Gaye does not rake the world, his own or ours—it is not in his nature. He does not beautify bad feeling to make it (and him) worthy of your attention. Not exactly. He does not want to describe agony, or anatomize it. His vulnerability is not dramatized, or exhibited *in vitro* as an object of special value to the curious. His operation is rather more nuanced and purposive than that. What he does is make an offering.

Gaye is best understood as a sacramental artist in the Christian tradition, but one whose conviction is subject to doubt. He is an uneasy votary. He grew up in Washington in a fiercely Pentecostal family headed by the pastor Marvin Gaye Sr., who exercised his disciplines physically. Marvin Jr.'s strongest work arises from those things about which he feels intensely (and usually badly)—betrayal, sex, the environment, social injustice, personal commitment, romance, crime, his marriage—and he represents the agony of it all in beautiful terms, as if the act of offering all this transforming beauty will somehow heal those multiple wounds. No attempt is ever made to represent agony agonizingly, or to impose agony upon the listener.

He is no more interested in excruciating his listeners than J. S. Bach is in-terested in meting out actual physical punishment when he spends three hours enacting the Passion of Christ. Because such a gesture could never be effectively votive, or consoling. It would offer nothing worth having *instead*.

I have on my office wall a reproduction of the fifteenth-century Flem-ish artist Rogier van der Weyden's *The Descent from the Cross*, an altarpiece painted in the 1430s for the Guild of Crossbowmen in Leuven. It has fol-lowed me around for years in one format or another, since I was a small boy, when I was first unconsciously struck by its weird tensions.

This strangely claustrophobic image depicts the moment when the form of the expired Jesus, sheet-white and near-weightless, his feet still nailed together, is gently lowered from the cross, hand over hand through a tunnel of opulent fabric, and entered into the embrace of his mourners—as well-heeled a knot of late-medieval Flemish burghers as ever wore ermines and silks.

Formally, the image is all about crossbows (the shapes configured by the cadaver, the hand-wringing Magdalene and the insensible Virgin all echo the shape of a crossbow in various states of tension). Thematically, it is about grief. But psychologically, *The Descent* is entirely concerned with the confinement of intense feeling into a box, a box that contains and then transforms grief into beauty. That the containment is "impossible"—the ten figures are rammed into a shallow, gilded embrasure with the use of false perspectives to fool the eye—only ramps up the intensity of the emotion, which is conveyed realistically by the faces of the mourners and theatrically in the weave of their gestures. There is literally no room for anything on this tiny, shallow stage other than the swirl of revealed emotion, itself rein-forced visually by the linear swirls of the composition. In other words, the intense feeling is not negated by the spatial artificiality and the "impossible" confinement: it is concentrated by it, into an overwhelmingly intense dis-tillation or essence. All the better, you'd think, for the making of offerings.

So it was with Marvin Gaye's canon, and never more so than in the spellbinding error of taste and judgment that was his 1978 "divorce album," *Here, My Dear.*

It remains the strangest album deal ever struck, as well as one of the more peculiar divorce settlements. That settlement's terms stipulated that Motown's slightly faded and reliably unreliable leading man—at that point wholly displaced as the label's banker star by Stevie Wonder—would remit to his estranged wife Anna Gordy the label's $300,000 advance against the new album plus the first $300,000 it would inevitably turn in profit. Presumably, Anna figured that a nailed-on six hundred grand, proceeding directly from the one thing Marvin might be relied upon to deliver, amounted to a better bet than a million in cash on an airy promise.

What followed was even weirder.

Let us put ourselves in Marvin's shoes. Faced with such an imperative, most of us might well quail, dig our heels in, utter a few resentful oaths, and then knock out a routine piece of work in double-quick time, fulfilling the letter of the contract but no more—not least because the stark reality of the situation was, in this case, that there would be no meaningful financial reward accruing for whatever work was done, even if the thing did sell by the hatful.

Not Marvin. Marvin decided that the righteous thing to do was to use the opportunity to write a poison-pen missive in musical form to punish the ex-missus in public for the sheer effrontery of making him somersault through legal hoops over the finer points of the divorce—and presumably for the impertinence of wanting out in the first place. He would justify himself with the indignant thought that Anna was denying him access to their child. The album he would make would give a summary account of the breakdown of the marriage calculated to cause maximum hurt to Anna and embarrassment to her brother Berry, who was nothing if not entangled in the greater complexity of the situation, both emotionally and financially. Marv got down to work in 1977.

His biographer, David Ritz, was an astute observer of the Marvin method, and his take on the transformation that took place as the singer immersed himself in the project rings true. "In the course of creating this ode of rebuttal and revenge," he wrote for the most recent reissue of *Here, My Dear*, "something very different happened. Art overwhelmed anger, and healing, the by-product of courageous introspection, was miraculously achieved." Which is another way of saying that what came out at the end didn't exactly match up with what went in at the beginning.

Here's Marvin himself: "I figured I'd just do a quickie record ... Why should I break my neck when Anna was going to wind up with the money anyway? But the more I lived with [it], the more it fascinated me. Besides I owed the public my best effort. Finally, I did the record out of deep passion. It had become a deep compulsion. I had to free myself of Anna and I saw this as the way ... So I had [the engineer] open up the mics—I sang until I drained myself of everything I'd lived through."

Here, My Dear is as self-pitying and self-serving a work of art as can be imagined. It is inconsistent in its perspectives, indulgent of its maker's religious sentimentalism, deluded in its prospectus of what a marriage can be. Some of it is juvenile. Much of it is coldly bitter. It is saved from being pusillanimous only by the determination of the wounded Marvin to be as big-hearted as he could bring himself to be in the circumstances, and by the courage he exhibited—perhaps unwittingly—in revealing his own weakness of mind. The album is one long baroque non sequitur, as full of self-loathing as it is of befuddlement, as smirkingly patronizing as it is revealing of its author's own self-knowledge deficit. It is also fantastically lovely.

Formally, *Here, My Dear* represents a kind of apotheosis of the gospel-soul tradition, in which sophisticated, toweringly elaborate vocal harmony stands for the outreach of the human spirit in the general direction of the ineffable. This is Swan Silvertones and Soul Stirrers territory but transposed to a new location, in which the fan vaults and flying buttresses of quintet gospel are put to the service of a less than heavenly project: the secular realm of Marvin Gaye's muddled psyche. Instead of the ineffable, the one-man vocal quintet of *Here, My Dear* is reaching for the guts of an emotional experience, subdividing itself endlessly and unanalytically, as if the subdividing were itself part of the process of offering and avowing, as if the breaking down of self into its constituent voices were the point of the exercise: the essence of life, even. The album is an exquisitely laid description of emotional fragmentation.

And what began as a vengeful act became in the end, in its creator's mind at least, a votive act of self-mortification and prayer—an act of rescue. What really drives *Here, My Dear* is not a weak man's need to get even but his need to feel better. All that stacked-up, improvised, lambent beauty—all those trailing sad voices—do ultimately say something worth hearing. They say: I may be many things of little or no value to you, or to anyone else for that matter, but at least I can do *this*. This is *precisely* how vulnerable I am—and if you listen hard you may find yourself making a breathless new contract with the scope of your own vulnerability.

GRACE NOTES

ARETHA FRANKLIN: "OH ME OH MY (I'M A FOOL FOR YOU, BABY)"
Atlantic Records, 1972

There exists marvelous film footage of Aretha Franklin listening to play-backs in the studio in the late 1960s—a few seconds of it are often deployed in documentaries about the history of soul music, montage style, for texture and to insulate against charges of inauthenticity. The filming was proba-bly done at Atlantic's New York studios, rather than at FAME, in Muscle Shoals, Alabama, but you can see the Muscle Shoals Rhythm Section there, behind their instruments, and producer Jerry Wexler, behind the glass. The color is rich, the lighting naturalistic, the texture grainy. The scene is not staged. Aretha stalks the floor in a smart white shirt, under the gables of her 'do, one arm crossed under her breasts, the other held straight up from the elbow, supporting a cigarette in two fingers like an antenna, tuned in, her head down, face frowning. Sometimes you get her in profile, revealing the curve of her beautiful Egyptian nose. It is an image of the gravest concen-tration you can imagine. She looks invulnerable.

Franklin is as adamantine in the history of black American music as Duke Ellington, Miles Davis, and James Brown. She is a fundamental. A big boulder. If they ever get round to carving an African American music Rushmore, she'll be up there for keeps, in all weathers, her nose throwing out rain like a flume. She has earned her formal title, the Queen of Soul, and will never have to face a succession crisis.

Her status is unyielding in part because of her deep association with the Baptist church and its driving role in the civil rights movement of the 1960s—the kind of respectability that can only be earned by doing hard, hard yards. She is famously agoraphobic and certainly did not network her way to reginal glory. Also, Franklin has endured her fair share of personal agony, of both the romantic and the parental kind. Hers has been a life every bit as emotionally fraught as materially successful and, even now, she cuts a remote, troubled, slightly forbidding figure in her gathering age. But of course the chief reason her status is so high is simple: it is because of her voice, which has come to stand as a sort of sonic archetype of the soul of African American aspiration. It has shape, trajectory, and reach. It arcs over the lively waters of the 1960s/70s popular- and countercultures like a great bridge.

This is remarkable, given that it isn't a particularly beautiful voice. There have been richer, warmer, funkier, beefier, subtler, smoother, coarser, sexier, kinder, and more intimate voices in R&B. There have also been more elegant ones, and voices that suggest deeper tracts of worldly experience as well as gospel intensity and emotional sophistication. But so what? Pure aesthetics and facile characterization are barely relevant to this calculation and, besides, no voice in any musical style has ever cleaved as closely to the spirit of ecstasy and its close associate, rapture (plus all the bits that break off ecstasy and rapture and fall away to collect in little regretful heaps). This was a voice born to sing both of God's love and of human love, as if the two were somehow connected.

Back to old footage . . .

Film of Franklin doing it during her great period between 1967 and 1973 is fairly rare and usually delicious, provided she's switched on. Hers is also one of the most watchable voices ever. She is a vivid singer, who, when she's fully committed to what she's doing, lives the song from the inside out, in a way that really does reach out to meet the eye. She is never less than serious, even when miming. In most cases, you could probably get a perfectly viable reading of the undercurrents of whatever song she happens to be singing just from watching her sing it with the sound down. She doesn't semaphore the contents of a song or dramatize it or embroider it; she simply lives inside it and gives you the option to get in there with her.

It's worth pointing out, in that case, that what we get to observe, when we do our looking, is actually a repertory of involuntary physiological presentations—meta-articulations, if you like—which suggest by their very nature that what we are hearing when we listen is a form of existential "turning out." Aretha sounds like soul but she looks like it, too. She is all involvement, completely whole in her singing; graphic but not histrionic, minutely articulate at a level of phraseological detail that serves to create the illusion that time is both elastic and, when occasion demands, static (I'm thinking here of some of her live gospel recordings which hold the moment with withering aplomb). As a result, it is extremely hard for the listener not to become equivalently involved, and to be led down exciting paths.

Here's a short list of her more obvious physical mannerisms. There's the tipping back of her head and the pushing up of her shoulders while pinging top notes; the raising of her eyes to heaven perhaps in the hope of catching, as she sings, a momentary glimpse of the path to transcendence; not forgetting, in more considered moments, the knitting of brows and the opening of hands, in a gesture of welcome; and, most compelling of all, the curious compression and popping forward of her entire facial mask while she locks on and then holds fast to an extended cadential phrase, as if every last fraction of an inch of Aretha, right to the tips of her nose and lips and eyelashes, is being pinched, pushed, squished, and squeezed into the act of going all the way, to wring out the last drops. It is a miraculous and beautiful sight.

Most of these presentations will have arisen as a simple by-product of her schooling at the New Bethel Baptist Church of her father, where the young Aretha first copped her chops and learned to display a resolved humility in front of a grown-up congregation; all the better, you'd think, to facilitate her tuning in to higher impulses. The gospel method does not permit self-conscious showing off, nor preening.

Yet all of what comes naturally to Aretha in church transposes to the secular music world with a kind of magicalized authenticity, and no loss of crunch for making the journey. Indeed that transposability is the key to her appeal. She brings the otherworldly intensity of the Pentecostal church to bear on secular concerns and, without dissipating the impact of all that holy wallop, makes it palatable. She never seems pious, nor sanctimonious. She doesn't come across as prim. Her gravity and physical restraint—even when uncomfortably trussed in a tiny metallic 1960s minidress—always get the better of any impulse she might feel to put it about a bit for the cameras. She is queenly but human in her dignity.

Which is perhaps partly why, when she manifests it, Franklin's vulnerability is so subtly compelling. It is veiled by her dignity and fierce physical involvement and so you, the listener, are always taken by surprise to feel your own vulnerabilities so stirred by her. Aretha's vulnerability is unexpected, but not as much as yours.

Her first Atlantic album remains one of the great essays in vulnerable love. It's called *I Never Loved a Man the Way I Love You*, and it was recorded in the aforementioned Muscle Shoals studio and then New York, in 1967, following modest returns on her initial early-sixties Columbia-sponsored pop career.

It is made of simple enough parts: the title track, followed by "Do Right Woman—Do Right Man," "Respect," "Baby Baby Baby," "Don't Let Me Lose This Dream," "Soul Serenade," "Drown in My Own Tears," "Dr. Feelgood" . . . It just goes on and on being what it is: one of the perfect mid-century genre collisions—turbo-powered gospel conviction hitting small-scale romantic R&B-pop midships and not sinking the boat, instead joining forces to create some new kind of hybrid vessel that just . . . well, it just *sails*. I think the record contains some of the most nakedly thrilling singing ever sung.

It is very easy to be misled by the sheer gusto of the thing. It's a loud, bright, muscular, physically close record. The arrangements are pretty much ad hoc but they are also utterly clear. The playing is gusty and limber—as it should be: the Muscle Shoals Rhythm Section were well-fed young men in the prime of life—but it is also exquisitely restrained (there is no blokeish grandstanding permitted in this studio) . . . while at the technical level, *I*

Never Loved a Man is captured to tape brilliantly: the music punches out of the speakers at any volume you choose to play it, and nothing in the sound seems unbalanced or extraneous; there are no loose notes, no unconnected levers.

And so it might seem odd that such a full, uninhibited blast should come with such a delicate subtext attached. But there it is: it does. *I Never Loved a Man* also has a wistful dimension to it, despite all that gusto and all that power. It droops a little; it trails a gossamer dragnet of woe. For such brightly forward-looking music, it also seems somehow to *refer back*. To what? To prior experience? To deeply felt animal doubt? To what? There's nothing in the sound of the music that you could point a finger at, or cut out with a knife. But it's there—hovering wanly in the spaces between the interlocking mechanisms of blatting horn, bass, and dry-popped snare drum. And that thing, that gossamer dragnet, is the key to Aretha Franklin's genius: her vulnerability.

It's always there, in all her best recordings. "(You Make Me Feel Like) A Natural Woman" and "I Say a Little Prayer" are both sterling, declarative records, but they are also performances which balance their carnality and romantic excitement with an awareness of what lies on the flipside of both carnality and romance: the trace of a worry; the fleeting hint of an alternative outcome; the abiding sense that what goes up must come down . . . None of this doubt is expressed overtly—she's probably not consciously aware of it herself—but you the listener sense it and find yourself snared in the doubt, too. It's an agonized form of dramatic irony, in which you fear for outcomes that she's not even hoping you won't have considered. You are half-privy; she might not be. That ambiguity is what makes the recordings so spectacularly vivid.

However, it is not one of the big hits that shakes my soul-ambiguity tree down to the ground, but a B-side: the reverse of the 1971 top-tenner "Rock Steady" and the opening cut on the gorgeous *Young, Gifted and Black* album of the following year—a song so suffused with both joy and vulnerability that even now, more than thirty years after I first heard it and loved it, I still want to cover my face and bite the edges off my fingers whenever I hear it.

"Oh Me Oh My (I'm a Fool For You Baby)" is a funny old song for a gospel-soul diva to be singing in the first place. It belonged then (if it belonged to anyone but its writer Jim Doris) to Lulu, the Glaswegian belter of *Eurovision* and "Shout" repute, who'd recorded it at Muscle Shoals for her 1969 debut on Atlantic's subsidiary label, Atco, and done a pretty good job with it, all things considered. Lulu's version is sturdy and without secondary inflection. Aretha's is nearly all secondary inflection. It begins as so many of her great records do with Franklin's own piano, meandering wistfully with her right hand against flicked percussion and Donny Hathaway's hushed organ chords. Instruments drift in delicately, as if entering the room discreetly on tiptoe, one by one, to make themselves comfortable for the telling of a sweet story for children.

And they're right, both to be delicate and to be whisper-discreet about it, for "Oh Me Oh My" in Aretha's hands amounts to nothing if not the equation of romantic hope with the exercise of make-believe and self-distraction—an entire song devoted to rapture as a form of innocent play. There is no sex in this story.

A ballet is staged on a tabletop, with fingers, the accompanying music a happy emanation from her lover's eyes. Then a genie emerges from blown cigarette smoke to conjure a magic-carpet ride to heaven knows where—but somewhere nice and sparkly with unicorns, probably. And henceforth it's up to "our smokey friend . . . to keep us side by side." "Come on, let your love light shine on me," sings the Queen of Soul, supported by the Sweet Inspirations in the role of heavenly choir. This is a projection of love's excitement so insubstantial in its foundation that fag smoke plays the role of narrative anchor.

Meanwhile, Arif Mardin's strings have entered the room and whisked up a brumous storm, the bass line has begun to plunge up and down like a boat on choppy waters and to conclude, as the vessel pitches and yaws, Aretha's voice disappears into the saturated ether like a seabird's cry.

"Oh me, oh my, I'm a fool for you, baby. Oh me, oh my, I am *craaazy*, baby."

There it is. She's craaazy, baby. She knows it and she fears it, but there is nothing she can do about it but buy into the distracting illusion a little bit more, because it's the buying-in that makes the thing real in the end, isn't it? That's what playing and make-believe is: buying in. Having faith. It's as if romantic love, for Aretha, is actually analogous with the heavenly love we all know is perfect—perfect because ineffable and inevitable. And, although not as inevitable as the heavenly variety, the romantic kind is at least manifest in the world and you kind of know when it's *there*, in the play of eyes and smoke and fingers and the eternally vulnerable emotion of hope that smashes through your nervous system and threatens to burst your heart.

This "Oh Me Oh My" is the love song of a woman who fears that the only one you can really trust with your heart is God, but wants desperately for that not to be the case . . . Because God is everywhere, isn't he? Even in the childish hearts of men. This song says that it is—but you can hear the singer making the effort to suppress her concern that it may not be true.

THE RAMONES: "BEAT ON THE BRAT"
Sire Records, 1976

Sometimes vulnerability manifests in places—and in ways—that you would not entirely expect, or even recognize at first. The Ramones, for instance.

When they lit upon the English ear in the late summer of 1976, the Ramones were all that the new idea of "punk" had to offer in its most concentrated, unrefined form. Belligerence, cogency, brevity, energy—drums, bass, a single chainsaw guitar recorded loud then fiercely compressed, as if contained within a subterranean concrete bunker with meter-thick walls. And driving it all, an apparently mindless muscle-twitch. No time for reflection; no room for emotion . . .

Except that the voice surfing all that noise betrayed vulnerability in a way that even then, in the first amphetamine rush of the nihilistic punk idea, smote the heart.

Joey Ramone's voice was the cry of a fat baby seal stranded limbless on a floating ice shelf, abandoned by its mother. It was the most truly plaintive sound going that year and for many years after it, a sort of reproachful bark shading into a wail and a gulp. The brat being beaten in the song might have been another individual for the purposes of the group narrative but, in the head of the listener, it was all Joey.

The Ramones were the sound of bullying, from the point of view of the bullied.

MARY MARGARET O'HARA: "BODY'S IN TROUBLE"
Virgin Records, 1988

I saw Mary Margaret O'Hara sing three times in front of an audience. I saw her in a small club in Toronto, in a small West End theater in London, and then finally, and heartbreakingly, at Hammersmith Odeon in 1992. I never saw her again after that because she ceased to do her own stuff in front of live people—in the UK at least.

"Body's in Trouble" was the song that always moved me the most, whether as a single release or in the context of her one and only album *Miss America*, or as a live performance. The recorded version is amazing.

It's a slow waltz. Slow as in chained up. Guitar, violin, bass, and drums negotiate a path through the song and give it shape at the same time—brilliantly economical playing at an almost unplayably static tempo. Meanwhile, in the fissures between the instrumental parts, the strange perforated ululation that is Mary Margaret's singing voice bobs and weaves, twists and lurches, hooks, snatches, and grabs at the melody, such as it is, as if trying to peg up heavy sheets in a howling gale and the washing line's too loose, won't hang still, and the sheets keep snapping in her face and snagging round her body and being snatched from her grasp and heaven only knows what next . . .

The song is about how the body will not always conform in its actions to those actions which are desired by the mind, sometimes leading the mind or even deserting it; a song not only about inhibition but about involuntary action and physical disarticulation. It's about falling through the cracks and things not being squared up and the desire for everything, dammit, just to *hold still*.

Yet it is also about the joy of nothing holding still and the wonder of all that disarticulation and cognitive dissonance. It's an extraordinarily simple song about a problematic way of being and it is hauntingly lovely, provided you are not disturbed by its fundamental gesture, which is to admit vulnerability as a galvanizing creative force.

Mary Margaret frequently doesn't finish sentences and even words, either in conversation or in song. Her words get split up and subdivided and sometimes disarranged. Sometimes you only get the first syllable. Sometimes the middle one. This is partly because she has a very fast-moving mind, but also, I suspect, because she has limited trust in what language can do for her. And so she presents as an extremely vulnerable individual who is always on the hop, one jump away from full flight.

The third time I saw her, at Hammersmith Odeon in that summer of 1992, things would not square up for her at all, nor hold still. She couldn't get her strange, rabbity, hippety-hoppety sense of rhythm to mesh with what her band were doing; she couldn't get her voice out at all, as far as could be told—she'd start songs and not finish them, and sometimes she couldn't even start them. It was lurch after crash after stumble. I have no recollection of whether or not she did "Body's . . ." but I imagine she did, in some disintegrated form.

At all events, after an uncomfortably long period of lurching and crashing, some bright and doubtless well-intentioned spark in the dress circle yelled "Come *on*, Mary—get it *together!*" And that was that. Within minutes she was gone, with a flap of her hand and a shake of her beehive, probably tripping over her feet as she flumped into the wings, distraught. Her body in trouble.

Get it together? Someone was missing the point, I think.

And she hasn't been back since, except in a supporting role, where another body has to shoulder the burden of scrutiny. But for a while, her vulnerability was the most thrilling thing out there. Thrilling not in and of itself, but in the way she used it to make things happen, and then rejoiced in it, as if vulnerability were the most human quality of them all.

4

Class Acts

I am at the counter of the local hardware store with my daughter.

"A bag of nails, please," I say, confidently, shifting my gaze over the racks and drawers of metal things. "Short ones, if you've got them. But it doesn't matter if you haven't. Any old size will do, really, as long as they're not too long. And they're pointy." I feel it is sensible always to share the full range of one's technical expertise with tradesmen, because they will only respect you for it.

The proprietor turns away and begins to rummage behind the counter. I feel a nudging in my ribs. It is my daughter.

"Arsenal," she whispers.

"Oh, give over, B," I mutter, trying not to sound irritated.

I buy the nails, which look ideal for the job I have in mind. Then, as we walk back to the house, I remember that we are short of milk and bread and so we stop off at the grocer's. The grocer is a man of few words, so we execute the transaction without unnecessary discussion—he says nothing as he pours change into my open palm, coin by coin, as if begrudging every copper penny. I squeeze out a gracious "thank you" and we move on.

"Double Arsenal," says B.

"Rubbish," I splutter, indignantly, once we are out in the street. Really quite crossly, actually. "Complete and utter nonsense. That was a completely

Arsenal-less moment—there was literally no Arsenal in it. I said "Thank you" and that was all. Two syllables. How can that be Arsenal?"

"You didn't say "Thank you," Dad. You said "'ank yew'—and don't pretend that you didn't. It was a Double Arsenal and you know it."

"Darling, that is utter—"

"No, no—" she's holding up her hand now—she can be really quite forceful when there are points to be scored. "No. It was a Double Arsenal, and that's my last word on the matter. End of." She fixes me with her best screw-face and dips her head. "You feel me?"

I harbor fears that she will grow up to be a lawyer or a gangster or possibly both, because as usual she has a point. She caught me at it again—"doing an Arsenal," which is short for "doing an Arsenal voice": her way of calling me out on the slight plasticity that modulates my utterances every day of our life in London, depending on social context, mood, and location. She is accusing me of fraud.

But I have "done an Arsenal" every day of my life since I was wee and cannot change. I see no reason to change, because it is just the way I am and have always been. Besides, I wouldn't *know* how to change. You see, my voice seems to fit itself, automatically and without any conscious bidding, to my surroundings. I have no way of stopping it from doing so. It just happens, as it has always done.

It's called doing an Arsenal because the wretched girl initially clocked it as an epiphenomenon when I first took her to watch football matches at Highbury when she was but a tot. And even then it was not as if she hadn't had the opportunity to observe it before. But perhaps my Arsenal voice was more, as it were, pronounced at the football; perhaps I spoke louder or more uninhibitedly at Highbury, or maybe it was my participation in the general atmosphere of unbridled coarseness—she loved football swearing from the off—that made something snag in her steel trap of a mind: a drawn-out vowel here, a dropped consonant there; the deepening and roughing up of my usually dulcet middle-class baritone into something else. Well, kind of else.

Fair cop. (In fact, good girl! Keep up the close observation, rigorous social criticism, belligerent bullshit-detection and so on—it will serve you well in life, *if* deployed with tact.) But I do insist that the voice she noticed on that occasion wasn't all that different to the one I use to speak to her grandma, say, or the Queen, when she comes round for tea. The fact is, I don't do a football "accent" at football matches. I don't talk all cock-er-ney in the pie shop. I don't adopt a whole new persona to echo my surroundings. My voice just changes ever so fractionally. It modulates into something a little less conspicuous. It tucks in. Essentially, I continue to talk in my usual domestic voice but with it switched to a slightly different mode, as if adjusting tones on an amplifier. It's still my source signal, my voice; not something I import or download for the occasion; it's not an effect. It's not something I *put on*. It's still me talking in *my* voice. I am certainly not imitating anybody else. No, I am sewing myself into the fabric.

What I am trying to describe here is something subtler and more abstract than "accent"; something to do with the tiniest differentials of intonation, amplitude, rhythm, attack, timbre, texture, vowel-stretch, consonant-squish, and throat-gurgle. Something to do with the plasticity of my very identity. For identity is right at the center of this, historically as well as psychologically. You see, I was first mocked, and even thumped, for sounding "like a snob" (i.e., middle class) at Infant School in 1966—which was of course the point at which I began to sound less middle class and learned to adapt my voice, automatically and without thinking about it, to fit with the prevailing tonality of whatever environment I happened to be in. 1966. That was fifty years ago. It's a long habit.

So, yes, sadly, I have reluctantly to admit that my daughter has a point, technically. My voice does seem to modulate a little according to context, when I can be bothered to notice, which isn't that often at all. On those occasions it is possible to observe myself saying "'ank yew" in shops, and hear my vowels lengthen and my consonants blur in situations where I don't want to be mistaken for a "privileged" middle-class wanker-insurgent.

As a result of this, a very large part of me wants me to hang my head in shame. Oh yes. I pride myself on my personal integrity—call it "authenticity," call it "honesty," call it "psychological correctness" if you really want—and it is not an idle or narcissistic pride. I believe that it is important to be true, wherever possible, to your sense of self. You will not catch me, ever, pretending to be other than what I am, which is a middle-class London family man with a decent arts degree from a respectable red-brick university and parents who worked in academic libraries and publishing.

But another part of me bridles at the crypto-snobby priggishness of the first part. This second part says, don't be pathetic—what is there to be ashamed of? So you adapt yourself to fit inconspicuously into your environment . . . So what? Are you trying to deceive others or misrepresent yourself when you do this? Do your minutely flattened vowels stand as an attempt to manipulate people and events to your own ends, to pull wool over eyes or to lie, dissemble, and ensnare? Or are they evidence of a subconscious desire to make sure your environment does not react to you with hostility (as, I may add, you yourself take exception to the uninhibited braying/drawling of public-school gobshites in public spaces)?

Hmm?

It's a tricky one. The human voice is nothing if not a gaping wound. Often it seems to me that there is no quicker way to get turned over than to open your mouth.

* * *

At the beginning of the 1960s, the surest way to have a hit pop record in the UK was to sing like an American.

Actually, that's not quite right. Let me rephrase.

The likeliest way to have a hit in the UK was to sing with an American accent and with vaguely American phrasing. Everyone did it as a matter of course. And why not? Pop music was American, as Flanders and Swann were British. That was the pleasure of it. Pop's very American-ness meant that, above all things, it was not English, and that very non-Englishness formed a significant aspect of its appeal: the warm, energetic, unthrottled voices of Americans did not sound remotely like Flanders and Swann or, for that matter, like any other of the many iterations of postwar received-English

poshness then available as an example to young English boys and girls. Indeed, you might hear in pop's New-Worldy vowels and bright, unrestrained
vulgarity a rejection of all that was stuffy, austere, class-bound, and self-
consciously proper. Or cartoonishly cockney. Or gauchely "northern." Or
chippily "Scottish" or "Welsh." The American pop singing voice was beyond
region and beyond class. Just for starters, you might hear in it blackness and
energy and irreverence and closeness; even real intimacy, shading into the
warmth of proximate lust, which you could never get from English voices.
Not from Tommy Steele's, at any rate, or Cliff Richard's. Put the Marvelettes' "Please Mr. Postman" on your Dansette in late 1961, if you were hip
enough to actually own a copy, and you might hear the voices of young,
black, sassy, independent, uninhibited, classless, excited but self-possessed
individuals who sounded not like accomplished musicians cleaving to the
regulations of their time-honored art but like real people having fun, now.

John Lennon may or may not have been the first Englishman to sing
American-derived pop music with an English regional accent, but he was
certainly the first Englishman to do it as if he meant it and it was a serious
business: as if he was not doing a parody and the music was absolutely indivisible from his selfhood, like his flesh and bone—as if he *lived* it. We can
only wonder now whether Lennon was aware at the time, when he began
having hits with the Beatles in late 1962, of the gravity of his situation.

For here is the most important thing about John Lennon's singing. His
voice was free in a way that he, the individual, felt that he was not. That fact
must have disturbed him almost as much as it thrilled him.

Lennon's life story, to that fission point in 1962, was not a happy one.
As is well documented, he was brought up by an aunt in lower-middle-class
suburban purdah in Liverpool following the collapse of his parents' relationship when he was but a tot. At the age of six he was required to choose
between an unreliable but charismatic mother and a seafaring father, and
he failed in that instant to be decisive (which is six year olds all over, isn't
it just?)—hence John's subsequent removal to his Aunt Mimi's would-be
bourgeois fastness on the edge of the countryside. His dad then disappeared
completely from his life, while Aunt Mimi's husband, the benignly encour-

aging Uncle George, died when Lennon was a young teenager—followed shortly afterward by Lennon's beloved if wayward mother, Julia, killed in a road accident. By the age of eighteen, young John was an unreliable, sardonic, vulnerable, cynical, shortsighted, jealous, gurning, would-be hardcase with a soft underbelly and not much serviceable armor on top. He had, however, developed a purist's feel for rock 'n' roll and its English derivative, skiffle, thereby fortifying himself with thick coatings of the brand new sound of invulnerability. He was determined that no one was ever going to hurt him again.

And if all he'd ever done of worth in a studio with the Beatles was to record an end-of-session cover of the Isley Brothers' hit "Twist and Shout," as filler for the group's first album, he'd still be regarded as the greatest rock singer ever to be English. He'd be a cult figure. Literally dozens of people would employ hushed tones to mutter his name at conventions. A wizened Lennon himself might emerge periodically from behind the pumps of his Bootle hostelry to appear on sixties nostalgia tours with the surviving members of the Swinging Blue Jeans.

"Twist and Shout" was startling. The Beatles were by then a barely-off-the-road, new-in-the-studio unit of rowdy crowd-pleasers with a reputation to make—sufficiently tuned-in among themselves to be able to knock out a high-energy performance in a spare half hour of studio time at the end of a long day, but also still awed enough by the Abbey Road environment, its ghost army of white-coated engineers and their twitching needles, to want to oblige their producer George Martin and his thoughtful procedures, even when knackered. To which good-natured end, the band bomp through the instrumental backing of "Twist and Shout" like true entertainers, playing vividly, broadly, confidently (you can tell they're not doing the song for anything like the first time), pushing hard at the expressive limits of what can be achieved with a small ensemble recording three-chord R&B live to tape in an early-sixties British studio. It is by a distance the most energizing bit of pure playing on the Beatles' first LP.

But good as the playing is from the "feel" point of view—the music contrives somehow to both bounce and swing, as if the group are trying to elasticate the song's four-square arrangement—it's the singing that takes "Twist and Shout" over the top into new-thrills territory.

Picture the scene. It was the end of the working day, past 10 p.m. The ghosts in their white coats were looking at their watches. The group was pooped and Lennon's voice shot, the vapor of their collective sweat still souring the air. Nevertheless, at Martin's behest, they resolved to make the most of the minutes and seconds remaining to them and agreed to knock out one more number from their Reeperbahn-honed live repertoire. It is said that Lennon drank warm milk to soothe his throat and then removed his shirt to max out on his inner animal. He then virtually tore his larynx from its moorings, bellowing at his imagined "twisty little girl," that she should shake it up, twist, shout, and work it on out, right now, and all for his personal benefit. *Right* now. It was as if she, the twisty little girl, were some recalcitrant alloy and he a blowtorch. And as the song progressed, the singer's bent notes flattened and flattened until the melodic curve existed barely as a curve at all, but as some sort of torn-up straight line. By the end it was all one note—and hardly recognizable as a note at that. The up and down steps of the tune had devolved into the sound of torsion: a twisting, ripping, tearing laryngeal spasm . . . And then finally, when no breath remained to push out with any more force, refuge was taken with the other fellows in a wobbly but successfully stacked three-voice vocal arpeggio up the ladder of the dominant-seventh chord.

And end.

"Yay!" yells someone, off-mic.

* * *

The first pop record I ever owned was bought for me by my parents in 1964, for reasons that are semi-mysterious given that my parents professed not to like pop music. I was four. It was an EP containing four songs. It came dressed in more or less the same livery as the *With the Beatles* long-player, the four members of the group photographed on the front in ordered chiaroscuro splendor. The songs were extracted (with one slight variation in take) from the group's first two Parlophone albums: "All My Loving," "Ask Me Why," "P.S. I Love You," and "Money." They constituted the first music I ever owned—which is to say, the first music I ever considered mine to do with as I please. I consider myself fortunate indeed that this was my first material brush with pop.

It didn't thrill me, of course. I'd already been scared by the Rolling Stones on television and knew the difference between being thrilled and pleasantly entertained. But the *All My Loving* EP did compel attention. It entertained well. Most especially, I was struck by how two of the four songs differed from the other two in one very particular but hard-to-think-about way.

Of the four, "All My Loving" and "P.S. I Love You" were clearly sung by one singer and "Ask Me Why" and "Money" by another. One voice was soft, cottony, felted even, melodious, open-throated, warm, radiant, friendly, outreaching, solicitous. Lovely. The other was narrower, slightly nasal, appraising rather than embracing, less reliable-sounding, and much, much less friendly. The first voice sounded accomplished, as if tutored; the other was an untutored emission, an emission freighted with what we would now call "attitude." You might say, with sophisticated hindsight, that the difference between the two was one of cultivation, but I didn't think like that when I was four. All I knew was that one voice got my attention in detail and the other didn't, and that was all.

Paul McCartney has a lovely voice indeed. It's sweetly flexible in a way that very few true rock 'n' rollers' voices are (perhaps, of McCartney's rocking elders, only Elvis, Orbison, and Charlie Rich can claim to have more naturally euphonious pipes). He can rip it up like Little Richard or he can slick it up like Rick Nelson and do both with equal aplomb. Equal conviction, too. But on the *All My Loving* EP, McCartney occupied space somewhere in between the two: his voice was bland with conviction. "P.S. I Love You" and "All My Loving" offer a sort of chirpy yet soft-shoed exercise in period pop ingratiation. Both songs are sweetly sung. Both are addressed earnestly to "you" and Paul sings them warmly and humorously. You'd like him, you really would—he probably gives great cuddles, especially to your mum.

"Ask Me Why" and "Money (That's What I Want)" do not offer cuddles. The latter was plain nasty, in a jokey, chippy, bitterly deprecating way. The ripping sound of bad faith. The former was described by the great Beatles analyst Ian MacDonald as "the first of Lennon's exercises in the style of Smokey Robinson," which is a stylistic observation only, telling us nothing of what lies behind the style. Yes, formally, "Ask Me Why" is a sort of earnestly loping Latin-soul ballad evoking the brittleness and muddle—not to mention the insatiable gaucheness—of young love in all its ferment. It's a slight piece in most ways. MacDonald is sniffy about the arrangement and its "fumbling" ironies, and he is right to be. But at the time, in 1964 and, for that matter, throughout the rest of the decade, I wasn't listening to the arrangement. I was busy soaking up the voice. I was busy enjoying being invaded by the uncertain, wounded, slightly cranky feeling that is etched like dirt into its grain: it seemed to be expressing the idea that being in love is a reason to feel sad. No, not just sad: pissed off. In "Ask Me Why," the sardonic would-be hard-nut dispenses with the armored impersonality of the rock 'n' roll scream and animates, quietly and not at all confidently, the beginnings of a singing voice with content, a voice capable of expressing feelings which contradict each other—a *true* voice. You can actually hear Lennon thinking about what he's singing and how it makes him feel to sing like that. The performance isn't ingratiating. It is not an exercise in pleasure-giving. In fact it sounds rather less like a performance than the simple expediency of a man finding out, for himself, where his heart isn't.

Lennon's heart was all over the place, of course. He was not, by most accounts, a very considerate young man. Charming, yes; funny, intelligent, principled, charismatic, talented, and all. But also, when the feelings took him (and they appear to have taken him quite often), churlish, bullying, unkind, competitive, spiteful, and wildly, aggressively jealous. Given his childhood, it doesn't take a great leap of deductive imagination to see why that might have been, nor is it a stretch to figure that the newly minted social unit of the pop group might be an appealing one in which to, as it were, explore that emotional landscape. The exclusively masculine group environment, governed as it is by role-play, competition, and masking insincerity, provides plenty of opportunity to try things on for size; to just, as the idiom has it, try things on.

Throughout his career you can hear Lennon trying things on virtually every time he opens his mouth to sing. He does it with passion, ferocity, tenderness, levity, even kindness sometimes. ("Nowhere Man" contains some of the kindest singing I know—and it is reasonable, I think, to suggest that the object of that kindness is Lennon himself, who wrote the song in a blizzard of intractable mid-twenties depression.) His voice is always free of inhibition and obedience—or it at least sounds that way. Over the course of more than a decade, he lays out a moment-by-moment account of his selfhood that comes over as relentlessly authentic and hard to bear at times, not least because it comes in so many pieces. Sometimes it barely makes sense. Often it is contradicting prior iterations of itself.

Sometimes the pathos is in the slide between voices. The distances traveled can be tiny or epic. For every "Twist and Shout," there's an "Ask Me Why." For every "I'm a Loser," a "Nowhere Man." For every "Being for the Benefit of Mr. Kite," a "Mother." For every "Strawberry Fields Forever," a "Working Class Hero." For every "I Feel Fine," a "Revolution #1." I am hoping that you, the reader, can summon to mind the tone of each of these songs and can register within yourself that emotional slide as real feeling. Because these aren't contrasts in style; they're facets of an emotional landscape. Not masks but revelations—of new faces, new feelings, new angles on the tricky experience of being alive. Some of those angles are subtle, others less so. It is one of the more painful listening games you can play, juxtaposing Lennon voices as cruelly as you can. Try it some time. It'll make you feel queasy. How about "This Boy" and "My Mummy's Dead"?

But it will also make you realize, if you were not aware already, that back in his time Lennon's was a new kind of voice. If the primary objective of 1960s American pop vocal style was to offer a representation of a moment's authentic feeling, distilled and fortified and made rock-solidly vivid as an archetype of a recognizable emotion, then Lennon's departure (as was also, more or less simultaneously, Bob Dylan's) was to suggest that that moment's feeling, however psychologically truthful it may be, is always contingent in detail; contingent on who the singer is, where he sits, what he sees of himself in that moment and on all the invidious, terrifying, thrilling possibilities implicit in the way others might be seeing him as he sings.

Lennon expresses this sense of self-conscious contingency like no other, apart from Dylan. Listening to him now is no less gripping an experience than it was at the time, with the singular difference that, at the time, no one had sung like that before—not to us, not of himself, not in that way.

It should perhaps not come as a surprise, then, to learn from one of Lennon's post-Beatles recording engineers that the singer would come to loathe his own voice. He could not bear to hear it relayed back to him dry in his studio headphones, and so he always insisted that the signal in his cans be compressed, distorted, and drenched with reverb to the point of artificiality—otherwise he would find himself simply unable to sing. To be himself sufficiently to sing truthfully, he needed to not sound to himself like himself.

* * *

It seems unlikely that the young Mick Jagger was ever beset by such doubts, nor that he was ever much of a martyr to his own emotional instability. His infancy is not as mythologized as Lennon's but it has never been veiled in secrecy either. There is certainly nothing much to hide. He was born into middle-class suburban sufficiency in Dartford in the Thames Estuary, three years after Lennon, during the latter stages of the war, the son of a PE teacher and a hairdresser. He went to the local grammar school and then the London School of Economics. He was smart and capable and utterly adaptable to his environment, as he would need to be when living in squalor with the nascent Rolling Stones.

But then, if the 1960s was the decade of anything profoundly significant in the UK, it was the decade in which social mobility became fashionable. Pop and rock musicians did the most vivid, in-your-face lobbying on behalf of this transforming new zeitgeist, but footballers also did their bit after the World Cup win, as did television and the movies and fashion and even, in a more rarefied and exclusive way, the art world. Advertising was immeasurably important, too. And in a peculiar inversion, the English Establishment contributed plenty of impetus to the new sense of social and economic liberation by contriving to stay remorselessly out of touch with the times, as if gripped in a rigor of pantomime conservatism. What better mechanism can be imagined to guarantee the attractions of social mobility than the spectacle of those endowed with hereditary power *simply not getting it*?

Yet, in Britain, the new liberty bought by new relative wealth acted as an agent not of social revolution but of intensified social scrutiny, appraisal, and subtle shift. Social mobility meant several things, but most of all—on the ground—it meant "getting a look in." As barriers came down metaphorically, British people took not to the barricades, but to each other's berths in the class system, albeit on a strictly just-visiting, suck-it-and-see basis.

Over the decade—a decade bookended by two Tory prime ministers (Macmillan and Heath), but dominated politically by Labor's Wilson— wealth differentials narrowed significantly and the social classes eyed one another's attributes with new curiosity, shifting their relative footings uneasily but keenly, as far as seemed seemly or groovy or just plain possible in the circs. Toffs got their hands mucky with fashionable scruffs. The middle classes played slippery new status games amongst themselves while ensuring, of course, that they had enhanced access to all other areas at all times (the late-sixties middle-class hippie was ostensibly a committed downward mobilizer). Meanwhile, individuals of working-class origin stormed the citadels of money, culture, and fashion with ladders constructed out of whatever came to hand—which as often as not involved a great new classless music soundtrack as existential support. No, this was not an overturning of the social order—not even close; but subtle and not so subtle shifts were taking place all the time in between the girders of the old structure. What made the 1960s exciting was the thought that the place you began need not necessarily be the place you fetched up.

It might be argued that British pop's primary job was to give voice to this evolving model of social consciousness in all its grabby, evanescent individualism—both the freewheeling, free-enterprising aspect of it all, as well as the existential stuff. And it did so brilliantly. Pop did it by being loud, pithy, and abrasive, for sure, but much more importantly by making its utterances in voices that were articulate in new ways. I don't think that it is too far-fetched to suggest that our society in the 1960s was being re-animated from within by a colloquy of new voices. Certainly, pop voices seemed more real than any others, somehow—more so at least than those of the "proper" singers and crooners of the era—and they sounded free in a way that their owners could not, in all conscience, claim to be in person. In the music of the period you hear voices relaxing as the decade progresses, relaxing and multiplying and spreading out like milk spilt on a pantry floor, seeping into the cracks and creeping under fixtures—and then up them by strange capillary action—until, by the end of the decade, it was as if the British pop voice were a fluid capable of going just about everywhere and saying just about anything, in addition to stinking the place out.

* * *

That self-festooned pirate Keith Richards once described Mick Jagger as "an interesting bunch of guys." It's a memorable phrase because it rings so true. And Richards probably felt entitled to utter the phrase since so much of his own psychic energy is given over to ensuring that he is perceived as rock's greatest singularity. Keith has an awful lot invested in always appearing to be "himself." To be able to do that is one of the signal privileges of rock-star wealth and status.

The original context of Richards' observation about his sometime friend and creative partner's multiple natures is lost to me, but it was probably uttered glibly as a throwaway to a clever journalist probing into the dynamics of one of the late twentieth century's most successful joint enterprises—an enterprise formulated to a large extent on the sardonic-but-sincere assertion of the primacy of individual dread, desire, frustration, anxiety, and appetite over all other conditions in life. This was the enterprise that gave the world "(I Can't Get No) Satisfaction," "Gimme Shelter," "You Can't Always Get What You Want," and "It's Only Rock 'n' Roll (But I Like It)," an enterprise that for a decade at least was consistently self-aware and tonally apposite in its descriptions of the world around it, as well as in its account of itself. And though it is tempting to interpret "an interesting bunch of guys" as a subtle put-down by a singular guy of another guy afflicted with the scourge of multiple personalities, the truth of it is likely to be a lot less schizoid than that. What "an interesting bunch of guys" really means is "an adaptable guy, a smart guy, a slippery guy: a guy you can take just about anywhere." It's an acute description of a guy who would surf the decade of social mobility like a pro.

Nevertheless, from the very beginning, Jagger was faced with an intractable problem: he was simply not gifted by nature with a voice that fitted naturally to the kind of music he wanted to sing. Not one habitué of the Chicago freight yards sounded, as Mick did, as if he grew up in the suburban badlands of the Thames Estuary; no recording on the Chess label featured a holler quite so edgy, shallow, grammar-school-educated and—not to put too fine a point upon it—white. Muddy Waters, Etta James, Howlin' Wolf, Little Walter Jacobs, Sonny Boy Williamson, Jimmy Reed, even that verbose mere "vocalist" Chuck Berry . . . they all carried themselves in their singing voices in ways that the young Michael Philip might only entertain in his dreams.

What was a boy to do? Jagger was clearly too hip by instinct, even in 1963, to be content with merely pastiching the greats of the blues. But at the same time he was in no position to trust to his own chops, let alone the technical sophistication of those who might record them in behind-the-times British studios. It must have been a strange feeling indeed, singing "the blues" in that kind of vacuum—an absolute vacuum, let us not forget: there was at that stage literally no convincing home-made model of blues authenticity available for young white British boys to ape, apart from the real thing as it was imported from the US—but then that was the point. So to begin with, Jagger's voice barely existed at all as a thing in and of itself, as a vessel of quality and reach. He made a sound, all right—a loudish, abrasive, reasonably cutting sound—but it was not a sound that communicated much; it merely filled the space at the front of the band's sound, a sort of sinus-y cipher of teenage energy, lust, and chutzpah. No real blues to it. Barely any man. It is interesting to note, in that light, that the needlesome young Lennon experienced very little difficulty in finding a flexible, authentic-sounding voice for himself almost straight away, whereas the self-confident Jagger has spent decades putting on voices like costumes.

He has often likened the process of singing in a rock band to that of acting. Yes, there are the dressing-up and prancing-around aspects of rock singing which we can all register easily enough as a kind of acting—acting of the showing-off kind, of course, but acting nonetheless. And it's significant, I suppose, that in his heyday Jagger's performances were documented in the media chiefly as a kind of theatrical turn, in which his prancing, costume, and interaction with band and audience were the only real events of interest. Everyone with a typewriter during the 1960s and '70s wanted to describe Jagger the ludic satyr; no one was all that interested in Jagger the singer. And yet the reality is that his voices accounted for an awful lot, once he arrived at them properly and sorted them out and learned how to rig their attributes for maximum impact.

Where to start?

Well, the Stones' first ever record, a cover of the minor Chuck Berry whinge "Come On," is a jumping but throwaway jitter of a performance of less than two minutes' duration, complete with ghastly key change, fitful "black" American accent, plenty of reverb sloshed all over, and what sounds like doubletracking applied to Jagger's comfiest high-baritone range, to lend more presence to what is really a thin streak of sound. He does OK. Even at this early stage, it is quite clearly the same voice that Phil Cornwell would parrot in *Stella Street* thirty years later—a sort of quacky yowl from the inside of a watering can or, if you prefer, in the words of Mick's Stella Street neighbor, Al Pacino, "a bowling ball full of snot": as much a word-rich sound effect as it is a vessel of emotional expression.

And so it went, for as long as the Rolling Stones remained a punky covers band: yards of tearing calico and yelping standing in for the vocal identity of a Thames Delta bluesman, relieved only by the occasional apt impersonation. (In 1964 the Stones covered Don Covay's "Mercy, Mercy" rather nicely, and Mick had the ineffable pleasure of imitating a black singer who already sounded quite like Mick.)

But then songwriting dawned—in particular "(I Can't Get No) Satisfaction"—and an interesting bunch of voices was born.

What makes "Satisfaction" the striking thing that it is—certainly as much as Richards's hooky fuzz riff, Charlie Watts's bouncing on-beat and the Dylanesque parade of colloquial language—is Jagger's abandonment of any pretence at R&B authenticity. "Satisfaction" is quite clearly not an imitation of a man singing from his heart but a performance governed by personal identification with the subject matter in the song. Never mind R&B authenticity; "Satisfaction" has psychological authenticity.

* * *

Jagger's vocal begins as a pseudo-*sotto voce* butter-wouldn't-melt singsong croon, of the kind that bad grammar-school boys use over tea with their parents in the headmaster's office (and Jagger would use again a couple of years later, when debating permissiveness on TV with a bishop and the editor of *The Times*). It then quickly ascends the dynamic scale to a full-bore, open-throated shout of sardonic irritation, a sort of bellowed one-note recitative in which the singer goes through the inventory of his dissatisfaction item by item, room by room: this, that, and the bleedin' other, just one damn thing after another . . . A protracted, plateau-shaped climax following one of the neatest dynamic step-shifts in all pop history. Meanwhile, the rest of the Stones blat away coolly behind him like Booker T's MGs.

The upshot is pop articulacy.

"Satisfaction" was not the first pop record I ever heard but it was certainly the first one that ever excited me out of my wits, way beyond the compass of mere entertainment. It was also the moment in which Jagger's vocal penny dropped. In "Satisfaction" he may have been using elements of black R&B style to get his mojo working, but he was by no means making those elements the point of the exercise; crucially, there was a groundedness to the performance predicated not on the thought "I hope I don't sound too honky," but in the confidence that this was a role he could inhabit with absolute conviction. *Yeah.* I can do that. I can *be* that.

I *am* that.

The result is not so much impressive singing as terrific vocal Method Acting, no doubt partly founded in Jagger's certain knowledge that, if you are not endowed with the kind of vocal timbre that leaks emotion through its very pores, then you have to do some other kind of work to get the song across. You have to become your voice on a case-by-case, role-by-role basis. It should be lost on no one that Otis Redding's cover of "Satisfaction" sounds shallow and lightweight next to the Stones' original—and who among us would dare to claim that Redding's voice didn't positively squirt emotion from its pores?

And so "Satisfaction" became the portal through which Jagger and the Stones passed to become truly articulate. What, given the group's new-found, if reluctant, identity as avatars of the zeitgeist, would happen next?

What happened next was "Get Off of My Cloud," a chunkily buoyant teenage sneer of disdain, followed by "19th Nervous Breakdown," "Paint It Black," "Have You Seen Your Mother, Baby, Standing in the Shadow?" and "Let's Spend the Night Together"/"Ruby Tuesday," which taken together stand as one of the great hit clusters (each of them reached the top spot in the charts, or came close to it, between October 1965 and January 1967). Not one of them is a truly great record in itself, but all of them, moment by moment, add important new tonalities to the sixties Babel, Jagger's curious slack-faced whisper-and-bawl sounding an insolent and/or mordant note at odds with the general warmth of the Swinging London era.

Here were the real voices of a juvenescent New British society, a society bristling with uncontrolled energy, hormonal, bolshy, smart, sardonic, and resolutely prepared to not observe traditional values—the sound of appetite unadorned with an ingratiating smile. In fact it was all too easy to respond to this clamour resistantly, as if it were not a collection of voices belonging to one individual but those of a tribal chorus—a sort of football chant hollered by a tribe of class-amorphous art-school hoodlums with a fetish for America and one rancid eye on your daughter. The songs certainly served the Stones' manager's purpose in positioning the group in that shadowed alley of the parental mind in which terrible nameless things might occur in the name of, well, in the name of *modernity.*

But perhaps the most interesting Rolling Stones records of this period were not the crotchety, rebellious hits but Jagger/Richards' Dylan-inspired attempts at sharp social observation—their little contributions to the sex and class conflicts of the era.

"Mother's Little Helper," "Under My Thumb," "Sittin' on a Fence," "Play with Fire," "Miss Amanda Jones," "Lady Jane" . . . Actually, there were many such gestures on the albums and B-sides of the period, some better than others, many of them proto-psychedelic in tone, some of them pseudo-baroque, few of them owing very much at all to the blues, several of them open to charges of puerile misogyny, all of them acquitting themselves at least nominally as grievous little stabs at the hypocrisies, empty conventions, and vanities of the day. Some of them were unquestionably ugly—there is perhaps no uglier stain on the middle years of pop's 1960s than "Under My Thumb"—but all of them are demonstrations of Jagger's "acting" ability, his capacity for assuming skins. Here was the sound of what's really going on in modern life, sugared only with lashings of youthful sarcasm.

Then, following this bright Anglocentric moment—and following the group's notorious brush in 1967 with the legal arm of the Establishment—other, more exciting things started happening in American music and the authorial gaze turned west once more.

* * *

Music history makes much of the sound of "Jumpin' Jack Flash," as it should. It is a stupendous piece of work, both dynamically and in the way it remade the group's sonic signature. It was, to say the least, a major overhaul: psychedelic frills, crisp tempos, and pop articulacy displaced by hard riffage animated from below with savage rhythm; swamp R&B up to the neck and no floral accessories. And the fact that Keith Richards got the finished riff together by recording a pair of acoustic guitars into the microphone of a cheap Philips cassette recorder is always worth repeating—this was no thought-through marketing strategy but a bright creative idea hatched serendipitously one morning by a switched-on artistic mind.

Mick Jagger has a new voice, too. Gone is the playful rue of "Sittin' on a Fence," the urchin reproof of "Play with Fire," the insincere boudoir simpering of "Lady Jane." The poisonous little shit who voiced "Mother's Little Helper" so priggishly is nowhere to be heard. Instead Jagger executes an electrified dog yawn, drags his syllables out like a tape measure, hissing his s's and lolling his tongue, and in doing so contrives a pretty convincing approximation of how a rock 'n' roll Mephistopheles might figure in the after-dark imagination, bony beckoning finger, dripping lips and all—the voice as theatricalization of a sexual nightmare.

Judged solely on its lyric content, "Jack Flash" is actually a pretty terrible song and, as such, it serves as an apt demonstration of the old truth that, in rock, it isn't what you're saying that speaks, but the oomph in your sound. And what the Stones now sound like, in 1968 (see also "Sympathy for the Devil" and "Street Fighting Man"), is a potent rhythm juggernaut fronted by a dancing, flickering, jabbering figure sufficiently protean to embody the spirit of whatever dark and lustful thoughts might be already lurking in the recesses of your intoxicated mind. Jagger's version of authenticity is now meta-psychological—it seems to manifest psychic disorder while simultaneously making observations about the nature of that disorder—on the basis that all young souls yearn primarily to be, like, y'know, *out of it*. It was a canny move, given the times.

The times subsequently produced such bacchanalian wonders as "Honky Tonk Women," "Gimme Shelter," "Brown Sugar," and "Tumbling Dice," not to mention four brilliant albums'-worth of A-grade Anglo-American raunch, as pregnant with anxiety, death, disappointment, and mistrust as they were with decadence, sex, and lordly insouciance. Indeed, as much as the 1965-to-'67 run of hits, from "Satisfaction" to "Let's Spend the Night Together," was a shout of uncheckable youthful exuberance, the latter batch of louche chugs represented the fag end of a decade's barely restrained social slippage and fragmentation—funky as all hell but contrived out of the stuff of worry: the rhythm of a social group concerned that it might be dancing off to hell in a handcart.

But hold ... There were, in the murk, glimmers of another, less stagily dark strain of soullessness, something less worldly, less sophisticated. More heartful. "Moonlight Mile," on *Sticky Fingers*, is not as "enacted" as most performances in the Jagger canon, even if it does come decorated with theatrical whimpers and moans. This is not the flickering Mephistophelian Mick of "Jumpin' Jack Flash," nor even the baleful herald of countercultural doom who allowed Merry Clayton to steal the big thunder in "Gimme Shelter." This is existential Mick. Could it even be Real Mick?

Essentially, "Moonlight Mile" is a Keith-free trudge of a ballad driven instrumentally by Jagger's own chopped-out "Japanese" acoustic guitar figure and then shaped by an absolutely brilliant string arrangement composed by the Stones' favorite charts man, Paul Buckmaster, which grows around the song like a hull.

The lyrics describe weariness and ennui not as a metaphor but as an actual physical feeling that is as enervating as any cocaine comedown, the protagonist slumping after "another mad mad day on the road," abraded by the unending sound of "strangers sending nothing to my mind," longing to be "by your side"—the sound of a great weight of emptiness bearing down. What begins in physical torpor evolves over nearly six minutes of ratcheting, chromatic tension-and-release into a rage against loneliness. The moonlight mile is the distance traveled home in the imagination, describing in its silvered hallucinatory swoop the hope of arrival and the end of all emptiness. When he moans that he is living only to be lying by her side, the closeness of "lying" to "dying" in the cavern of Jagger's mouth is surely not accidental.

"Moonlight Mile" is not on paper a scintillating or remarkably original piece of writing, but it is unusually touching for a Rolling Stones song because of Jagger's retreat from his usual professionalist policy, which was to write *good Stones material*. The song may be no more personal than the better-loved "Wild Horses" from the same album, but it feels like it. It certainly does not come on like a ballad classic by design, as "Wild Horses" sometimes seems to. Toward the end of "Mile," at 4:12, as Jagger slogs through another of his plateau-climaxes, repetitively bellowing the syllables "down the ro-o-oad" over a series of electric guitar chords belted out studiously by Mick Taylor, I never fail to shiver—at perhaps the only occasion in the Stones' career where it seems possible that the singer's heart might actually be breakable. No, really. You shiver, of course, at the neural reward offered by the successful cadencing of a long musical pattern, but you also shiver in empathy.

Which is unusual. One does not expect to feel the world as Mick Jagger feels it, to identify personally with him, to look through his eyes, to feel the heaviness in his arms, legs, mouth, and spirit, to actually *be* Mick Jagger for a moment, with what disappointingly little that may actually entail. One does not expect to enter his gates. But in "Moonlight Mile" we do get to go inside, briefly, or so it has always appeared to me, invited not all that enthusiastically into a room in which the pissed-off author yearns painfully for the simplicity of home (or whatever it is that "home" stands for)—a longing that seems as plausible in that moment as it had seemed inconceivable in other moments that he should ever be really touched by anything remotely resembling common human feeling, by the snarls of love or the impossibility of justice or the perils of conformity or the ecstasies of intimacy or any of the sensations that must arise from the solidly held conviction that you are the subject of somebody's else erotic nightmare.

Just for a change, "Moonlight Mile" is Mick Jagger not subletting himself to *good Stones material*, but acting the reluctant host; not offering all-areas access to the delicate and/or dreary soul guarded so punctiliously by the Interesting Bunch of Guys, but certainly admitting that he has his vulnerabilities, and that these are communicable feelings, not some smart, worldly attitude adopted strategically in a cool moment. And it was possibly the first and last time he ever managed such a gesture convincingly, with the noble exception of much of *Exile on Main St.*, which followed "Moonlight Mile" the next year and is notable for some of the grumpiest and most unbated vocalizations Jagger ever committed to tape. *Exile* was not a happy experience for him, but it did, interestingly, result in a lot of unmediated singing—just one of the reasons it still stands, for me, as the apex of the group's creative output.

For the remainder of his career, though, all the way up to the present day, it is fair to say that what we listen to when we listen to the Rolling Stones is Mick Jagger parodying Mick Jagger doing an interesting bunch of voices.

* * *

A final thought.

The high level of actorly artifice evident in Jagger's vocal performances has never bothered me as much as it has some. To me, it's what he does—and I love the sound of it, so long as the performances don't stray into cheap minstrelism (as they sometimes but by no means always do after *Exile*). I would not argue with those who insist that the Stones' music is essentially heartless, but I would say in response to such a charge that hearts are complicated and they come in all shapes and capacities and sensitivities and resistances. Also, hearts are not always relevant. Not to everything.

Rock music, as construed by the Rolling Stones for the British audience and then a wider international one in the 1960s, was never a music of intimate connection but an animated description of life as it is lived on the edge of its own times. The Stones' music was an account of an experience, not an appeal to the heart; it was a direct stimulus to the mind and the body, not an invitation to share an emotional and/or imaginative landscape. The Stones left that territory well alone to those who could do better with it, most notably in white rock music to the Beatles and, in a different but equally impressive way, to Bob Dylan. But no one, not even the Beatles and Dylan, could make you feel as the Stones once did, that you were dancing—flickering, jabbering—on the very edge of life.

Which is perhaps why it has been such an unedifying spectacle watching Dartford's finest chug on through middle age into their autumn cadences, as if their discourse might still have something useful to express to the world around them. Bless them. All they can do now is entertain and make money. They are still pretty good at the former and excellent at the latter. But they do not dance on the edge of their times, and nor do we when we trouble to turn up in our hordes to observe them pantomiming their back catalog. On those occasions, we dance only on the edge of our wallets.

So it is a basic misconception, I think, to damn Mick Jagger's singing for its "lack of soul" and for its thespy qualities. Or for its campness. Totally invidious too to claim that he is a failed white-boy R&B impersonator (it was nearly always his intention after 1965 to use R&B, not to *be* it). Praise him instead for his adaptability, his stylishness, his originality, and his vividness; for his ability to suggest that all may not be as it seems, that mystery is afoot and that worldliness is not a sin but a condition to be endured with the exercise of sense and sensuality, not to mention a keenly appraising eye. And praise him unstintingly for his unending desire to make a vocal line dance.

And then forgive his transgressions in taste.

Besides, it was never his job to unveil his heart for the edification of the masses. That was Lennon's—and Lennon only did it because he felt he had no choice in the matter. They were a complementary pair, but not like Flanders and Swann. Between the two of them, they combined to make 1960s Britain articulate without first having to observe the rules of beauty and propriety—because the rules of beauty and propriety would get you nowhere near to what is true, given what we were beginning to know back then. They sang that way just because they could, and no one had the faintest idea how to stop them.

GRACE NOTES

THE KINKS: "WATERLOO SUNSET"
Pye Records, 1967

There is no more touching scene in English pop than that of Terry and Julie crossing the dirty old River Thames at the chilly-chilly end of a long black-and-white day.

To do what, though? To become fuller realizations of themselves? To become anonymous statistics? To become Julie Christie and Terence Stamp?

Who cares what they became. To ask what became of them after the end of the song is to miss the point. The point of "Waterloo Sunset" is to experience the moment, not examine its consequences. These are the 1960s, after all. And it is not Terry and Julie that the listener identifies with but the delicate feelings of the wistful spectator whose gaze we follow so epically yet humbly across the span of that handsome bridge.

It is impossible now, anyway, to make a valid reconstruction of the intimate long look described in "Waterloo Sunset," not with any hope of encountering the same view, peopled with anything like the same folk living remotely equivalent lives. London's twenty-first-century skyline is a metaphor for the capital's own metamorphosis into an armored neo-liberalist homeland, and there is precious little room in it for the meanderings of the world's Terrys and Julies across its for-profit-only real estate. Central London is not the same place any more and the essence of the new place is expressed in its phallic architectural boasting. See how big we are, and how powerful and how rich! Excuse us while we fuck the sky!

"Waterloo Sunset" does not fuck the sky. It beholds the sky as a benevolent if slightly lowering canopy beneath which small lives scurry with living weight and privacy. I have never figured out whether Terry and Julie are crossing the bridge in a northerly or a southerly direction, or even if they're crossing the bridge at all. Not visibly. Maybe it's something they'll do later, out of shot . . . After all, what kind of vantage point would you need to observe both the entrance to Waterloo Underground station and the pavement over the bridge? But I have never minded about that small difficulty, because of the beauty in Ray Davies's voice.

You want undiluted, unembellished English pop singing?

Get Ray. The jiggling, slightly over-busy instrumental intro to the song sets him up. Its too-many notes articulate the frenzy of the too-many people pressing into Waterloo tube station: drums hustle, electric guitar jibbers, acoustic guitar slashes across the auditory field like traffic. Human ciphers dot and press. And then Davies comes in at an angle, following a downward trajectory, as light and wistful and artless as a boy from Muswell Hill can make himself sound. And it's important that he finds a way to be light and artless, because the essence of the song is its detachment, its atmosphere one of concentrated distraction. Indeed, the voice of "Waterloo Sunset" lives in the listening mind so vividly not because of the voice's expressed desires or its appetites or its wounds or its entitlements but because of the greater life it perceives in the world outside itself, in the hurry-scurry of the end of an ordinary day. It is a voice aware of its own existence but not, for this moment, interested in it. It is distracted into rapture. It is William Blake's voice, perhaps.

So no need for American phrasing here, or accent. No need for inner pain/ambition/rage/appetite expressed with soul. An uncultivated north-London suburban whinny will do just fine.

DAVID BOWIE: "LIFE ON MARS?"
RCA Records, 1971

But what if artlessness were death? What if life were actually experienced most truly—or least mendaciously—in the artful? What if the identity you ascribe to yourself feels more real than the one with which you are already endowed, by nature, by nurture, and by mediated socialization? What if there is life on Mars?

"Life on Mars?" was recorded and first released in 1971 on the *Hunky Dory* album, a passing contract-filler of a long-player that was seen at the time by Bowie's management, or so it has been said, as an interim, impetus-boosting measure on the road to the forthcoming main event, *The Rise and Fall of Ziggy Stardust and the Spiders From Mars*, scheduled for release in a few months' time. It's hard to think of it like that now: *Hunky Dory* has "Life on Mars?," "Changes," and "Oh! You Pretty Things" on it.

Perhaps its nominal throwaway status was the reason "Life on Mars?" only became a hit eighteen months after the release of its mother album, when it was hustled out as a follow-up to the two top-three smashes from *Ziggy*'s own follow-up, *Aladdin Sane*, "The Jean Genie" and "Drive-In Saturday" (things were made to happen quickly and in any old order in those days, in case the audience blinked). Whatever the reason, however random the strategy, however purely serendipitous the sequence of releases, it worked. "Life on Mars?" made the top three too, in the summer of 1973, and then stuck around for a lifetime.

To a rural boy of thirteen tender years, listening hard to his bedroom transistor for signs of extra-rural life, "Life on Mars?" hit like an asteroid. "Drive-In Saturday" and "The Jean Genie" had already been a sensation in my sanctum, but "Mars?" seemed to emanate from a different part of the universe altogether, a cosmic fold in which strangeness was a comfort, surfaces were soft, girls had mousy hair on their heads, and their breasts harbored catlike resentments, while cavemen . . . Well, just look at how they go about their business. It was not to me a song about stardom and ambition and the sale of life, but a song about the act of watching the self as it watches life unfold—so enthralled and so contingent. Again: detachment, self-absorption, and half-understood longing described as if life were best experienced in the form of an enacted dream.

The song has, on occasion, made me cry. It has done this when it has taken me unawares by creeping out of a radio speaker like a tiny alien invasion, as it did when I was young. I have always found it histrionically tender, shrill and over-colored. The tears come even now, I presume, because my nervous system is still wired to welcome that invasion, even though the rest of me knows full well that I have traveled way too far down life's path for that kind of self-watching to be useful. But there it is.

It is acknowledged fact that "Life on Mars?" gets its basic harmonic structure from the original French inspiration for Frank Sinatra's "My Way," written in 1968, one of those stately step-by-step chord progressions that were the bedrock of the baroque. Rick Wakeman's cultivated piano is as important to the atmosphere of the piece as the towering string arrangement composed by the Spiders' guitarist Mick Ronson. But the song has survived like a perfect building because of the elements of its basic construction: the rock-solid relationship between vaulting melody and stepped bassline—and because of the trail left behind by Bowie's streaking voice.

It's an English voice, no question: a bel canto Anthony Newley. It is pinched thin and careful to begin with, softened with open vowels and even the odd moment of involuntary gentility: I always think Bowie utters the line about the "seat with the clearest view" like an elderly customer asking for a table in a Yorkshire tearoom. How thrilling, then, that the very moment in which he asks for an advantageous position in the tearoom, a mere twenty-seven seconds in, is also the first snatch in the ignition sequence that will result in the slow launch into the stratosphere of one of the great rocket-propelled pop performances of all time.

I always used to marvel as a kid at the sheer slowness of Saturn Five rocket launches: how the rocket—a huge, heavy, boiling, sky-poking tower of a thing—would lift itself into the air so torpidly, so grandly, so effortfully, and yet so inch-by-inch *gradually*, as if steadied and eased upward by giant invisible hands. What a spectacle. A cathedral taking flight. Explosive power expressed in slow motion, with a grandeur that in other contexts might be deemed operatic, but in the context of the early 1970s found artistic equivalence only in the drawn-out, stately ascension of an unusual pop record. "Life on Mars?" is literally the best British pop record ever made about going slowly upward.

Bowie's vocal performance is utterly stable, pitch- and yaw-perfect in its curving ascent, never hasty but holding steady under massive thrust, shedding redundant stages as it accelerates, gaining height and impetus as it becomes smaller and smaller to the listening mind, dwarfed in the huge empyrean of the song's arrangement but somehow still focal . . . until it disappears completely and lingers only as an echo of itself in the mind's ear. A lost dot of light and energy. And it does all this while remaining steadfastly a property of the south London suburbs, a prisoner of nothing on earth but its vowel sounds. How could it not linger for good and all in the nervous system?

If the phrase "stark reality" has any application in the realm of Bowie's early 1970s *oeuvre*, it is manifest here. The stark reality of "Life on Mars?" is simply that of the south London suburbs going into space. How could we not be moved?

It is worth noting here, I think, the extraordinary outpouring of grief amongst a certain age group, of both genders, on the occasion of Bowie's death in early 2016. I was no different; I felt it too. And I was taken by real surprise by how much I had to struggle to maintain an even disposition while the issue was discussed over the kitchen tables of my peers.

It seemed clear to me both at the time and now, eight months on, that here was prima facie evidence that voices do not exist merely as emblems and symbols of our lives, but that they have a function: they are vessels—carriers, vehicles, safety deposit boxes—in which we deposit our profoundest, most elusive feelings for safekeeping while we proceed with the tricky procedures of life.

ROBERT WYATT: "SEA SONG"
Virgin Records, 1974

Both feebleness and grandiloquence proliferated in much of the psychedelic/progressive singing of the late 1960s and early 1970s. This may have been because it was felt at the time that it was important that the music sound as if it had sprung into the world without reference to America.

But there was more to this than mere bolshy un-Americanness. There was intent too: a sort of positive ideological intent to do with how you go about doing music, and why. In the prog purview in particular, the singing voice was taken to be only one constituent element in the overall musical gesture of the collective group sound, and not the dominant feature. There were to be no hierarchies. What the singer had to express was no more nor less important than that which was being expressed by the multi-keyboardist or the bass player or the guy with the Tibetan glockenspiel. In such a fierce democracy of sound, the voice must enjoy no special prominence or privilege or license but must earn its corn as an effective conveyor of incidental melody and text. That was its job. Psych/prog had very little interest in the private emotions of singers.

And text was no small matter either. Psych/prog lyrics had more in common with free poetry or classical fable or prose whimsy than they did with Holland–Dozier–Holland and so did not lend themselves easily to the guttier kind of emission. But they did need to be delivered somehow.

The upshot was that the psych/prog world was fraught with over-singing and under-singing and rather a lot of uninhabited singing and singing by numbers—but very little cogent singing.

It is hard to argue the case that many more than a couple of genuinely memorable voices emerged from English psych/prog. But the owner of one of them was certainly Peter Gabriel, whose dry-as-toast, throaty English-ness, and his willingness to strain himself in the cause of artistic reach, attached no little theatrical passion to the early works of Genesis and then animated a long and fruited solo career.

The other unarguably great one was Robert Wyatt. Wyatt was never a prog-rocker, nor an acid-head, but he was as deeply attached to the "progressive" methodology as he was to his Coltrane records and to the tenets of Marxist materialism. His voice was first broadly heard—"broadly" is a relative term, and so is "heard"—in Canterbury's beloved The Soft Machine, a sort of avant-psych-jazz experiment in hippie Pataphysics, involving language, rhythm, and electronics. But it was not then a distinguished thing, his voice—nor, it should be said, was it striving to be. Being distinguished was not the point of the exercise.

And so it was not until Wyatt fell victim to a terrible accident and found himself permanently confined to a wheelchair that his voice came to be heard as a vessel of even vaguely conventional song, cushioned at low amplitude by agreeable synthetic textures (plus other suitably restrained "organic" ones) and freed from the obligation to explore tricky time signatures at the most awkward tempos imaginable.

"Sea Song" is the opening cut on his brilliant solo album from 1974, *Rock Bottom*, and it contains English singing quite as lovely and expressive as any of the period.

What is being expressed? Well, it depends on who you are, I suppose, and how you were made. And what you value in life. But I hear love and wonderment and a sort of tenacious wistfulness in his wavy phrasing, halt though it is and shallow its dynamic range. It is thin and fibrous, Wyatt's voice, but it is beautiful. He is like seaweed in a current, anchored at one end, free at the other, and he undulates with the subtle movement of the melody as if happy to go with the prevailing conditions of his environment and to offer no more resistance than is necessary for life. When conditions are favorable, it is possible to imagine seahorses nodding in his fronds.

RICHARD AND LINDA THOMPSON:
"DIMMING OF THE DAY"/"DARGAI"
Island Records, 1975

The story of English folk-rock is a parenthetical old yarn. It's almost as if English folk-rock were a sincere aside in the comic after-dinner speech that is the history of English pop—the bit in the story when the narrator has to give some kind of solemn account of what English pop came to mean in its relationship with native English custom, before getting back to the main theme of the evening, which is the story of aggressive English modernism in its relationship with American culture.

The late 1960s and early 1970s were English folk-rock's heyday, and what a day it was. It gave rise, on a very small front, to some lovely, heartfelt, imaginative music, the occasional screed of fine writing—and a very small amount of great singing.

By common consent, the doyenne of English folk-rock singing was the late, lamented Sandy Denny, who rose from middle-class suburban folkie beginnings to pull the stumbling Fairport Convention into focus, to make a commendable hash of her own group Fotheringay and then to pursue a solo career of fitful creative brilliance. Hers was certainly a brilliant voice, a silken pennant swirling in a furious English breeze, when it wasn't huskily fumbling for the gap in the medieval wall-hangings which brought warmth and insulation to her troubled inner world. She was an authentic tearaway and her cult is justifiably extensive.

But I always preferred Linda Thompson. Thompson was Denny's friend and sometime vocal partner, and the long-suffering wife for the duration of the seventies of the guitar and songwriting genius, Richard Thompson— and oh, how I longed to rescue her from that fated match. This preference of course says more about me than it does about the respective merits of the voices in question. But let me frame it this way: one voice was big, exuberant, lyrical, forthright, silken, extravagantly impassioned; the other was small, hesitant, anxious, prosy, aching, cotton-kind and intimately warm, and it pleaded for rescue. Where Sandy's lofted pennant can make me break out in a cold sweat even on a hot summer's day, Linda's can break my heart on any old day of the year.

"Dimming of the Day" is emblematic of the Linda thing. It is a plea for closeness and warmth in a cold, uninterested world, sung in a warm contralto with all the dolour that a soul can contain, quiet as anything but somehow engulfing in its wounded humanity. Meanwhile, her genius husband accompanies her exquisitely with fingerpicked Anglo-Scottish-Arabic folk guitar in a slow, twanging pavane—oooh, those naked fourths!—which gives into a voiceless but independently titled coda that seems to turn away from the sorrowing Linda as it engrosses itself ever more deeply in its own brilliant patterning. By the end of "Dimming/Dargai'"s seven-minute duration, she is quite forgotten.

Nevertheless, some of us will carry her voice around in our pockets for the remainder of our lives on earth and we bring her out occasionally, even now, to remember how we once felt like men of heart.

KIRSTY MacCOLL: "THEY DON'T KNOW"
Stiff Records, 1979

As punk shaded into the several things that followed punk, a certain interest was renewed in pop's fundamental features: beat, melody, and guileless innocence—a real back-to-basics move to soften the times after all that sound and fury. *Nostalgie de la whooooooo!*

In timely fashion, "They Don't Know" came out on the Stiff label to a welter of critical approval. I was nineteen. Read the review in the *NME*. Had to have the record. Got my hands on it on the day of release as I was working in a record shop in town to fill up my gap year with music. And I've still got it somewhere, in its original picture sleeve: not exactly treasured but certainly *retained*. It would have been a hit too, were it not for a strike at the distribution company, which stopped copies from reaching the shops. They couldn't get enough of it down at Radio 1, but no ordinary punter was able to buy it after the first week of release.

"They Don't Know" has beat, melody, and guileless innocence in abundance. But it also has MacColl's voice, which surges over the tinkling retro instrumentation like molten chalk, like Milk of Magnesia, sometimes self-harmonized or buoyed with a hint of doubletracking (although that may be just my faulty hearing), but always, always, always driven from note to note by the flow of her language and not by any desire on her part to communicate the intricacies and subtle shadings of her inner life. Its warm, spiky detachment is mesmerism in a loop.

I still think of it as a perfect pop record and will defend it as such until my dying day. And not just any old perfect pop record but a perfect English pop record.

Why English? Well, mostly because you can hear Croydon in it—its breeze blocks, its overpasses, its underpasses, its traffic islands. But also because of the way MacColl refuses to let her voice stray far from its psychological anchorages, in the playground, at the bus stop, down the café, in bed, or sprawled prone on her bedroom carpet, her mouth slightly ajar, one ear pressed to the speaker of her tinny bedroom stereo while Motown plays, the other one alert and responsive to the *scritch-scratches* and *wooshes* of life as it continues its whirl beyond the membrane of her bedroom window.

All good pop records are snapshots of a moment's feeling. But the very best ones tend to be snapshots of a moment's contradictory feeling. In this case, the contradiction is plain: the melody, the beat, the language, the forward thrust, and tonal uptilt of the music—together they say "yes" to love and its many hills and valleys. But the voice . . . Well, the voice says something else altogether, something quite elusive, to do with resentment and anxiety and doubt and defensiveness and resistance to the onlooking gaze. It speaks of shyness and embarrassment about even being here doing this now. This singing.

THE SMITHS: "GIRLFRIEND IN A COMA"
Rough Trade Records, 1987

A song about emotional detachment.

I know, I know—it's serious.

A song in which the narrator contemplates the slightness of his own empathy as if it were a charming pebble picked up on the beach. Or a stain on the arm of a sofa. The girlfriend in the coma might just as well be roadkill.

And to animate this most uneasy of scenarios, Morrissey deploys his noblest, most caring voice—a rather beautiful baritone at the very top of its range, close to falsetto, slipping betwixt and between in a sort of tenderized whisper, before gliding into a more familiar chesty ululation for the bridge passage, as if real feeling has flickered into life just for a moment. Only a moment, though. Pretty soon he's whispering his last goodbyes to the stricken figure in the hospital bed, sweetly and martyrishly, as if it is actually he and not the insensible girlfriend who has been grievously inconvenienced at this time. But then it's always politic to make a show of kindness when terminating a relationship with an unconscious person in hospital.

Distinct English pop and rock singing was never a single style, whole unto itself and discrete from its American counterpart. It has only ever been an attitude at the microphone, born of cultural relativity (we are not American—ergo, we must make a conscious decision to sound either American, kind of American, or not American at all) and expressed through the agency of a certain self-consciousness and contingency, some of which has to do with class.

"Girlfriend in a Coma" is all self-consciousness and contingency and nothing but. Even the jaunty bouncing shuffle of Johnny Marr's arrangement stands at an oblique angle to both voice and text, as if it wished it belonged elsewhere (in a song about dogs biting postmen, perhaps). But the ironies implicit in "Girlfriend" are too layered, too unattractive, too self-satisfied to be happy, and it should come as no surprise that The Smiths ceased to function as a band almost as soon as it was recorded—clearing the space, half a decade later, for the rise of Britpop, the most self-satisfied of all the musical "movements" in the history of postwar pop.

5

The Urge for Going

Joni Mitchell was admitted to hospital by ambulance last week. She had recovered consciousness by the time she got there, but things didn't sound too promising.

Social media immediately went into overdrive, as they tend to in such circumstances. Favorite Mitchell songs were posted. Get-well messages were exchanged competitively. And there was great speculation as to the nature of Mitchell's incapacitation, based on no medical information whatsoever other than the fact that the musician/writer/painter is known to have smoked like a chimney since childhood and suffers from a self-diagnosed but not medically recognized condition called Morgellons disease, which creates in its victims the illusion that their flesh is infested with parasites.

There was superheated prose knocking around, too. Eve Barlow, writing on the British internet platform *The Pool*, threw herself down upon the cold linoleum floor beside Joni's bed in Intensive Care: "We haven't exhausted her candid wisdom yet," she keened. "Joni knows us better than we know ourselves. She's our mother, complete with answers to questions we haven't yet thought to ask. I'm intimidated just writing down the name 'Joni Mitchell.' She would write it down better, somehow making the words even more profound."

Me, I just felt sad—but also slightly confused and disorientated, as if

"sad" were inadequate somehow. In fact I felt really quite odd. I got pictures in my head of Mitchell coming to in the ambulance, her pharaoh's
overbite working crossly and her pale eyes flashing distress, one hand—her
better hand—perhaps flapping impatiently at the non-arrival of the words
she wants to say. I wondered what she registered in that moment of regained
consciousness, and whether she thought about herself in the second person.
I wondered whether she was filled with poetry or just curses and banality,
the whole damn farrago being one prosaic experience too many, not to be
dignified with careful language. I got into my car to go to Sainsbury's and
listened to *Hejira* to remind myself of her genius.

It didn't help. *Hejira* just said the usual stuff, about flight, about sex,
about the urge to keep on going. I pushed a trolley around Sainsbury's
and experienced the low-frequency hum of anticipatory mourning while I
counted bananas. How does one lament the passing into shade of a force like
that? How does one let go of Joni Mitchell?

With difficulty, I find, because she has seemed so real and concrete
and permanent in life, so much a part of one's own fabric, and yet also so
manifestly a creature of invention, her own diligent invention: a woman apparently self-conceived and created and then reimagined by herself over and
over again in her slippy fight with her self-loathing, almost as full of detail
in the memory as one's own mother. Not that I have ever felt mothered by
Joni. Over the decades she has seemed as narratable as Helen of Troy, but
rather less warm to the touch.

In fact, to be entirely fair, I have never had any interest at all in her
personal life and still less any authentic concern for her legend, which has
seldom seemed all that attractive to me, expressing, as it does, so many of
the least appealing aspects of West Coast American countercultural celebrity. Despite the feeling that I "know" her well, I have never felt the slightest
inclination to wonder what she'd be like to have as a friend or neighbor in
some parched canyon, still less felt sexual stirring at the thought of her. I
haven't always liked her voice much either. I have been wholly immune to
her as a person and have only ever taken in her songs selfishly.

Yet she has occupied my psyche for nearly forty years with a tenancy more robust and demanding than that of any other singer-songwriter. She has occupied it passively, but tenaciously. I cannot shake her out of there. She will not leave. It's as if she took up residence in my chambers at some unnameable point in the distant past and just settled in, with a sense of entitlement you might expect only from family. Heaven only knows what I'll feel when she actually dies and leaves me to deal with what's left behind. Doubtless, it will amount to more than a terracotta army of pot plants and a manky cat.

* * *

Mitchell settled in the imaginations of pop listeners in the early seventies. In the UK, "Big Yellow Taxi" was a biggish hit in the summer of 1970, its glassily sardonic reflections upon humanity's relationship with the environment marking out the flaxen-haired Scando-Canadian hippie-chick who sang it as a poster girl for a certain kind of wholesome big-R Romanticism. She was fey, frowning, Nordically bony, the perfect package for the deal: a one-take archetype. What the songs didn't articulate and the voice didn't swoop upon like a slender bird, the hair flowed over in a river of molten gold. Like nature busily abhorring a vacuum, Mitchell flooded space that ought perhaps to have been filled by an array of other women before her: the role of thoughtful, poetically articulate, unsentimental, insubordinate, self-expressive female countercultural pop icon. It was a tough job and maybe Mitchell didn't ask for it, but she certainly got it and then did it with never less than questioning commitment.

She'd already done the itinerant North American folk thing for most of the previous decade—silvery footage of her tooting "Urge For Going" on mid-sixties Canadian folk TV is easily traced on YouTube. But she was already leaving that world by the time David Crosby of the Byrds hitched her to the Californian counterculture wagon. By then, other people had had hits with her songs—notably Judy Collins's "Both Sides, Now"—and LA's Laurel Canyon had become Mitchell's home and her cathedral, along with the rest of her adopted tribe of nesting longhairs. As a kinship group, they were quietly intent on contemplating the devolution of the sixties "dream," cannily accepting their status as seers of a disappointed new age and settling into mellow self-absorption, as into a great wicker armchair on the stoop at sunset. Mitchell seemed at the time to be the established priestess of the tribe, consecrated into her role.

But she was nothing of the kind. She had management—Elliot Roberts and David Geffen—and she had an urge for going.

Blue in 1971 is where you feel the clutch start to bite. It is a stark record for a golden girl to make. It came out the year after "Big Yellow Taxi" was a hit and it became an instant archetype of the "confessional" singer-songwriting style (a term Mitchell despises, incidentally, for its implicit associations with guilt and religious coercion). A cult arose around it. If Mitchell herself represented a certain archetype of hippie femininity, *Blue* was an archetype of female expressivity: inward-looking, self-exposing, delicate, emotionally forensic, anti-triumphal . . . On first contact with it, you feel almost obliged to sit down and close your eyes, hands together, head inclined, all the better to experience the searching sensitivity of it all. And while it's true that *Blue* contains passages of brilliant writing and is without real rival for the rawness of its excavations of the soul wounded by love, it is easy now to feel that it was always destined to be *une vache sacrée*. Perhaps even that it was designed that way. Some of the melodies feel arched for display, like the tail feathers of a courting bird; some of them skim the ceiling of the singer's vocal range and threaten to leave by the window, as if the real motive for their creation were to demonstrate that Joni's supple contralto had other more exciting places to go than might be reached in all our dreariest two-a-penny dreams. Beat that, it seems to say. Try going *there*.

It's also a record that extended the range and depth of Mitchell's pianistic songwriting. Writing at the piano (as opposed to guitar) makes different demands on the compositional mind. You can hear her on *Blue* adjusting her methods to put "The Last Time I Saw Richard" and "My Old Man" together—sitting there on the piano stool, poised in a pall of artful creativity, breaking the chords into arpeggios, fingering them methodically out, trying to think big and artistic as befits the elevated status of the ivory keyboard.

Please do not misunderstand me: I think *Blue* is a marvel. "All I Want," "A Case of You," "River," "Blue"—these are songs for the ages. If she'd stopped there, *Blue* would surely have been sufficient to cement Joni into the structure of her times. But she didn't stop there, because she had much bigger explorations to conduct and longer roads to travel. Other places to reach.

For the Roses appeared the following year, and it sounds like what it is—a hard second-gear acceleration for the horizon. This is no gilded folkie delving into the ruins of her life from the comfort of the wicker armchair but a woman feeling a need to accord with expectation. Mitchell now has jazzers and cellists at her disposal. And she has a selfhood to firm up. We are ushered into a room in which we observe a proud, assertive, judgmental Joni at the piano, exploring the spread of her poetic reach as if it were fanned out in front of her like her hands at the keyboard. The tunes and their arrangements are artful. The voice swoops imperiously. She has plenty to lament. Robert Christgau wrote in the *Village Voice*: "Sometimes her complaints about the men who have failed her sound petulant, but the appearance of petulance is one of the prices of liberation." He loved the record.

Meanwhile, on the inside of the gatefold sleeve, an apparently naked Joni stands on a rock, one knee crooked, gazing out into the Pacific, a West Coast parody of Friedrich's Alpine *Wanderer Above the Mists*—or perhaps a reverse angle on Botticelli's *Birth of Venus*. On the record, she sometimes addresses herself in the second person. She is beginning to enjoy her sophistication.

Then, in 1974, came *Court and Spark*, which took sophistication by the hand and led it into a newly landscaped uptown park, where it spread out a giant square of French linen on the grass and hosted it to a picnic, a proper West Coast *Déjeuner sur l'herbe*. The sessions were held with an array of fully clothed musicians, some of them kind-of-jazzers, some of them sort-of-rockers, some of them a cultivated hybrid of the two, and they locked into the uptown-downtime groove like men of the world. What a picnic. Mitchell's voice now found itself, by its own volition, at the center of a high-tone ensemble and the tastefulness all around was as a frame to the naked elegance of her phrasing. The cellos were joined by reeds. The reeds were teased out into choric eloquence by arrangements that might have sat well with Sondheim. In fact it now appeared that Mitchell was unable to cadence a phrase without approaching the notes like a hostess at a cocktail party, swooping up to them with a swish in an airburst of expensive perfume.

Court and Spark is a brilliant parade of accomplishments, both musical and literary. The album radiates a cool, artful, bodiless glow, making a case for itself as the most *soigné* musical achievement of its era—so knowing and refined is its range, in fact, that it's not always possible to hear where Mitchell's internal landscape ends and where LA begins. It's a continuum, from she to shining sea. The songs might profess disdain for the superficial and the shallow but both irony and sincerity, as well as old-fashioned heart, are sometimes lost in the shimmer. The voice merely hosts the soirée—and swoops graciously up to its desired notes from below, to remind you of its silken command.

* * *

Just what was all this sophistication *doing* in 1970s mass-market rock music anyway? Was it just hanging around, hoping to be admired? Or did it have more sinister things in mind? Was this "rock music" at all, in fact, or something else altogether? It certainly had nothing to do with "folk," and not all that much in common with "jazz," despite one or two superficial borrowings from the book of jazz texture and harmony. It certainly didn't swing. Perhaps this was some new departure into a void that had always existed in between the real stuff and the even more real stuff—a sort of musical half-world where genre lines blur to the point at which nothing can be seen clearly any more, just vague shapes and hinted-at implications, neutered sensations, half-glimpsed exits and redrawn lines in the sand: the encroaching fog of fusion. Perhaps bodiless was the new naked.

While I am meditating so indulgently upon the nature of the prevailing musical zeitgeist forty years ago, it might also be worth pausing to reflect for a moment on where popular music had been since that first outbreak of teenage rebellion in the 1950s. Perhaps it might help to describe, in the lithest possible terms, the trajectory of the arc connecting Little Richard and Bony Joni—from camped-up male hysteria to tasteful female self-contemplation.

You might say that, in psychological terms at least, pop had undergone a quite logical, even systematic process of maturation, and taken its time over it.

It had enjoyed its first unfettered hormonal outburst in the 1950s, the decade that began with austerity and concluded with the first exploration of outer space. That furtive probing of the cosmos had reached an early climax with Yuri Gagarin, the first cosmonaut, and coincided with pop's sudden retreat from the rock 'n' roll *esprit* into showbiz convention and the cult of the hygienic juvenile lead. Pop was then in the earliest stages of its own industrialization and was hugely self-conscious and in no sense prepared to go all the way with anyone—not if it was to maximize its social appeal. The very early sixties, then, was an era of light petting enjoyed by girl gangs and boys with drippy voices plus insistent, barely audible offstage noises made by the ultra-lively but still largely segregated "race market." Plus novelty instrumentals.

It took the intellectual clout and independent-mindedness of the Beatles and Bob Dylan, not to mention the rocket-fueled counter-corporatism of Motown, to change the picture, by which time in the middle of the 1960s it was feasible for any self-respecting twentysomething pop consumer to feel that his or her needs were being addressed, face to face, *mano a mano*, man to woman, and not in a patronizing way. Pop was no longer an exclusively juvenile preserve, nor were the strings of its industrial control quite so visible, as creative power devolved more and more conspicuously in the direction of artists, producers, and their personal advisers and away from the chubby fingers of corporate management and its agents. By the middle of the decade, pop looked like the only game in town worth playing, and such was its social and cultural cachet that even corporate management bowed to the time-honored reality, observed by parents of every generation, that if your baby has outgrown its childhood, then you must, perforce, give it a measure of freedom—otherwise you might lose it altogether.

Meanwhile, ordnance rained down upon the Far East. There was fighting on the streets of Europe. Americans were preparing to set foot upon the Moon. Blacks and Irish still weren't welcome in parts of Cricklewood. Pop music gave rise to rock, and rock's social and intellectual scope sought new horizons to expand into. Sex was no longer hidden, and barely even encoded. Books were read and regurgitated in the name of self-affirmation. The psychedelic playbook gave way to folk mythology and then to darkening personal angst. New chops and styles and attitudes toward creativity were co-opted from classical music, folk and jazz, and from public schools. Meanwhile, the music created by African Americans was consumed for the first time in largish quantities by white people. As one decade gave wriggle-room to the next, rock and soul were bywords for seriousness and reach—far more so then, incidentally, than they are today—and they appeared for a season to be singing from the same hymn sheet.

It seemed then, surely, that even if the Age of Aquarius were not about to dawn any time soon, then at least the age of majority was about to come to popular music. Now, the kids who'd bought Elvis records in 1956 and then Kinks records in 1965 were churning through their thirties. And the hipsters who had bought Miles Davis records in 1959 were even older than that. And they still had money. In fact, in very many cases, they had a lot more of it than they used to have. By the middle years of the 1970s they had children of their own, too, or were thinking about it, or had decided not to have them and were enjoying their money in all its exciting disposability. They felt grown-up and as if they had arrived in life. They had survived the wilding of the previous decade and now they were ready to claim the ultimate prize in a socially mobile world in which old class barriers had been breached or blurred or simply flattened. In 1974, the ultimate prize of any newly formed adult, whatever his or her station in the class system, was the feeling that he or she might at last have earned the right to feel sophisticated.

The markets responded. They responded by conceding that it must surely follow in any mature discourse about the serious things in life—as well as the somewhat melancholy nature of life itself—that women really ought to be involved.

Women had of course been involved in pop all along, once the initial testosteronal rush of rock 'n' roll had dissipated. True, they had been in an extreme minority, but they had punched above their weight in the great song factory of the Brill Building (thank you, Carole King, Ellie Greenwich, Cynthia Weil . . .) and they had fronted up the pop conceits of male producers, composers, and arrangers since time almost immemorial. Some had even achieved diva status (Dusty, Dionne, Diana . . .), capable of timeless statements of great artistic authority but without proper authorial control over their singing careers—and without the license to sing unequivocally about their own lives from their own texts. By the end of the 1960s, women who were visibly in creative charge of their own texts were long overdue in pop.

But once the door had opened a crack, they were through in a flash. Lots of them. The social modulations of the previous decade had counted for something at least. Pop had grown up at last. And by the middle of the 1970s, authorial women were everywhere and they were making a huge difference to the way pop sounded. They were even accorded their own designation: "female singer-songwriter."

Joni Mitchell, the doyenne, even produced her own records. This was not usual.

* * *

I was fourteen when *Court and Spark* came out. In 1974 I was still a creature of English prog rock, glam, and the Rolling Stones; Joni Mitchell was not speaking to my desires at all. Yet, through the agency of friends and their elder sisters, I was made aware of the album. I wasn't all that impressed. In fact I despised the musicians who played on "Raised on Robbery" for their flappy, uncogent rocking; disliked their employer for sponsoring such a feeble parody in the first place. Sophisticated worldliness meant little to me—almost as little as the inner worlds of females. And so I disregarded the shimmer of *Court and Spark*, as I disregarded many things that appeared to have no direct bearing on my immediate experience.

Then, right at the very end of 1975, when I was fifteen, *The Hissing of Summer Lawns* came out.

Hissing changed the picture, and not only because my hormones had settled down somewhat and I had given the prog project the old heave-ho. There was more to it than that. This was not for me a political or a feminist moment, but a moment of authentic enquiry predicated rather less on ideological rectitude than on the pleasure of self-exploration. Not so much "how do women feel?" as "how do I feel about how women feel?"

My great friend Lorry—himself a Joni neophyte—was the first to lay out the sterling. And I followed, entranced by the shifting, fruited tonality of the new music, its ambiguous minor keys and Mitchell's newly levelled-off melodic style. There was no preening on *Hissing*, no self-congratulatory jumping through melodic hoops to show the extent of Joni's reach (precious little, once you'd got past her exuberant opening gambit, "In France They Kiss on Main Street"); she seemed to be fashioning the music out of some need not to fulfill expectation but to settle, searchingly, into melancholy, as if abandoning a raft for the deeper draught below. This music had body. It snaked, much as the anaconda on the cover snaked, in and out of the grasp of its portaging "natives" on the very edge of the jungle, close to where it becomes a city.

And for once, the tunes and the heft of the voice and the swirling musical arrangements were not the only objects of scrutiny: I found myself listening with attention to the stories *Hissing* contained about women, about Scarlett and Edith and the "anima rising" of "Don't Interrupt the Sorrow," which sounded to me like a description of magma pushing through the chimneys of the Earth. I listened to them and wondered. These were not politicized stories, exactly—not overtly, anyway—and they were way too thought-through to be exhibitions of petulance. They seemed to be more like the exercise of existential feeling through acute observation: descriptions of used women, kept women, women who are willfully trapped; women with "impossibly gentle hands" who "must have everything"; women who note the bubbling of their magma as a matter of daily routine. Most of the songs did not seem, on the surface at least, to be about Joni at all. *The Hissing of Summer Lawns* felt immensely real to me, and not like some position. It felt grown-up.

Both Lorry and I later congratulated ourselves on our unexpected but entirely genuine enjoyment of the record, and chiefly on the personal sophistication we felt bubbling in our own flues and chimneys as we listened privately to the music; and we mesmerized ourselves with the thought that perhaps we were beginning to know everything.

Of course we knew nothing. We weren't even born.

* * *

Within days of finishing my A-levels in the summer of 1978, I left the family home wherein I'd done all my growing up since the age of four. I moved into the box room of a semi-detached dump on the very edge of town, where the city's sprawl gives way to nothing whatsoever, and began immediately to feel the loneliness of freedom. I was living with a couple of friends, and glad of it; really very happy to, in fact—I was more than weary of the routines and constraints of family life. But it was still a leap into the unknown.

I had decided to defer my university entrance for a year and was determined in the meantime to acquire a job in town that would get me into the grain of things, get my hands dirty-ish. And miraculously, I'd landed a gig working in the back room and sometimes behind the counter of the best record shop in town (there were, on retrospective calculation, at least seven record shops servicing a town populated then by perhaps 90,000 souls). I was extremely pleased about this. It felt as if I had arrived at some new gateway in life that just required a push and I'd be on my way, if not to untold happiness, riches, and high social status, then certainly into the grain.

But the box room in the dump on the edge of town was tiny and cold, even in summer, and it remained for a few weeks more at least the official residence of another guy, who was due to move out soon—but would I take over the lease while he enjoyed the rest of the summer elsewhere in warmer climes? I think his name might have been Chris; it usually was in 1970s East Anglia. So I duly moved in and sat on Chris's cream candlewick bedspread and felt the world gape. And for the first few days all I could listen to was *Hejira*, which had come out a year or so after *Hissing* and felt, at least nominally, like *Hissing*'s slightly less gorgeous older sister. This temporal paradox did not stand up to much scrutiny, of course—but nothing else in my growing record collection seemed right for the moment, so I listened and listened.

It may not come as a surprise to you, dear reader, if you are yourself sophisticated and already familiar with the nature of *Hejira* and its relevance to my new situation, teetering as I was on the very edge of the rest of my life, as well as the edge of the bedspread—but I was clueless. I'd heard the thing on numerous occasions since its release and had acquired the record only a matter of weeks before—and I had got nowhere near to coming to grips with its expressed themes, let alone its deeper psychological swells. I was into Siouxsie and the Banshees, not psychological swells. I certainly had no idea that *Hejira* was precisely the music that a "sensitive but not entirely unworldly" boy ought to be listening to in the moment of his leaving home. So I listened to it in total innocence, as one listens at first to most pop music—as a textural adjunct to life in the hope that the new texture might make life feel more textured for a moment. In addition, I listened to *Hejira* for its beautiful, comforting sound and for its openness and slowness and for what impressions I could scrape together from my half-focused apprehension of Mitchell's words, which on first, second, third, and even ninth contact appeared to be mostly about what fun it is to travel, and to have sex and not have sex with people you meet while on the hoof.

I observed the vapor trails of 747s. I listened in on the ghostly clatter of old Beale Street, Memphis. I imagined what a chicken must look like as it scratches for its immortality. I appreciated the soft, low undulations of the music and the way it seemed to elicit a rocking motion in the narrow spaces contained within my body. I particularly appreciated the importance of Jaco Pastorius's fretless bass as a vocalistic counterpoint to the quartering melodies of Mitchell's voice on top, a voice that was no longer swooping from a regal height but moving carefully forward in simple strides, inviting you to follow. I heard in the thrum of Mitchell's open-tuned guitar the thrum of wheels. My listening was uncomplicated. I did not imagine that this was the sound a woman makes when she is doing the greatest thing she will ever do.

"Hejira" (or Hijra or Hegira) is an Arabic word associated with the journey of Muhammad from Mecca to Medina. It means flight from danger or trouble. It implies that flight or the act of travelling away from a threat is itself an activity alive with special meaning. *Hejira* the album was the by-product of a return journey made alone in a car, in Mitchell's own elasticated time, across country from New York back to her usual place of residence, Los Angeles. She did not travel in a straight line. It was not clear what, if anything, she was in flight from. But, after a fashion, she was quartering America.

So far, so conventional. This "lighting out for the territory" (à la Huck Finn) had been a trope of American literary self-esteem for decades; arguably for centuries, if you want to go back to the foundations of an American literary and song tradition which abounds with accounts of journeying into the wilderness beyond the ordered, familiar world to embellish existing myths, to establish new ones, and perhaps to enable a spot of personal myth-burnishing on the way. Jack Kerouac had done precisely that in the 1950s and his literary shadow lay long over American pop culture, with the result that both average and much-better-than-average songwriters had for years, long before the arrival of *Hejira*, exercised their right to self-actualization through the idea if not the actuality of American exploration—Bob Dylan being but one of them. Indeed, it was a widely held assumption that the US cultural imperium was itself in part built on that kind of impulse, the solitary soul finding itself alone in the expanse of the American heartland and calling it—and the soul—into being, by narrating it. The actualization of Manifest Destiny.

But *Hejira* is not a narration of the American heartland, or of any of its other expanses, for all the vividness of its burning deserts and farms and its wistful imaginings of Darktown society in old, concreted-over Memphis. *Hejira* narrates the revelation of a woman's selfhood as she discovers it through the abandoned act of hard, solitary travel. In this vision, it is fugitive movement, not love, which brings the woman to herself. The travelling entailed might just as well have been done in rural France or the Greek islands—both favored Mitchell destinations of the past—or it might have been on the Moon, but it would not have altered the substance of the discovery. Place is not the discovery. The heartland of the self is. America is only the incidental location of the story. The agency of Mitchell's self-discovery is not place but flight, not location but locomotion. And the point of the story is to explain the soul's long-abiding "urge for going" not as a neurotic desire to escape from the world but as a need to turn to face it more honestly: the only place she can be truly at home, in "the refuge of the roads."

* * *

Not everyone likes Joni Mitchell's voice. In fact, in my experience, most people don't. "Yeah, she's great, I can see that," people often say, "but I just don't like her voice."

I know where they're coming from. I don't always like it either. I am certainly not fond of the prim trill with which she elucidated her concerns in "Big Yellow Taxi" and "Both Sides, Now," while the desperate alto-to-soprano arcing of so much of *Blue* does not encourage me to enter the bounds of her broken interior so much as create objections to my entering it, on the grounds that I may be too coarse a bacterium for that inflamed and lesioned place. And I have always hated her singing on *Court and Spark*. There, I've said it.

But suddenly, on *Hissing* and *Hejira*, everything changed. It was as if the Scando-Canadian ex-hippie woman of means put everything she'd learned behind her and began to sing with a new voice, one she'd been driving toward but never yet found the courage to use: a voice not stretched by the agonies of failed love or burnished into stylish self-parody by the imperatives of sophistication; a voice matured out of all recognition from the girlish purity of her folk beginnings. It's just . . . her voice, a *true* voice, or so it seems: a deep, linear, narrating voice which succeeds in conveying you first, in *Hissing*, into the inner worlds of other women and then, with *Hejira*, into the real world of the author's flight—the world as she experiences it literally in passing.

The tunes on *Hejira*, though shapely, exhibit none of the heart-monitor spikiness of prior creations. Instead they drive with great suppleness and candour into the substance of real thought and feeling, as if this too were a place, just like America, the voice following the contours of the melodies without apparent effort but amazing metrical precision—not for show but to get the substance of the songs across, quiet and clear, to the listener. What we're listening to here is not the careful enunciations of a poet, keen that you miss none of the nuances of her language, but the deep moment-by-moment involvement of the soul singer who wants to feel the click of those nuances herself, as if she needs to actually live them out to force sense out of them. It is, in the end, the singing of a woman who has arrived at her idiom—a mode of self-expression that appears to come to her as naturally as breathing and does not belong to any other creature in creation. There are no arch-backed vertical takeoffs in *Hissing* and absolutely nothing in *Hejira* that even hints at a swoop.

But there is a song on it so marvelous that it can make me weep, mostly, I think, because it is so marvelous. It's called "Song for Sharon" and it finds Mitchell recalling the day she went to Staten Island to buy a mandolin. While there, she saw a lacy white wedding dress in a shop window, waiting quietly there like a magnet to draw the inchoate cravings of "some girl"—and out of that passing snapshot, a skein of reflection looped Joni back into her childhood and her friendship with the eponymous Sharon, and then deeper into her own "illusions" about love and craving and the futility of craving. It is one of the greatest songs of reflection ever written, not only because of the poetic quality of its observations or the rawness of its honesty about matters it is very hard to be honest about, but because of the way the song and its singing make you *feel* the slippages implicit in every syllable of Mitchell's thinking and feeling. Somehow, you register the song as a sequence of emotional and intellectual events in real time, and as you go, you experience those ambivalences as if they were your own. You are not excused from any of it.

It isn't all dismal stuff either; not by any means. The landscape changes with the shifting of the recollective light. There is even a little buck up, when, at the start of the fourth verse, Mitchell explains to Sharon how she separated from "my man" at a rail station in North Dakota prior to heading for New York, and for the duration of that three-bar incident, the drummer—who has hitherto done nothing much apart from click along in time—syncopates the kickdrum and hi-hat barely perceptibly into a quirky hump of subtle new rhythm. Just for a moment. Mitchell responds by riding the hump as if it belonged to a camel. She goes with it, swings with it effortlessly, and the entire complexion of the song changes for perhaps five seconds. It is the tiniest, least exuberant expression of joy I think I have ever heard in music, but it casts its patch of light across the undulations of the song like a break in cloud.

And then it's gone.

What do I mean, "arrived at her idiom"?

I suppose I mean that, with *Hejira*, Mitchell alighted on a form of musical expression that agreed absolutely with the content of what she had to say, so that no seams were visible and the showy stylistic mannerisms that had lent so much exaggerated shape, intensity, and high tone to earlier works just melted into nonexistence. Irrelevance, even. In this new account of the world there was no need for such self-conscious artfulness, no need for show. Whether this departure was the result of stratagem or serendipity is moot and not all that important, to my mind—although it is worth noting that, because the songs on *Hejira* were all written "on the road," Mitchell was forced to put them together on guitar alone, without the option of retreat to the highbrow fastness of the piano.

Should one be bothered to notice such things? Possibly not. But it is certainly worth pointing out that this "idiom" was in part shaped by the necessity of having to play guitar in a variety of open tunings; the result, or so it has been said, of childhood polio, which limited the dexterity of Mitchell's fingering hand. Certainly there is a kind of chord voicing that can be identified as Mitchellesque, though you'd need a musicologist to demonstrate what those augmentations and diminutions are, precisely. Yet still, still there's more to the Mitchell sound than the pitch of the notes themselves. The physical impact of her playing—the way she strikes the strings—carries a shaping force that orders the overall sound and camber of the music as substantively as, say, Keith Richards' string-striking used to shape the sound and camber of the Rolling Stones. It is *that* important to her music, her guitar-playing. Or at least it is on *Hejira*.

But, again, when I refer to Mitchell's "idiom" I don't just mean sound: I also mean what we conventionally think of as content—the substance of her lyrics and the style of her writing. The songs on *Hejira*—even the more stylistically biased ones, "Blue Motel Room" and "Black Crow"—lay themselves out before you with an even distribution of weight and beauty as if they had been discovered, not composed. There is, on *Hejira*, a sense that Mitchell's block of sheened, translucent marble has at last been chiseled down to its essential form; that all extraneous material has been removed to reveal the meat of the matter, the poised and tensile figure that lies on the inside of every virgin block of stone. This is the essential Joni. These are the stories she has it within herself to tell most cogently—the result of willed detachment from the familiar world and its expectations, its obligations, its vanities, and its responsibilities.

* * *

It is three weeks—no, four—since Mitchell was carted off to hospital, and there has been no further word about her condition, apart from the usual dead-bat assurances from her people that she is making good progress and that all will be well. In that time I have listened to *The Hissing of Summer Lawns* and *Hejira* at least a dozen times each, and mostly in the car when making spiritual journeys to Sainsbury's or transporting the family to the Heath for a compulsory stroll under filthy London skies.

"C'mon!" chorus the other occupants of the car as "A Strange Boy" unwinds to its non-resolution, "haven't you had enough of her yet?" To which I reply that, no, I haven't. But, I say graciously, I will change the record if they will only stop complaining and tell me what it is that makes them so inhospitable to Joni.

None of them can ever say, though. Neither wife, nor children. It is as if Joni belongs to another universe, a universe that runs parallel to ours and is, by definition, not only not available as subject matter for discussion but is in fact by definition not a viable topic for discussion, like the Holy Ghost.

But I am pigheaded and stubborn.

"Come on," I say. "You can give me more than that. Of course you can. If you want me to turn Joni off, then before I do so you have to justify it—I want to hear actual descriptions of how the sound of Joni Mitchell causes you pain and dissatisfaction."

There usually follows some mumbling about Joni's voice and how she sounds unrelaxed and swoony and a bit over-intense and such an obvious hippie, and how her tunes are long and wordy and artily shaped and they never seem to stop unwinding, as if the pain of life is unending and "she's just pouring it out of a big jug" and couldn't we have something on just a bit more cheerful and fun? Even jazz?

"It's just not happy music," says one naysayer, certain of her own co-gency; then, convinced that this will nail it: "Plus, it doesn't speak to *me*." And I find it necessary at last to point out that a much younger Joni Mitchell than this one discovered that she was pregnant by an ex-boyfriend in her very early twenties, back in 1964, and that, after giving birth, she gave up the child for adoption because she was unable to provide for it and because there was enormous stigma back then attached to mothers who gave birth to children out of wedlock—and that every song she ever wrote after that was an act of expression growing directly out of an inability to talk to the one person in the world she wanted to talk to—but couldn't.

The car fell quiet after that.

Then, after a while . . .

"So, Dad, why do you like it so much, then?"

And for once I realized that I had nothing relevant to say.

GRACE NOTES

JACKSON BROWNE: "FOUNTAIN OF SORROW"
Asylum Records, 1974
The same year that Joni Mitchell's *Court and Spark* alighted so graciously upon the world, another album made itself available rather more somberly but with no less sensitivity: Jackson Browne's *Late for the Sky*.

Late for the Sky was not really meant for fourteen-year-old English boys and it should come as no surprise to the reader that fourteen-year-old boys in England did not show much interest in *Late for the Sky* either. In my city, we all became aware of it a couple of years later, around the time of the onset of punk, when we were sixteen and beginning to engage with girls in a way that they might not find wholly repellent. I am sad to say that the coincidence of punk made it very difficult, even quite shaming, to like *Late for the Sky*, despite the manifest attractions of its mournful, elegiac sound.

How come?

Let me offer you a brief account.

Jackson had long glossy hair, off-centrally parted. He was pretty. He looked incredibly clean. He read books. He sat at a piano as a poet hunches at a lectern. And all of this superficial image stuff stood in analogic relation to his music, which in turn stood for his social meaning. Jackson's music was gentle, melancholic, wholesome, and full of words of regretful reflection—and there were loads of them. He appeared to be sensitive and generous spirited. He understood that perhaps he had made mistakes in life and that, where he hadn't made them, fate and "changes" had intervened to bring disillusion. He lacked irony. Furthermore, he lived on the West Coast of America and appeared also to regret the lost hopes of the 1960s. He recorded on the Asylum label. He also had form, having written songs for the Eagles. And his voice was deliquescent like melting butter. Worst of all, girls found him desperately attractive and played his records in their bedrooms as auditory totems of their own sensitivity and availability to the right kind of chap—a chap like him, not you.

So chaps like me scorned Jackson Browne for a good couple of years, until it was safe to emerge as newly matured near-adults endowed with both the palate and the sophistication to accept that there was room in the world for both Siouxsie and Jackson. Interestingly, and no doubt purely coincidentally, this moment corresponded in life with the onset of rather more sex.

"Sophistication" is one thing, "melancholy" quite another. But it is in the work of Jackson Browne above all that we find the latter expressed not as a cosmetic feature of the former but as a driver of it. Oh dear, he seems to be saying, I know too much of the world and of you and of myself, and it is grievous to be so burdened. As a result, I am suffused with a close-to-biblical sense of helpless sadness that is, in fact, entirely secular and subtly political. Indeed my melancholy is the only thing that fits me for the world. Melancholy *is* my sophistication.

"Fountain of Sorrow" is a wonderful, insightful song, even as it is also a tiny bit self-romanticizing. A tiny bit? Completely self-romanticizing, actually, in a way that Joni Mitchell would no doubt scorn on grounds of ickiness. But that roseate, self-critical glow of sadness so beloved of Jacksonites is what makes the music sing, even as it soars unaided on its updraughts of not-wholly-repressed narcissism. This really is a beautiful song, whichever way you slice it; and Jackson really is a beautiful guy, however many pieces you want to chop him into.

It clicks along like the Eagles sometimes used to, on a propulsive West Coast piano, bass, acoustic guitar, and drum chassis. It has a high rate of harmonic turnover with an absolutely exquisite improvised Stratocaster descant looped and tied on top by regular Browne sideman David Lindley. (I recollect discussions taking place in pubs and sixth-form common rooms, which revolved chiefly around the unadulterated musicality of Lindley's playing—it was much easier for an eighteen-year-old chap to engage with that than with the content of the songs. Some might say that Lindley gilds the lily unnecessarily, but I would argue that there is not a lily lolling around in a field anywhere in the world that would not be enhanced by a garland of Lindley—even if the lily were already as pretty as the twenty-five-year-old Jackson.)

The song tells the mournful story of the singer's discovery in a drawer of an old snapshot of an ex-lover, and the array of challenging thoughts that arise from this chance encounter with his smiling, doubtful past—not the least of those thoughts being that the gaze is always contingent. "I was taken by a photograph of you," he sings, managing narrowly to avoid sounding pleased with himself.

And there, right there, is the essence of JB: the deliquescent voice of sophisticated melancholy melting into seductive elegance before you've had the chance to feel anything real yourself. There is certainly very little pur-chase to be had in the moment-by-moment experience of Browne's songs. You don't enter them in any mode except that of the admiring emotional spectator: here be "sorrow," and there be "regret." See that purple passage over there? That's "real emotional insight," that is. It's as if a deal has been struck: Jackson will do the thinking and feeling and phrasing and mourn-ing for us, and we'll play his ruminations back to ourselves in confirmation of our own sensitivity—and perhaps as a caution to ourselves to be more sensitive in the future.

When Jackson sings, we listen hard. But we do not experience his world so much as admire his account of it from a distance: it's a world we might only aspire to be part of on our very best, most sensitized days. Jackson Browne certainly makes the world a better place, if "palatable" is what we mean by "better."

PAUL SIMON: "HAVE A GOOD TIME"
Warner Bros. Records, 1975

At what point did rock music reach full maturity? Or, to put it more mod-ernly, when was Peak Adult in pop? You can certainly make the case that Paul Simon's 1975 album *Still Crazy After All These Years* was a spike.

Just look at that title. Just look at Paul on the cover in pouchy, pock-etless jeans and fedora, leaning proprietorially on a New York fire escape with his sleeves rolled up neatly above the elbows, arm akimbo, a worldly man of all worlds, a thick moustache crawling across his face on its way home to the joke shop. All the image of Paul lacks is a portfolio of holdings (maybe it's just out of shot, resting against the rungs of the fire escape). As for the graphics . . . Tinted photographic sepia on a beige ground? Epistolary script? You can't get more *Hannah and Her Sisters* than that—and *Hannah* wouldn't be out for another decade. Paul is smirking, literally smirking, with delight at his own sophistication.

He actually turned thirty-four in 1975, the year in which he declared that he was still crazy after all these years. All thirty-four of them. Then there's "My Little Town," which reaches all the way back to the place of the narrator's upbringing in another smaller time, in another smaller place, a long time ago when things were so much smaller. And "Night Game," which casts a rheumy eye over baseball's ghosts, and "50 Ways To Leave Your Lover," which is a hymn to sexual knowingness, and "You're Kind," which is a hymn to sexual self-knowledge. The musicians? They are top-liners from all over the country: mature, multidisciplinary exponents of the sessioneer's craft, as much at ease with a genteel boogie as they are with difficult time signatures and sprung meter.

The point of all this? Partly, it would appear that the point is to assert the possibility that high-end contemporary pop music might take "maturity" and "sophistication" as themes, in addition to the music being itself mature and sophisticated. *Still Crazy* may or may not be pure memoir (I am pretty sure it isn't), but it shows no interest whatsoever in that primary pop concern, the cult of youth; and having taken that decision, it shows real determination to wear the gesture as lightly as you might wear a fedora on a fire escape. To be sophisticated is to *not* be heavy. And so it is important, as the song says, to have a good time, while lolling on a counter-sunk Latinized funk groove propelled by Steve Gadd and Tony Levin, with a chorus of horns. God bless our standard of living, for it is the cornerstone not only of the American way of life, but of a developed sense of irony.

And never has Simon's boyish acorn-cup of a voice sounded so insouciant a note. How do you trust so mature an innocent? "Have a Good Time" is worse than Randy Newman for not keeping you quite in the picture, by skewing it, by forcing your gaze to slide across its surface; it's Randy Newman with the existential agony extracted with fine-pointed instruments and replaced with choirboy cherubism. Who's really talking here? And does he mean what he says?

Simon is "voicing" a character, for sure, but he's doing it so blithely it's hard to tell whether he thinks shallow, consumerist complacency is a cancer or a boon. Or maybe it's both! How's *that* for sophistication? Perhaps he feels that we'd all be so much better off if only the shallow and the complacent among us would take responsibility for themselves and become sophisticated, just like Paul. The point is rammed home at the end, when the last word goes to an unresolved alto-sax cadenza by the venerable bop musician, Phil Woods. He rips into eternity without support, without explanation. The passage is open-ended, complex, linear, somehow obliquely ironical in the context, yet coolly effortless—and you really can't get more sophisticated than that.

RICKIE LEE JONES: "THE LAST CHANCE TEXACO"
Warner Bros. Records, 1979

Vulnerability. Soul. Sophistication.

Bring me a pretty—but not too pretty—white woman who can embody all three of these qualities in a single persona with lashings of authenticity and hip charisma, and I will sell a million records for the company!

You can imagine the head of Warner Brothers' A&R operation in the late seventies saying something like that to himself. Certainly Lenny Waronker, who had the job, pretty much fulfilled that aspiration when he signed Rickie Lee Jones. Warners had by then taken over from Columbia Records as the principal fount of sophistication in pop, and a lot of that was down to Waronker's artist-centric A&R policy. He was a real old-school music guy, in it for the long haul, interested in quality over novelty—a man for his time, as the industry struggled to counter the global slump in sales that had turned the end of the seventies into a mire.

If indeed that mythical siren was what he was looking for, he found it in Rickie Lee Jones, a blonde waif of a neo-beatnik from the palpitating heart of LA's hipster scene. She was talented, gawky, wayward, and wore a beret. She smoked cheroots. She had benefited from all the dubious endowments of the itinerant hippie childhood and was the very definition of the expression "footloose." And you could hear in her massive breakout hit, "Chuck E.'s in Love," a kind of ditzy jazz-spiritedness that might parlay well into the highly evolved studio-production values in which Warner Bros. had invested so much in recent times. She was soulful, all right; she was vulnerable as cobwebs. And, framed with just the right degree of delicacy and dry candor, she would appeal to sophisticated tastes.

"Chuck E.'s" is charming, of course: a syncopated, swinging, elusively warm mumble of a record, big on heart, but equally big on Waronker's (and his co-producer Russ Titelman's) fabled production translucency. That entire debut album stands to this day as a minor classic of the kind of pre-digital close-miked technical perfection that made the LA sound of its period really sing. The production invited you to smile and feel warmth. But Rickie Lee's voice made you shiver.

We're all different, and we all have our own projections of how things really are. But for me the very center of the album, and therefore of the entire Rickie Lee *oeuvre*, is not "Chuck E.'s" or the tragic epic of lonesome inconsolability "Company" but "The Last Chance Texaco," which drifts into your presence on wistfully strummed minor chords on acoustic guitar and then stalls into silence a little over four minutes later like an expired engine.

It is among the very greatest car-metaphor songs ever written and sung. You'd have to be made of something very stern and innately unresponsive not to be transfixed and perhaps a little humbled by this achingly sad failure to be straightforward about things.

The song is ostensibly a description not of the motive power of an automobile but of its familiar tendency to break down, the certainty that its fuel will run out, the unassailable truth that batteries die, and the creeping knowledge that rust will eat underpinnings until bits fall off. And yet . . . And yet there is always one last Texaco gas station, offering one last chance to get the old heap bodged back on the road—and the temptation to pull up on to that forecourt is impossible to resist, despite the sure knowledge in your breast that, this time, the game really is up. It's over. Finished.

She's talking about relationships, of course.

But she sings from the very bottom of her well of feeling, her high, keening, boyish wisp of a voice creeping out at first and barely enunciating the words—no one has ever rolled syllables around in her mouth with such a combination of hunger and suspicion—responding only to the pulses of emotion within her body. The music is sophisticated, tasteful, melancholy; the voice is raw vulnerability and very little else, for all its huge dynamic range and tensile strength. And at the end, she squats down on the edge of the forecourt among the weeds and tires, half in and half out of the light, and watches other, more reliable cars speed past her and vanish into the dusk, going about their business.

"Niiiiiiaaaaaoww," she goes. "Niiiiiiiiiiiiaaaaaooooowwww."

STEELY DAN: "HEY NINETEEN"
MCA Records, 1980

There's another kind of sophistication: let's call it "a sense of irony that runs so deep it no longer knows what sincerity is or what purpose it serves or how it feels to actually feel it." In fact it can't get it up for sincerity at all. But it can watch. In the case of "Hey Nineteen," it's an aging hipster—the former "dandy of Gamma Chi"—watching a nineteen-year-old girl dancing to 'Retha Franklin at a party, as if that is all he has left to connect him to the non-ironical realness of the world as he possibly once experienced it.

"She don't remember the Queen of Soul."

The Steely Dan joke has grown comfortably old without straining itself. Everyone's easy about where Steely Dan is at now, ain't they, now that Steely Dan are old too? Less of a rock band than a high-concept exercise in sophisticated, multi-level irony, no? After all, the Dan were only slightly more of a "band" back in 1972 in California when they first appeared to be one, than they were eight years later when "Hey Nineteen" bobbed so hygienically out of the shower cubicle of their seventh album, *Gaucho* (still half a decade shy of the widespread adoption of digital compact disc but recorded, for the most part, with OCD-ish proto-digital cleanliness in NYC), a band in name and more or less in conception, but in reality not a band at all. In fact after 1974 Steely Dan were not even pretending to be a band, and were quite content to be recognized as a conjuring trick performed by a pair of darkling sixties hipster-nerds who'd met at "liberal arts" college: Walter Becker and Donald Fagen. What a pair. They liked modern jazz a lot, and they thought there was a lot to be said for reflecting sardonically upon the layered superficialities of American materialism, as if they loved it all really. And in a way, they did love it really. In a way. In the same way that you love the bits about yourself that you hate the most.

So naturally Americans bought in at face value. And why wouldn't they?

The Dan started out sounding like a smooth West Coast pop operation but they evolved very rapidly, with the deployment of tricky jazz chords, supra-articulate guitar solos, and drummers who can really swing, into a generically slippery high-end rock band and then into the most perfectly buffed example of deluxe jazz-funkified studio art ever to be experienced on expensive hi-fi. Why wouldn't you get from "Rikki Don't Lose That Number" the idea that all American lives, whether affluent or not, have the potential to be low lives? Huh?

Naturally, that neurotic technical perfectionism plus the narcotics and the industrial-strength hipster cynicism put a terrible strain on Becker and Fagen's relationship, and it all came to grief in 1981. But for the best part of a decade Steely Dan's was the best-kept secret joke in American music. And the funniest thing about it was that, even if you didn't get the joke—even if you, the listener, were oblivious of the game being played and you took the Dan's oblique songwriting strategies at FM radio face value—as a classy pop soundtrack studio-crafted for deluxe people—then you could still feel worldly as you listened. And that was all because of Donald Fagen's voice, which was about as full of spontaneity and joy as a tapir nursing a headache in a shed.

He hooted and he sneered and the arrangement of the skinflaps around his larynx (not to mention the moisture content of his sinuses) ensured that no note ever went unsmeared. It was a sort of anti-cologne, Fagen's voice. It splashed human corruptibility across the polished surfaces of Steely Dan's music and ensured that no one ever came away from a Steely Dan record feeling anything less than the million dollars that they rather wished they hadn't left behind by mistake in a plastic holdall in the wrong room in a motel on the beat-up side of town.

6

What Is Soul?

The first soul record I ever bought was not a single, as it should have been for true propriety, but an album. The album was called *This Is Soul*. It was a cheap compilation licensed for the British market in the late 1960s containing perhaps a dozen Stax/Atlantic classics by such monsters of *el mondo chitlin* as Wilson Pickett, Arthur Conley, Eddie Floyd, Otis Redding, Carla Thomas, Sam & Dave, Percy Sledge—people like that. I no longer possess it, sadly, although I have no recollection of disposing of it either. But I do recall the strange sense of transgression I experienced in forking over the 50p the album cost secondhand in 1974. Long-haired East Anglian prog-rocking teens were no more accustomed to buying soul records than they were to combing their oily tresses. Buying *This Is Soul* felt weird.

The cover art was different to what I was used to, too. It wasn't really "art" at all; certainly not in the way a prog-rocker thought of art. It was a commercial design, pure and simple: design that was clearly saying something. But what could it be saying, apart from "buy me!"? What was its secret message? In the top-left quadrant of the cover, the album title was spelled out in a chubby orange and pink sans-serif font so redolent of the 1960s it struck a contemptibly nostalgic note in 1974. And that was it so far as typography went, apart from the handsome Atlantic logo positioned off-center at the bottom of the twelve-inch square. No mention was made of what music might lurk within, only the title assertion, *This Is Soul*, as if there were nothing else to say on the matter, no further information to impart. The rest of the space was filled to the edges by a roughly taken (with flash) snap of a thinly mustachioed black man in a leather waistcoat bawling into a pig-iron microphone with his eyes tight shut. The picture was evidently taken from a lofty position upstage of the singer, because the background of the shot was filled with an audience receding into darkness. It was composed mostly of white faces, faces observing the onstage action with cool indifference. A couple of them had their backs turned.

But what made the design compelling was neither the skin pigmentation nor the apparent indifference of the audience, nor the expressed passion of the singer in the spotlight, nor even the offensively nostalgic pink and orange typography. It was the grid of jigsaw-puzzle shapes superimposed in white onto the photographic image. Here was mystery interlocking with enigma. The singer's face was positioned stably enough bang in the middle of the grid, but it was graphically subdivided by the edges of no less than four jigsaw pieces, their central nexus located above the crease defining the singer's left nostril. Meanwhile, over his left shoulder, one of the jigsaw pieces was filled by the expressionless face and dishevelled bouffant of one of the spectators. She was turning her head over her own left shoulder to face the stage in desultory fashion and it was more than possible to suppose that her thickly kohled gaze was actually drawn not to the singer working his mojo so manfully, but to the lens of the camera.

It seemed to me that the allegory of the cover of *This Is Soul* was profound but elusive. The best interpretation that I could muster then was that it all had something to do with pieces "fitting together"; that soul music, like humanity itself, was a puzzle and that all you had to do to make sense of the puzzle was tip the pieces out of the box on to a flat surface and get down to work sorting them out. No? Maybe not. Or perhaps the jigsaw signified that, for all our divisions as a species, beneath the rigors of the regulating grid imposed by society we are all one: one heart, one spirit, one soul . . .

I remained agnostic.

Fortunately, there was a Ben E. King song on the album that seemed likely to help. It asked the difficult question to which the album, its title, and its jigsaw puzzle imagery sought to express an answer. The song was entitled "What is Soul?". It wasn't much of a song, but it had unequivocal things to say on the subject of what soul is.

"Soul is something that comes from deep inside / Soul is something that you can't hide."

Ah, *at last*. Thank you. That explains everything . . .

In the end, I came to the conclusion that soul is not something that exists *sui generis*, a discrete thing in and of itself, but is something that you recognize from previous exposure to things also deemed soulful. Indeed it seemed quite clear that "soul" in the musical sense was a quality, not an actuality—not even a form—and that it evinced properties that did not obtain in every walk of musical life, however much it might be the case that most serious musicians (apart from some radical modernist ones) tend to think that their music is always something that can't be hidden which comes from deep inside. "Soul" was a quality with very specific applications.

I ought really to have read a book about it, but in 1974 I was not aware that any such book existed. And so I organized my own interpretation. Soul was black. It was a vocal music of clarified song, not technical virtuosity. Its motions were continuous with those of the body. It took the passions and appetites as its primary subject matter. It took the emotions of the soul singer as the primary agent of that subject matter. It took what I understood to be the form and energetic spirit of gospel music and turned it, in a lather of sweat, to embrace the profane with lots of dancing, which I wasn't too keen on back then. It also wore smart clothes, which was also bad news.

That was what I inferred, impressionistically, from listening to *This Is Soul* and the radio and from reading music magazines. But actually, all I knew for sure was that I absolutely loved Wilson Pickett. I had no notion of what to think about the man but I loved his voice and its relationship with the rhythm that locked and pinned "Mustang Sally" and "In the Midnight Hour." I can't remember now whether both songs were on *This Is Soul*, or just the one. But Pickett was the reason I bought the thing so nervously from the record stall in the market square. I wanted him in my bedroom.

* * *

Although my definitions of what constitutes soul music have expanded over the intervening forty years, and perhaps become a little more sophisticated, I still stand by the notion that "soul" is identified principally by example and precedent. You *recognize* soul from what you already know. It's the way the thing is done, not the thing itself. It's a quality, not an actuality.

And the Wicked Pickett was the first to make me ask myself the Big Soul Question, so he remains for me the embodiment of all that the "soul" idea might contain. From the beginning I matched the sound of his voice to the word "soul" and so he is the model of it, the archetype. The lodestar. Soul descends like blood from him. He is the fount. Everything else I hear that aspires to the condition of soul is automatically weighed and measured against his voice. And of course hardly anything else ever does measure up completely to that example of yelling, grumpy, anguished, saturnine, wolfish, dangerously emotional masculinity. How could it? Only Pickett can sing "I'm in ... *LO-O-OVE!*" and make it sound as if the bottom of his heart is filled with rocks.

Does this mean that soul has to be yelling, grumpy, anguished, wolfish, saturnine and dangerously masculine to be properly soulful? Of course not. But it does mean that soul has, for me, to be expressed with an equivalent degree of expressive intensity, however conventionalized and mannered the style of execution (it is nonsense that successful soul singing can never be mannered; soul is itself a manner). It isn't the grumpiness and potential for violence in his voice that make Pickett soulful; it's his willingness to irrigate the feelings expressed by the song with his own feelings, the ones that reside within him already. Just listen to his notorious transformation of "Hey Jude" from a kindly portion of avuncular advice into a gnashing Alabamian haka. Be assured, oh tinies, that the movement you need is almost certainly not located on your shoulder. Soul, like all things, is always a matter of degree, of course, but when Wilson sings, you are left in no doubt that he not only means it to the max—whatever "it" may happen to be in that moment—but also that he is experiencing "it" powerfully here, now and in the rapture of the moment. He is close to bursting.

And yes, what about gender? Surely I can't claim a solitary male archetype for soul? It would not only be wrong but ridiculous to imply that soul can only be true when it has masculine characteristics. Wrong, ridiculous, and laughable. Soul always has a mother as well as a father. My soul mother is Gladys Knight.

Like Pickett, who hailed from Alabama, Knight was a child of the South who followed the well-trodden path from Georgia to Detroit, where there were both jobs to be found and relative freedom from at least some of the perils endured by blacks living south of the Mason–Dixon Line. In the end, Pickett returned to his Southern home territory to realize his honking, barking career as premier Soul Beast of the 1960s, but Knight stayed in the northern Motor City and became, with her family corps of backing singers the Pips, a second-tier act in the booming mid-sixties Motown enterprise.

She had been a child prodigy, her husky contralto winning prizes in public from a very young age—the classic tot endowed with a weirdly adult voice. But it was as a twenty-two year old in 1966 that she signed to Berry Gordy's Motown, with two cousins and a brother in tow as a straight-ahead R&B four-piece vocal combo. They were not very original, but they had soul in abundance. And they hit modestly with a blustering "I Heard It Through the Grapevine" the year before Marvin Gaye did, and then with a string of crossover successes in the United States at the start of the following decade.

Mainstream pop listeners in the United Kingdom did not really cotton on until 1972, when her darkly intimate reading of Kris Kristofferson's lonesome sleepover ballad "Help Me Make It Through the Night" slept over in the charts for what seemed like an eternity, and then stayed on for breakfast. I didn't like the song at all, but there was something about Gladys's voice that connected with my fundamental structures—something to do with its measured, thoughtful, huskily mournful warmth. She sounded wise and sad, and yet also as if genuinely in need; and I did not contest the real-world plausibility of a woman singing Kristofferson's highly masculine lyric, on the grounds that I was twelve and knew no better. The thing about it was, Gladys actually *sounded* lonely, and not as if she were just taking a position on the subject of loneliness. She made the sound of loneliness. I also loved the way she seemed to have to push hard sometimes just to get her voice out. There was a resistance there, in her tubes: you'd hear her push and then the voice would pop out half a second or more after the first moment of pressure. This I found wildly attractive. So I disregarded my distaste for "Help Me Make It . . ." as a song and enjoyed the sound of her voice as one can always enjoy the taste of food even when it has pips in it.

There are for me two signature Gladys moments. The one everyone knows is "Midnight Train to Georgia," on the Buddah label, which became a hit in the UK in 1976 following Knight's departure from Motown in 1973. It is an emotional tour de force of the kind that occurs in soul and very few other pop places—certainly not in country, Southern Soul's close cousin, where this kind of vocal animation of inner passion simply doesn't occur, however searching the lyrics of the song and however extrovert the attitude of the singer.

The song was written by a favorite of Gladys's, Jim Weatherly (for the record, a white Mississippian), and it tells in choked-off aspirational style of a woman deciding to accompany her man back to his homeland in Georgia following an abortive shot at "making it" in LA. It is a deeply conservative piece of writing in many ways and it appeals in part to the unrepentant provincial in me, as it seemed to appeal to something unrepentant in Gladys. But as an exemplar of how certain kinds of singing make you experience a semi-narrative song as a flux of real feeling in real time, it is hard to beat. The listener experiences every shift of doubt and misgiving in her, every one of them, yet you buy into her heavy-hearted exaltation and accept her decision as she spins the tale of how her chap sold his old car and headed off to the railway station to buy a one-way ticket back to his former life. (*Whoo-whoo.*)

The arrangement demands the muscular involvement of thick horns, rippling piano, a bobbing, pulsating bass, and the Pips in full Greek chorus mode, seeming both to echo Gladys and to stand apart, like a conscience as well as like the whistle on the train. Gladys herself is absolutely magnificent, addressing the conflict in her own heart with a fathomless combination of gospel intensity and mature acceptance as she realizes that, at bottom, she'd "rather live with him in his world than without him in mine." "Midnight Train" is not a classic of the feminist canon but you cannot help but believe in the authenticity of her decision. I am always utterly moved by it.

But the Gladys moment to define them all for me actually came out back in 1971, before "Help Me Make It Through the Night" added pop balladry to her list of accomplishments.

"I Don't Want To Do Wrong" never troubled the scorers in the UK at all, despite being a biggish hit in both pop and R&B charts in America and, on the face of it, the song does not have all that much going for it. Lyrically, it is at best a slight piece with a half-developed theme, and it depends for hooky color on an exaggerated blues arrangement for string orchestra absolutely drenched in pentatonic intervals. The song was co-written by Johnny Bristol and produced by him on an arpeggiated R&B chord sequence straight out of the 1950s street-corner songbook. So it's pretty much a genre piece, exploring the doubt and guilty anxiety precipitated by estrangement from a lover who has "been away" for such a long time that an emotional vacuum has developed in his absence. The song begins with a hesitant, torpid Gladys thinking about taking another lover but deciding that really she doesn't want to—she really, *really* doesn't want to do wrong. No, no, no. But one might easily infer from the texture of her worry that she has already fallen just a little and that "wrong" has already been done.

"I think I've lost this fight!"

Then, over the arc of three verses and choruses plus a breakout instrumental interlude in which the strings shoot to all four corners of the blue universe, she concludes that, such is her absent man's reluctance to communicate with her, perhaps the truth is that he has fallen out of love with *her*— as she has, indeed, fallen *in* love with someone new ... And then you realize, just as she does, that in the very moment of the utterance of the words, as she sings this very song, she is feeling the reality of it for the very first time. She has already crossed the line.

The Pips circle her like her crows.

And that's it. "I Don't Want To Do Wrong" is a snatched moment of time fraught with doubt and resentment and reproach and self-recrimination and, finally, self-knowledge, and Knight animates all of these coursing emotions over the duration of a little less than three and half minutes, as if a lifetime's worth of worry were compressed there between giant slabs of granite. The desperation is traumatic.

And yet the effect is consoling.

Gladys is as consoling as J. S. Bach. Her warmth, her wisdom, her sensitivity, her generosity, her sense of responsibility, her clear eyes, her deep, dark, justifiable yet controlled anger, her unabashed *seriousness* . . . These things are the very essence of consolation, as they are of soul, and it is not for nothing that I think of Gladys as my soul mother. The mother of all soul singers.

* * *

Soul mother? Soul daddy? Next thing I'll be constructing an entire new family for myself out of ennobling old-school R&B shouters . . .

And now that I've had the thought, it is worth pausing for a moment to consider the possibility that we do make new psychological structures for ourselves when we listen to voices. Voices are, after all, the first auditory signals that we associate with feelings of love and safety. They nurture. They cast a protecting veil. They chastise. They comfort. They stir. They are the vessels of family feeling. There have been occasions in life when I have been profoundly grateful that I have had certain voices to turn to.

And it seems to me no coincidence at all that, back in the day, while rock and its associate forms railed against all the institutions of Western bourgeois stability, and stood stridently against the social hegemony of the nuclear family and its ancillary structures, much of the black popular music mainstream in the 1960s and '70s (i.e., soul and funk) stood not only squarely behind the family as a structure but also for a greater sense of community and communitarian responsibility beyond the bounds of the home unit. Mainstream R&B has seldom evinced much interest in loosing anarchy upon the world, even at its most playful (which is not to say that it hasn't, from time to time, expressed the idea that anarchy is everywhere to be found—quite a different proposition). Soul music may in its period of primacy in the sixties and seventies have delved into torrid individual experiences as a matter of principle, but it always set those experiences in the wider context of the family, neighborhood, citizenship, and nationhood. Soul *encouraged* familial thoughts and feelings.

In real life I have two sisters, of whom I am very fond, even though I don't see them as often as I would like. But despite the physical distances between us, and the long history we share of petty bickering, they are also my soul sisters, after a fashion. They may not have neat equivalents in the realm of American R&B—Ann Peebles? Shirley Brown? Betty Wright? Mavis Staples? Nah, none of 'em, not quite . . .—nevertheless I do understand that they, my two real sisters, occupy a space and mark a presence in my psyche that might on other days be occupied and marked out by the sisterhood of soul. They are all female authorities of one kind or another, and embodiments of the female principle. They all exert their influence from a position of real-world stability and far greater maturity than I have ever mustered in my shallow life. And they are much better at arguing the toss than I am. I understand this to be incontrovertibly the case every bit as much as I understand my desire to confer the status of soul parenthood on Wilson Pickett and Gladys Knight.

And that's OK. I am very happy at any time to confuse my sister Deb with Millie Jackson. Or would be, if they were in any way confusable. The fact is though that Millie Jackson, for all her dissimilarity to Deb as an individual, sounds rather more as if she has a familial role to play in my psyche than, say, Grace Slick or Siouxsie Sioux or Lady Gaga have ever done. Soul always brings me back to what family means.

But sadly, I have been dealt a rum hand in this game of soulful Happy Families. I have no soul brothers. I have no soul brothers in the same way that I have no real brothers. Never have had them, never will; the role of soul brother simply does not exist for me. I can no more imagine what having a soul brother is like than I can conceive of what it's like to have a real one. And I suspect that one is contingent upon the other: I have no soul brothers precisely *because* I have no real ones. I don't know what brothers are like.

Yes, I hear myself protesting primly, but what about Al Green? You *love* him. Been sharing playful intimacies with him for more than forty years; looked up to him too for a while, after a fashion, as if he knew the world in ways that I might only aspire to. And Marvin? Love him too, despite his waywardness and unreliability and his many instructive failures of judgment. Paul Kelly, Teddy Pendergrass, Eddie Levert, Percy Sledge, Bobby Womack, Levi Stubbs, Otis Redding, Luther Vandross? Yes. They're close, all of them. I feel as if I have enjoyed at different times a personal relationship with every single one of their voices. They have been voices of consolation, pride, loss, indignation, lust, redemption, anxiety, pity, frailty, transformation—all of those things.

But not brotherhood. Not one of them. They have different roles to play. They are my soul dads, soul uncles, soul cousins, soul chums; perhaps even soul selves, for heaven's sake: figures of remote authority or renegade idiosyncrasy or masculine anguish or genial wisdom or near-identical frailty. They are not my brothers. I have no idea of what it is to have a brother. Where I should have a soul brother, or maybe two, there is only a void. Well, a state of wishful not-knowing.

*   *   *

But Sly Stone was pointing in the right direction, as usual. Soul is always a family affair, even when it isn't all that familial.

During the 1970s, when I was growing up in brotherless insularity on the edge of the East Anglian fens, white British mainstream rock and pop music played an interesting hand, by investing the social and economic fabric of the era with gala parades of home-grown would-be soul boys and girls. In fact, during that period "soulful" became the default setting on aspirational Brit-rock dials. If you excluded the era's art- and prog-rocking strategies from the equation, then British pop and rock vocal style in the 1970s remained as governed as ever it had been by the values, tropes, and figures of soul and blues, perhaps more so: such stuff as "classy production," American accents, syncopated phrasing, heightened emotions, torn throats, frayed edges, the struggle for sincerity, the renunciation of irony, the desire to get "inside" the emotion of a song and turn it out into the light through the expression of selfhood, as if the singer were making his or her own long-repressed emotions servant to the song, and they were all coming out, those emotions, at once in a rush. It was as if the point of soul and blues vocal style to white British singers was not the rapture of the instant so much as the opportunity the instant presented to get at stored-up emotional material that hadn't seen the light of day before. Not ever.

For years and years this presented a touching, if not always edifying spectacle, whether the musical performances themselves were good or not—and quite often they weren't very. Both male and female British nationals went to the well of black American vocal style and heaved up buckets of . . . well, what? What *did* they come up with?

If the 1970s were partly distinguished by numbers of white British brothers and sisters drinking rather self-consciously from the well of black American R&B, then who cleared the space for them to be there? Who did it first? Because, as sure as eggs are the fruit of a chicken's reproductive system, Paul Rodgers and Maggie Bell were not the first Brits with soul. Yes, the pair of them may well have taken their inspiration directly from records made by Otis Redding, Bettye LaVette, and some pompadoured Mississippian beau none of us have ever heard of, but neither of them brought themselves to bear on the world of British pop without precedent. They did not represent a point of origin.

I suppose the first star of English blue-eyed vocal blues to glimmer awkwardly in the pop empyrean was the towering six-foot-seven-inch enigma Long John Baldry, a Home Counties grammar-school boy and helpful sponsor of assorted fledgling careers in the early days of the British blues epiphany—most notably those of the Rolling Stones and, more conspicuously, Rod Stewart, whom Long John engaged as a second vocalist in his Hoochie Coochie Men after hearing the Mod-ish young tearaway busking

Muddy Waters at the railway station after one of his own gigs in Twicken-ham. Baldry's voice was a big, theatrical baritone, and he ploughed the tiny British blues field like an outsized Massey Ferguson. He chugged and roared and spluttered. He gouged at the sod of American black music with no great subtlety but great determination; he certainly turned more than a few pieties over. But the truth of it was that, booming out of Baldry's mouth, the blues sounded a rhetorical note shimmering with overtones of outsider panache and hints of transgression, plus lashings of barely suppressed camp—but not a whole lot of soul. Moreover, Baldry looked way too white and testos-teronal for the blues; too well fed and healthy. Irony seemed to glaze him, like sweat. Yet his voice was cavernous and sometimes close to unbridled. It's certainly worth finding on YouTube his lapel-clutching delivery of "Got My Mojo Working" for a Beatles TV special in what looks like 1964. It is a beast of a performance, as if Howlin' Wolf had come back to haunt the Old World in the upright form of a Guardsman-cum-honey monster, never actually transgressing the codes of TV propriety, but making it quite clear that you need only say the word . . .

Perhaps it should not come as a surprise then that LJB's one and only major hit was not a blues but a sonorous pop ballad, "Let the Heartaches Begin," a few years further down the line in 1967 when his relevancy had diminished somewhat and his light dimmed. It certainly owed about as much to the Chicago freight yards for its gestation as he did for his. Baldry never quite cracked the code—though it was not for want of trying and, in truth, in the context of his times, he could have done little more: a gay man functioning brightly in a social and legal context that denied him the right to self-reveal. But he did set an existential agenda for British R&B and it was a heartily irreverent one—one that insisted on the blues maintaining its edge and its abiding potential for transgression no matter what. Above all, he seemed to assert that the blues should always be engaged in the struggle to shake off the dragging chains of showbiz agreeableness. The blues should never be crooned.

But hearty irreverence, even all-out delinquency, does not get to the soul of the blues, as Messrs. Jagger and Lennon discovered for themselves when they were obliged to raise their own creative stakes beyond basic levels of pastiche, parody, and respectful knockoff. "Soul" might well be a manner, but if all you deploy in your singing are the mannerisms of soul and none of the supporting psychological substance, then what comes out of you will strike a nonresonant note, flat as a tin dinner plate. After all, if Ben E. King was right, then soul ought at least to *sound* as if it comes from deep within. Soul is a quality, not a thing.

And so the creative super-objective of British R&B vocal style became the discovery of its own authenticity, its own version of "deep within"— whatever the individual's chosen sub-idiom: purist blues, shouty R&B, or the newest melismatic flourish on the 1960s block, soul. You could be as irreverent and delinquent as you liked, but if you were going to convince listeners of anything at all, you also had to be *serious*.

The upshot was a generation of etiolated young white would-be stirrers getting down to work on their existential mojos, determined that, if nothing else, listeners should be under no illusion about the seriousness of their intent. (The vast majority of them were male, incidentally; for the most part, young women at this stage of the sixties were not allowed out of their frocks, or to sing from the gut—literally by order of management—any more than homosexuals were permitted to be gay.) And so what you heard at the time, and what you can still hear now in the recordings of the period, is not the sound of "deep within" but the sound of a generation of repressed, antsy, white, postwar class rebels discovering what it feels like to *think* a little about what lies deep within, and maybe to see what it smells like in there . . .

Some of these young men were scrappers, sonorous, raw-knuckled urchins, such as Newcastle's Eric Burdon and Chris Farlowe of north London, who scrapped their way out of their urban desolation with a combination of mordant, narrow-eyed bluesy phrasing and presentational grit. But soulful highmindedness was present, too, in small parcels: Van Morrison of Them and the Spencer Davis Group's Steve Winwood both deployed their keening vocal tone with a muezzin's combination of intensity and reserve, as if calling the faithful to prayer from a remote place. And there were suburban rockers who saw no discontinuity between the brashness of rock 'n' roll and the more testosteronal aspects of rhythm and blues. To hear Cliff Bennett and his Rebel Rousers now is to make an age-old connection with the unchanging vulcanism of young-manhood. Meanwhile, Steve Marriott's early undertakings with the Small Faces, before acid took an interest, vibrate at an equivalent frequency to Otis Redding's sock-it-to-me ravings. Not rock 'n' roll by any means, but music charged with rock 'n' roll's irrepressible vim, as well as a new quality: English suburban soulfulness.

And lest you think that this was an exclusive caste of gifted young technicians, there was no shortage in supply of other, less distinguished voices from the badlands of a withered nation, many of whom had precious little to write home about in the way of singerly grace but were certainly endowed with enough black-cat bone to get it on and then write home about that instead. Keith Relf of the Yardbirds and Phil May of the Pretty Things spring to mind. Same went for the fellows who bellowed in the Downliners Sect. There were others, too, coming in from other angles: Duffy Power, Jack Bruce of the Graham Bond Organisation, and Roger Daltrey of The Who, whose singing on the group's first *Maximum R&B* LP may not have been all that inhabited, psychologically speaking, but did at least crackle with unruly energy, as if audible electricity were flickering over the surface of the music.

Rhythm and blues, in all its generic subdivisions, was the motordrive of English pop throughout the second quarter of the 1960s, resulting in some of the most lustrous music ever made by anyone at any time, on this side of the Atlantic or the other. Think Tom Jones; think Lulu's "Shout"; think, above all, about Dusty Springfield's sublime massaging of the classic pop ballad with the oils of uptown American soul. As has been observed many times before, we Brits did a great job of taking black American music and selling it back to white America with a twist.

The suspicion has always been, of course, that that twist was a sanitizing one—and viewed purely from the marketing perspective, this was unarguably the case. The Rolling Stones, Dusty Springfield, and the Beatles did indeed re-present elements of African American music to white America without white America having to think troubling thoughts about where it had come from. To white Americans, R&B imported from the land of bad teeth and homosexuality was as amusingly exotic a proposition as the bossa nova then being washed up on North American shores from the land of the banana hat.

But for those who actually lived in the land of bad teeth and homosexuality, the story was a different one—it was a compelling new cultural narrative in which *we* heard *ourselves* for the first time in a completely new way. Here, all of a sudden—and no longer confined to the stage of the Royal Court—were voices suggesting that struggle, anxiety, lust, self-absorption, resentment, low mood, high spirits, bad faith, and recalcitrance were living manifestly amongst us in this very place, now and every day, as if these qualities actually belonged in the emotional curriculum of our own era, doing service in the frontline of British life alongside the stiff upper lip and the deferential simper.

And as the R&B-pop voice traversed the middle years of the sixties via hallucinogenic drugs and the psychedelic bypass into rock, the patterns it made became more diversified, even complex. Indeed, by 1968 the English psychedelic voice had separated itself from the rough corporeality of R&B style like egg white from its yolk and had reinvented itself as a genteel, supra-articulate poet's innuendo, all hissing sibilants and cultivated vowels. In the English garden of psychedelic flowers there was very little room for "raunch" or funky odors, nor for truck with an emotional world that is not entirely compliant with the rule of psychedelic lore: that wistful, Kenneth Grahamish sound of intoxicated semi-detached wonderment, as expressed most amiably by Donovan ("our very own Bob Dylan") or in the slightly more disturbing top-of-the-head wailing and whispering of Pink Floyd's Syd Barrett. Or, better yet, one of those chaps from Canterbury . . .

And why not, for heaven's sake, when you considered what lay at the rainy end of UK pop? Over there lurked a trainee gas fitter from Sheffield, Joe Cocker, a convulsive belcher of soulful truths. And, just as calloused but rather more swinging, the cock-rocker's cock-rocker, monobrowed Paul Rodgers from Middlesbrough, whose teenage posse of blues-rock formalists, Free, constituted one of the more convincing English attempts at making the blues sound both soulful and rocking, as well as English and modern.

Both Cocker and Rodgers assimilated the muscle and puff of American R&B vocal style wholesale (Rodgers, in particular, sounded like an honors graduate from the School of Wickedly Picketting), on the basis that rock, soul, and blues were American forms in origin and that it is *form* that brings heft to content, not personal identity. Not forgetting accent. Accent is an element of form. *You* try ransacking your dark interior astride a syncopated, thrusting, danceable pulse while vocalizing with an English accent. Yes, you'll sound like a pillock—not only to everyone else but to yourself as well. You will sound as if you are taking the piss, as indeed many were.

How symbolically loaded, then, the contrast with the other extreme of the Brit-vocal spectrum. How needful, too. At one end, stridently ablaze in its own passion, the forthright, "unpretentious" non-ironic first-person emotionalism of Joe Cocker's rehydrated American R&B; at the other end, a cloud suspended on gossamer threads in which floated the incorporeal voice of the far-from-confessional songwriter Nick Drake, whose toney, susurrant murmur prioritized lyric ideation and melodic shape over the exposure of the singer's own passions and whose identity as a musical force owed as much to the selfhood-effacing English folk tradition as Cocker's did to the gutty individualism of American rhythm and blues. It was a conviction of the post-psychedelic intellectual hippie worldview that life should be apprehended as a passing show to be observed in detail; as an ontological pattern, a waveform, a latticework of delicate significances; as a cognitive puzzle, not a sensory experience. And cognitive puzzles have no use for gutty emissions. Whereas your Rodgers and your Cocker were more than happy to experience their inner worlds through extroverted engagement with appetite, passion, longing, frustration, and resentment, Drake accessed his own "deep within" by other means and emerged from the dark interior with quite different trophies.

It is tempting but way too facile to define this division as a neat binary of oppositions: cognitive vs. sensory, mind vs. soul, authentic vs. "authentic," homemade vs. assimilated. It is certainly tempting to try to construct an equation that somehow faces northern/Celtic working-class soulfulness

off against southern middle-class existential fret. Tempting, facile, and just plain erroneous. But it would be ridiculous to pretend that such polarities did not exist in British pop music at the turn of the 1970s, just as it is impossible to ignore the uneasy fact that in a culture that is retreating fast from the repressions (a.k.a. "standards") of a monocultural imperialist past, the word "authentic" cannot have a single, irreducible meaning.

Indeed the self-consciousness engendered by that uncertainty of identity has never slackened its grip on our popular music, and it possibly never will. It might be argued that it is precisely this self-consciousness that defines our pop. What can be stated with some conviction is that after forty to fifty more years of Brits singing with American voices, semi-American voices, or assertively non-American voices, nothing at all has changed: it remains the case that when we open our mouths to sing, we do not make statements about who we know ourselves to be. Instead we open up a debate in time about who we think we might be, given the circumstances. And, of course, about whom we would like to be taken for.

* * *

It is really quite hard, then, a decade and a half into the twenty-first century, to recall precisely how 1970s white British R&B/soul impacted on the juvenile imagination in its own time, bearing in mind the assertiveness of its evolutionary competitors, glam-, prog-, and art-rock—not to mention its direct progenitor, black American soul, which reached the zenith of commercial appeal in the first half of that decade and in turn exerted an ever more probing influence on the bashful British inclination to be soulful. Speaking for myself, as a glam-, prog-, and art-rocking young teenager of the time (one endowed with a secret liking for American soul, to which I barely admitted even to myself), I am pretty sure that I registered the white British soul/R&B variant as a fatuous adjunct, an imposture, a sort of pointless stylistic sideshow irrelevant to the main events of the day—*real* soul, *real* glam, *real* prog, etc. So I gave little or no thought at the time to what white British soul people themselves thought they were doing.

But I liked Paul Rodgers's hyper-masculine Wilson Pickettisms. This was partly because they reminded me of Wilson Pickett and partly because they translated well to the formal requirements of guitar rock (as exemplified first by Free and then by his next group, the rather less funky Bad Company). Indeed, Rodgers was at the time widely taken to be the rock singer par excellence—a sort of model and archetype and *summa cum laude* all rolled into one tightly-trousered macho package (fly-buttons on the outside). This was how rock singing should both look and sound. It was felt, soulful, manly, and mostly interested in the expostulatory aspects of nonverbal language: the grunts, groans, and whoooaas that express what mere words never can. In fact, for all his lack of lyrical delicacy, Rodgers's was a rather beautiful voice, and it remains so in the second decade of the twenty-first century—although we might appraise it differently now if only he'd used it slightly less ruggedly back then. But there it is. If ruggedly sexualized indignation is what "deep within" means to you, then that's what it means. What is unarguable is that Rodgers did a lot of the early heavy lifting for what became the default setting for masculinist rock vocal style for the next decade and a half in a multitude of dead-end hybridizations. And that story—the story of how Wilson Pickett was transformed alchemically over time into David Coverdale—is a story that has never really interested me.

But what of those less elemental souls for whom a song was not an assertion of manly appetite so much as an exploration of selfhood or social style or the existential moment in all its heaving pregnancy? Did it have to follow necessarily in the 1970s that whenever white men sang "soulfully," some lady-love somewhere would be obliged to open up her love wings and let him in? No, it did not. Not always. Nor was it inevitable that white British women of soulful or bluesy inclination should torch the landscape like Janis Joplin—although many of them felt unable to swerve her influence entirely, just as the menfolk could never quite escape the shades of Wilson and Otis.

But surely too many members (and descendants) of the 1960s' white blues-wailin' tribe took the word "soulful" to mean "loud," "abrasive," and "stretched to the limits of endurance." What had begun in the previous decade as a concerted effort to explore the possible meaning of the words "deep within" in germane and spontaneous terms had, in many cases, devolved into an exploration of what it means to shout and strut in front of a large number of intoxicated and/or excitable folk, who are themselves also shouting reciprocally from time to time in an effort to strike the right Dionysian chord in return: the great rock 'n' roll whoop that remains, to my ears, the emptiest signal in all music history: "Whoooo! Ra-a-arck and *ro-o-o-oll*!"

Perhaps there is no better exemplar of this vector than the journey undertaken between 1965 and the mid-1970s by sometime-mod Steve Marriott, whose sharp, soulful underpinnings in mid-sixties R&B with the Small Faces achieved a tumultuous, whooping, overstated rock apotheosis with Humble Pie in the following decade—one of the primary reductions into absurdity of that occasionally absurd musical era. But then that's rock for you. It does do that if you let it.

But there were other impulses. And by the end of the first quarter of the decade, a number of soulful white British voices had scratched out a sound that at least looked like a roadmap to a new, green, and pleasant kind of Deep Within. Or at least a location in the vicinity.

* * *

I have no useful memory of Stone the Crows but it was always said back then (I may be paraphrasing here) that rasping Maggie Bell could sling an R&B phrase like a stone into a giant's forehead. She had grit by the shovelful. She had, in the excruciating parlance of the day, "balls." The group also possessed a singing bass player, James Dewar, who would later, as part of Robin Trower's Hendrixy power trio, go on to make unassertive but genuinely soulful sorties to the microphone while being jostled by his leader's churning Stratocaster.

Then there was Vinegar Joe, a straightforward British R&B outfit that galumphed around the UK gig circuit until 1974 and made three albums for Island. Vinegar Joe could boast no less than two standout voices of the period in Elkie Brooks and Robert Palmer, both singers of northern extraction and soulful intent but of very different style. Brooks was endowed by nature with husky bellows that in the context of Vinegar Joe owed plenty to Tina Turner but would later, during a rather less raucous but nevertheless passingly successful solo career, reveal a slight tonal resemblance to Billie Holiday. Consequently, Brooks cleared a space for herself as a talented framer of R&B-flavored torch songs for the adult weekend-hipster market. Her debts to both Tina and Billie were never, so far as I am aware, denied.

Palmer had a furzy, rather more "facial" voice but was no kind of R&B wild man. He wore a suit for the cameras and enjoyed a long and commercially successful solo career, transitioning from slick in 1974 to chromed in the 1980s, from the oiled Little Featism of "Sneakin' Sally Through the Alley" to the triumphalist "Addicted to Love" a dozen years on—a trajectory that spoke eloquently of his attitude to the deep within (i.e., slithering around elegantly on the surface is more fun) and possibly also of his own abiding handsomeness. For both Brooks and Palmer, the trappings of soul were a means to an end.

But to the Average White Band the trappings were of the essence. This woolly-headed Scottish rhythm combo experienced great success during the middle and latter years of the 1970s by focusing with real commitment on the exercise of R&B style. They were neither parodists nor pasticheurs, but earnest students of the danceable soul-funk manner. And though AWB were not equipped with a particularly scintillating voice up front with which to compel the listening mind—they shared vocal duties out unevenly among themselves—this was no more disadvantageous to the band creatively than the lack of a distinguished voice was a hindrance to any number of the great American funk outfits. Their groove was their voice.

Compare and contrast with Terry Reid, whose voice was his groove. Reid emerged from the East Anglian fens in the latter part of the 1960s, in some ways a sort of rural Steve Marriott, long on soulful torque, range, and throat-gravel, but perhaps not quite so lengthy on authorial acuity or commercial smarts—vocal charisma was abundantly present in him; memorable songs expressed with compelling and/or fashionable arrangements were in shorter supply. And so he lacked hits. For all his manifest talent and psychological realness, Reid seemed to pass by barely noticed at the time, lost in the crowd. Or perhaps, for his own reasons, he developed the habit of riding the wave behind the one everyone else was looking at. He probably did not know himself. Whatever the truth of it, he turned down the opportunity to become the lead singer of Led Zeppelin when first offered the gig by Jimmy Page in 1968—a decision he has always insisted he has never regretted— and did not enjoy much luck subsequently while making a series of records that varied in quality and grip but were usually worth the time of most days. *River* might have been construed as a sort of funky *Astral Weeks* redux had enough people been aware of its existence, and *Seed of Memory* is the definitive curate's egg, magnificent in parts. But still nothing much occurred in the way of sales and celebrity. History accords Reid the status of consistent nearly man. He, it is fair to say, has never been troubled by such perceptions.

Perhaps the same thing applied to another yeoman of the period, Jess Roden, who, following a traditional dues-paying passage through the estimable Alan Bown Set, Bronco, and Butts Band, spent the middle and later years of the 1970s making passionate, serious, physical music founded mostly in the black American soul-funk idiom. Roden possessed a burly baritone-to-tenor range that could on occasion slip without a great crashing of gears into a silkier, more intimate mode; and he exhibited excellent taste in judiciously picking top-notch cover material as salt to his own decent (if generic) songwriting. Furthermore, he had a band of players behind him that was wholly sensible of the importance of the instrumental groove supporting the voice—they were not perhaps quite as fluent nor light on their feet as the Average White Band but were nevertheless clearly in love with the economies and syncopations that together go to make music funky. Roden was admired, but his sales did not justify his record companies' investments—or at least that is how they would have put it to him at the time, as they failed to offer him a new deal.

Greater commercial success was enjoyed by the gritty Glaswegian, Frankie Miller, who at least had a decent-sized hit with the matey "Darlin'" in 1978 after a decade's hard slog on the roads to and from Ipswich

Gaumont or Stevenage Locarno. Glaswegians are not required by law to be gritty, but lore has different imperatives, and Miller fit the bill almost from the start. His clunchy oratory was hewn from the same Pickettian rock as Paul Rodgers's, and then buttressed with an undecorative stage presence and a characterful hat. Frankie was raw Glaswegian soul at its most concentrated, much less concerned vocally with the implications of phatic grunt than with "getting the song over"; in other words, a singer far less taken with the range of vocal effects at his disposal than with the substance of what brought him to this juncture in the first place, standing there under his hat in the spotlight with lowered lids, bellowing into a pig-iron microphone for the benefit of half-interested watchers with kohl-black eyes . . .

They were all good, after their own fashion, every one of those R&B shouters and soul belchers of the British 1970s. They were all sincere. They all had something of their own to impart. They all harbored authentically passionate feelings about the black American rhythm and blues from which they drew their inspiration. Not one of them, even for a moment, entertained the thought that the certain way to celebrity and riches was to steal goods from somebody else's culture. That wasn't the point.

The *point* was the question that was asked every time one of them went to the microphone, whether they were conscious of it in the moment or not. He or she would sidle up to the stage apron, take a deep breath, brace themselves, grab the microphone by the throat, and then ask the question of questions, as if his or her very life depended upon it, just like Ben E. King: "What *is* soul?" As if the answer to the question were to be found only in the act of asking the question the right way.

* * *

But in the end, if you confine yourself too often, for too long, and with perhaps too much puritanical zeal to an ideal, then the idiom in which the ideal is expressed becomes a trap. It ceases to be a vehicle for the things you have to say, or a device for addressing the questions you need answering, and instead becomes a prison incarcerating all your best expressions in a sort of dull stylistic echo chamber. In the end, your expressions are heard and appreciated only by fellow prisoners, the choir to whom you are preaching. Nothing really gets out. In the end, the question asked by would-be soul singers mutates into something altogether more plaintive.

"Is *this* soul?"

But then white British R&B never promised the earth. It did however once offer new experiential territory: not only a place where awkward young customers might go to get in touch with their most fiercely felt emotions, but also a place in which to feel that those emotions are actually admissible; that what you experience inside yourself has validity and weight and meaning. It's about growing up.

The problem is of course that "deep within" is not a place you can actually go to, any more than soul is a thing. "Deep within" is a conceptual territory you divine. Once you've divined it, you learn the lingo and the customs and that in turn enables you to be serious about yourself and the world in an attractive and stylish way. But it was never a place you might live on a day-to-day basis. You can't actually *be* a white suburban postwar British kid and a Chicago bluesman, not at the same time.

You can use your imagination, though. Wilko Johnson (born John Wilkinson) once said that his seventies Essex neo-R&B group Dr. Feelgood was constructed chiefly out of a fantasy that he and his best mate on Canvey Island, Lee Brilleaux (born Lee Collinson), used to indulge in on good days in the shadow of the seawall. The fantasy was that the two of them were, in reality, a pair of Chicago bluesmen imprisoned below sea level on the scrotty mud-pat in the Thames Estuary that they called home.

"It wasn't a designed thing, not as such," he said. "We just used to sit around, get stoned and have these fantasies—about ourselves as authentic bluesmen transported to Canvey. Which meant going down the market and buying cheap suits with narrow lapels—a bit like the Blues Brothers fantasy but before the film, y'know? We used to laugh until we thought we were going to die. The whole thing was a sort of projection of Lee's personality.

And there were just enough oddities in the landscape to fit in with that: the ships, the estuary, the oil refineries across the water—the big chimneys with flames making the sky go orange on cloudy nights . . ."

"It sounds infernal," I said in response, imagining smokestack lightning forking over the refinery towers.

"Well, I did grow up feeling slightly ashamed of coming from there," he went on. "You were definitely working class . . . You can't pass through Canvey on the way to somewhere else. It's the end of the road. You had to go over the bridge on to the island, and there we all were, below sea level. My mother always felt she'd been dragged down by having to live there. My dad was a gasfitter and it was all a bit . . . Lawrentian. He met my mother in an air-raid shelter in Sheffield, y'know . . ."

And there, it seems to me, is a perfect description of the conditions required for a convincing white-man's R&B: the sense of a dead end; a horizon begrimed; a need to feel that feelings count for something; the urge for escape; the urge to transcend (with laughter if necessary); the urge to identify with others whose horizons seem equivalently begrimed . . .

Dr. Feelgood's R&B was rock music, really; rock music executed with a rhythm and blues sense of discipline and economy and playfulness and bounce and structure. Nor was Lee Brilleaux a soulful singer; but he was a magnificent one, nevertheless, because of the raw conviction of his play-acting—the way his psychological climate created new weather wherever he cracked a snarl. His voice sounded metallic notes, in ship iron and rust. There was something mechanized about his phrasing, too, not in the sense that the singer imagined himself to be a machine but in the sense that he wanted to make his utterances implacable, repetitious, and dependably hard, all edge and dynamism and no heart at all. He spat words out like scurf, as if he wanted to get rid of them quick, before they got into his works and stopped the machine. He was not your friend. It was to be understood in no uncertain terms that whatever Brilleaux had to say about life and its monochrome treacheries, he meant it.

But you weren't meant to take Dr. Feelgood into your heart, any more than you were meant to take, say, the Rolling Stones into that warm, wet vale. Johnson and Brilleaux pretended to themselves that they were imprisoned Chicago bluesmen, and out of that pretense they convinced all comers of at least their hardness, their imperviousness, even as they almost believed it of themselves in the moment. For they actually had no interest in the soul question. They were interested in making an acute description of the world's lustful, wounding, laughable surface. They did not punch deep, not in the soul sense. They jabbed short, hard, and repetitiously. Here's Wilko again, from the same interview, conducted in 2004, a decade after the death of his former bandmate:

"I'd always felt that violent movement is exciting to watch and it just went perfectly with that sound. Enhanced it, even. And Lee, *cwoar* . . . he just had that thing: he just *radiated* violence and neurosis. And the thing is we kind of meant it. It was funny but real.

"How can I explain it? You know when you're a kid and you play cops and robbers? You remember that? Well, you're really firing that gun—even though you know it's not a real gun. And the guy you're shooting? He knows that you're not really shooting him—but he's really taking those bullets . . ."

* * *

You know when you're a kid and you sing blues and soul?

Well, you're really singing blues and soul—even though you know you're not a real blues-and-soul man. You know that you're not really, but in the moment you are. And the guy you're singing to knows that you aren't one, too—but he's really taking those soul bullets . . .

There was one white blues-and-soul man whose bullets I really took as a kid, first as an eleven year old in 1971, and then at fairly regular intervals for two or three years after that, before America became too attractive to him and he started making dull records in New York and Miami and LA. But that first run of singles—I took them all into my heart and as a result I bled real emotion, as if life were somehow more *feelable* while the records played.

Rod Stewart's sequence of nine hit singles from "Maggie May" and "Reason to Believe" in 1971 to "You Can Make Me Dance, Sing or Anything . . ." in 1974, accomplished with or without the instrumental input of the Faces, stands as one of pop's great artistic gestures. No, I mean it. It was a passage of music so poetically vivid in its conception and execution that it deserves to be accorded the same reverence and addressed with the same seriousness of mind as a passage of brushwork by a master painter or a magnificent sequence of paragraphs by a great writer—as an exemplary instance of inspirational flow.

I can't separate those records, not for emotional congruence. To my ever-willing ears—as much now as then—they strike me as component parts of the same socking great creative moment, a protracted exploration of a certain kind of being, accomplished not for once solemnly on stretched canvas or doggedly on milled foolscap, but joyously, in time.

"Reason to Believe," "Maggie May," "Stay With Me," "You Wear It Well," "Angel," "Cindy Incidentally," "Oh No, Not My Baby," "Pool Hall Richard," "You Can Make Me Dance . . ." Granted, yes, the last three felt a little more knocked-out than their six predecessors, even at the time—and now, with forty more years on their respective clocks, it's plain to hear that they lack the startling freshness and colloquial authenticity of that first brilliant sextet. But viewed retrospectively in the shadow of what later became of Stewart's career after he went to America to record *Atlantic Crossing* in 1975, all those singles are works of easygoing, slapdash genius; they constitute the most perfectly conceived and executed transatlantic articulation of the question: So what is soul if it's *me* doing it?

Which might seem odd because these were by no means soul records in the usual sense of the expression. Take the voice off any one of them and what you're left with is a scruffy but artful admixture of low-amplitude rock, blues, and folk, with a thud, a shimmy, and a shake built into the bottom end. They are all danceable records—even the Jimi Hendrix ballad "Angel" will encourage discreet undulation if you have the capacity for it. But they are also songs inviting the curiosity of an inquiring, feeling mind.

As productions—as *sound*—they contain themselves roughly within the dynamic framework of a 1960s Chicago blues record, the sort made by Howlin' Wolf. And they mostly describe a fairly flat trajectory—these are neither histrionic exercises in upsy-downsy melodrama, nor examples of the polished rock-into-popmanship in which Stewart would specialize toward the end of the decade: not by any means. Far from it. They are rough old dogs. They're played with jouncing rock 'n' roll enthusiasm. They almost merit the adjective "amateur" in its original sense. And they benefit roundly not only from the deployment of folk instrumentation but also from some of folk's textural finesse. The mandolin break in "Maggie May" is, in my ears, a true pop apotheosis, and that mandolin is pushed for both rightness and loveliness by the fiddle on "You Wear It Well." Indeed, it's that very textural folkiness that throws you off, that says to you "this can't be soul," as if a good-timey record with mandolins and fiddle on it has no business interfering with your deeper passages the same way that Sam Cooke did.

But soul it is, in all but name and outward form. As we have seen, Stewart copped his first break as a rhythm and blues shouter alongside Long John Baldry, and had since maintained his devotion to the high-end paroxysms of both Sam Cooke and Wilson Pickett, even while making loud rock records with Jeff Beck. Here was a voice capable of living with any instrumental configuration in any context, yet was always able to function as a vessel of real feeling, rough as hedgehogs on the surface but always suggesting the viable presence of an unvarnished sensibility beneath. Indeed, Stewart's croak was so highly textured, so fibrous that the illusion was sometimes created that he sang *chords*—not single melodic notes in linear sequence but clusters of them sounding all at once in fuzzy clumps. An illusion, no doubt, but I have always thought it a telling one.

Yet, for all his distinctiveness and controlled execution, Stewart was no technocrat. Essentially, his great insight was to uncouple the idea of soul from its formal grid and then reattach it without exaggerated mannerism— beyond a weird conviction that the word "realize" is spelt with an "o"— to the music that grew organically from the interests and capacities of his mates in and around the pubs and clubs of central and suburban London. He applied the principles of soul, as he understood them, to the stuff that came immediately to hand in his world. In doing so, he *expressed* his world.

It didn't hurt either that he often gave himself words to sing that lent themselves to the irrigations of the soul, even if they were not, by any stretch, conventional "soul" lyrics and sometimes even bordered on the sordid. The scenarios described by "Maggie May," "You Wear It Well," "Stay With Me," and "Cindy Incidentally" might not have suited Gladys Knight—the songs were mostly about the consequences of callow sex with older women—but they tripped from Stewart's fox-thin lips with a colloquial veracity that British pop has seldom since come close to approaching. The songs seemed to have been written straight out of real life—in the case of "Maggie May," while Rod was still putting his trousers back on—narrating events hinging on actions that were not fully understood, resulting in consequences that had never been given a second prior thought. The upshot is the presence of emotions of no clear definition but real heft—you *feel* Rod's blinking, blanked-out incomprehension in its life-and-death struggle with his bravado. Basically, the songs spoke of the feeling of vulnerability and doubt that gathers like smoke behind every cocksure teenage tearaway's gamey facade.

To eleven-, twelve- and thirteen-year-old ears at the time it was like listening to the world as it really is, and not as it's cracked up to be. And it went deep. It went miles in. I never for a moment felt that I was connecting with the rage in Rod's unruly soul (rage? What rage would that be then?), let alone to his trashed-up Mod-ish style- and class-consciousness, but only to his curiosity about what it meant to be himself in that moment of creation. It was as if you were privileged, for three minutes, to observe him reading for the first time from the book of his own uncertain feelings. And it did cause something to open up inside me, slowly. Something. Not much of anything really. But something. Just a crack, and then a bit more . . . and then more, until I pretty much gaped every time there was a new Rod single to be waited for patiently on the radio.

It was not a reluctant opening-up either: it was a keen process and a liquid one and, whenever it occurred, I felt that what issued from the fissure was an irrepressible beam of joy. I may even have kidded myself for a moment—just for a moment—that *this* is what it must be like to have a brother.

GRACE NOTES

DEXYS MIDNIGHT RUNNERS: "KEEP IT PART TWO (INFERIORITY PART ONE)"

EMI Records, 1980

Has any figure in British pop wrestled more earnestly with the question of what "soul" means than Kevin Rowland of Dexys Midnight Runners?

"Welcome to the new soul vision," he blurted, manifesto style, at the end of the group's third hit, "There, There, My Dear," as if he knew what he was talking about. The evidence is that he sort of did. Kind of.

For sure, the group had an overt sense of its own soulful identity, with a look (donkey jackets, woolly hats), an attitude (sullen, antisocial, contumacious), and an assumed air of authority predicated on a worked-out ideological stance vis-à-vis the real value of pop music in modern society. At one point, Rowland even imposed a total Dexys embargo on the press, following ribald and/or dismissive coverage in one of the music papers, preferring instead to pay for advertising space in the same paper in which to explicate (and obfuscate) his position in terms not entirely comprehended by everyone. In the great stylistic mash-down that followed the decline and fall of punk, your ideological dance stance counted for almost as much as your haircut.

But what Dexys lacked in *politesse*, modesty, and soulful reserve, they compensated for with a conviction that passion should be the engine of all value in pop; that, if nothing else, pop music should make you feel the same strong emotions as those felt by the boys in the band. And, boy, did they make a song and dance about it. They were ever so slightly oppressive—which was one of the reasons some music journalists were ribald and dismissive in return.

"Keep It Part Two" is a fanfare for the onset of depression, breakdown, and creative involution. It begins with blatting minor-key horns riding a seething Hammond slow-boil. It boils, they blat, the song cloaks itself in haughty but dismal shades. It then opens out into expansive chorus mode, achieving maximum load in its third minute with a full-bore horn play-out that multitracks trombone and saxes into extravagant cadential cascades. Both as a groove and as a mobile edifice it is magnificent—Booker T and the MGs could not have invested a state funeral with more simmering dignity. But it is the sound of Kevin Rowland's strangulated voice, thumbed like putty into the gaps in this noble musical structure, which makes a sturdy piece of songcraft into a broken window allowing a view into a trashed interior. It is dark as night in there.

"Keep It Part Two" asked the big soul question and then answered it, while gazing at its own penumbral reflection to make sure it looked and sounded soulful in the right way, not the wrong way. It represented in 1980 the absolute high-water mark for white British soul self-consciousness—so much so, in fact, that it bordered on the Gothic. Not for years afterward would aspirant soul boys and girls again feel that they needed to explain themselves with quite so much self-lacerating candor, nor make their pitch with so many laryngeal contortions. If a voice can be a watershed, then this was it. Rowland's doggish vocal is a stretched-out yelp of pain and manic anxiety, as if agonized not only in the moment but in the expectation that this feeling will last forever. Kevin has seldom known the pleasures of ecstasy. Not in his music.

Does it work? As a piece of Brit-soul *Sturm und Drang* it is pretty hard to beat and it stood then, as it still does, as a corrective to the idea that the authenticity of your soul depends on how stylishly you copy the American original. "Keep It" is British through and through and its soul is as murky and unsettled as a Black Country sky on a stormy November Thursday afternoon.

KIKI DEE: "ON A MAGIC CARPET RIDE"
Fontana Records, 1968

We have always strained in this country to be soulful—if "always" can be taken to mean "since the early to mid 1960s." That sense of strain is one of the defining cultural tonalities of the postwar period and, as a phenomenon, should always be addressed generously. "Soul" is a quality, not a thing, and, as such, its perceived nature depends on where you're positioned when you make that judgment. You might, for instance, be upside-down in mid-air.

We've all heard of Northern Soul now, haven't we? Northern Soul, for those who need a refresher, was not a genre of music but an attitude toward music, which grew out of the northern dance clubs of the 1960s and '70s and evolved through time into a full-blown pop cult dotted around the country. In fact it was an athletic-obscurantist pop cult: Northern Soul fans fixated primarily not on the soulfulness of "Northern Soul" records, but on their danceability. And if a record could be at once both danceable and utterly obscure, its Northern Soul value was doubled. As has been the case in hipster cults since the dawn of hipster time, it ain't what you know that defines you, but what everyone else doesn't know.

Musically, what was important to Northern Soul boys and girls was not the authenticity of the emotion expressed by the singer on the record but the energy expressed by the overall sound of the record. Particularly favored was a certain kind of banging, clattering, swinging cacophony of an on-beat vamp supporting a vaulting melody: the Northern Soul *bounce*, a sonic strategy typical of the early-to-mid-sixties Motown production model. Voices were necessary, of course, to carry melody and to signify the presence of a certain humanistic éclat, but they were not required to engage deeply with the emotions of listeners. What you're always looking for in Northern Soul is not its big beating heart so much as its big beat.

And what could be more obscurely desirable than a long-lost "Northern Soul" classic by one of our own? Native Bradfordian Kiki Dee's career as a professional singer has taken many turns in its fifty-year course, the most notable being the number one hit she had in the summer of 1976 jointly with Elton John, "Don't Go Breaking My Heart." But prior to that ought-to-have-been breakout moment, Dee had already put down a marker as one of the UK's gutsiest pop-R&B performers and as a balladeer of some style (her biggish hit "Amoureuse" caused my thirteen-year-old self to explore all manner of new sensitivities for a few weeks in 1973). Prior to that, Dee had been the first white English woman ever to sign for Motown and, before even that, had released a string of bouncy and occasionally soulful pop singles for the UK label Fontana.

Her 1968 non-hit B-side "On a Magic Carpet Ride" was rediscovered some time after the fact by Northern Soul collectors and accorded retrospective Northern Soul status. It has all the hallmarks: pulsating piano, drums that clatter, horns that toot, a swooping melody, and, above all, an excitable atmosphere, as well as near-total obscurity. It gets to the bouncing soul boy/girl in you quickly and then stays there for the duration.

But it doesn't rearrange the furniture in your most sacred chamber. It's not that kind of soul. It's Northern Soul.

TEDESCHI TRUCKS BAND: "MIDNIGHT IN HARLEM"
Sony Records, 2009

White Americans have striven to be soulful, too—since black Americans first showed them how to do it. But unlike their British counterparts, who were obliged to import their ideas about what "soulful" might mean, white Americans have grown up with it all around them. They have imbibed it with their mothers' milk. Not literally, of course, but certainly metaphysically. So whenever white Americans have drawn those slopping buckets up from the well of soul, they have been able to do so relatively unselfconsciously, as if it's all in a day's work and just part of the fabric of normal. For many white Americans, to be soulful is to be American.

It would entail the writing of an entire library of books to give an account in any kind of detail of the way in which African American music has been assimilated throughout the past century by white Americans, to the point where "black" and "white" have lost some of their usefulness as musical descriptors (and it should not be forgotten, while thinking about that, that for many decades one of the key engines of innovation in African American music was the drive to create music that cannot be easily appropriated by whites; hence bebop, hence hip hop . . .) And so there is an aesthetic ease to white American music that borrows from the African American tradition that just doesn't exist in its British counterpart.

For instance, there was a particular comfiness and empathetic confidence about Bonnie Raitt's take on R&B when she first appeared in the 1970s. It seemed to slip out of her without a second thought, let alone a third, fourth, and fifth. She sang the blues and a folksy kind of soul as if their textures were contiguous at the emotional level with her upbringing in liberal politics and the folk and civil rights movements, and in particular as if they shared hymn sheets with her version of feminism. Her voice was older than her years. The attitude expressed by her voice was tough-minded, but Bonnie was never, ever strident.

And just as it is possible to say that British R&B might not have enjoyed, say, Frankie Miller without Eric Burdon having cut up rough 'n' tough 'n' soulful first, so American music might not have benefited from the emulsifications of Susan Tedeschi if Raitt hadn't shown that it was possible for white women to go there and be soulful without a hint of stridency.

"Midnight in Harlem" is a song that speaks literally, if perhaps not intentionally, of the self-consciousness of white humanity's relationship with the concept of "soul." It tells the ostensibly romantic tale of a provincial woman in flight from destructive love, who finds herself in uptown New York City at the dead of night, face to face with the raw bones of her existence. But because it is Harlem, she is confronted with a different kind of reality to the one she is used to. It is sore and terribly real, Harlem; perhaps more rawly real, in the way it displays the relics of broken lives other than her own—and she is forced in the moment to see her own life anew . . .

Corny, yes. Sententious, maybe. Impertinent? I don't think so. In fact "Midnight in Harlem" stands as a rather lovely description of what white R&B has striven to embody down the decades: the sense that there is more to life than home territory; that reaching out beyond the confines of what you've been presented with is one of the best ways to find out about where you are; that the world of expressed emotion is a wonderful, revealing, exciting, energizing world; and that to inhabit others' creative forms fully, respectfully, and to the best of your honest ability is not, in the course of creative endeavour, the same thing as cultural appropriation. It's an expression of love.

Tesdeschi's voice is a subtle, controlled artistic tool. It is nicely husky but never stentorian. Indeed, so controlled is it and so circumscribed with good taste—and the awareness of its own good taste—that you might make the case on occasion that it is narcissistic. Sometimes the achievements of the Tedeschi Trucks Band sound as if they ought to be bound in leather and left for display on the nearest coffee table. But I do like to think of Gladys Knight listening to "Midnight in Harlem" in her boudoir and thinking, "Yes, well, that girl can sing."

7

Croon

Pity the mother who cannot sing to her children.

Mine certainly did. She sang to me in my high chair after lunch while she cleared up, to make me go to sleep. Nursery rhymes, jingles, "Zadok the Priest"—that sort of thing. By her own account she was no kind of singer at all—"The relationship between the key I started in and the one in which I finished was seldom close"—but she knew how to bust a classic. Croon "Baa-Baa Black Sheep" to me now while rattling the cutlery drawer and I go out like a light.

It's potent stuff, crooning. And it does not require of the crooner very much in the way of extravagant technique, nor great exhibitions of soul—although your crooner will never agree on either of these points. Crooners are nothing if not sensitive and they give the appearance of enjoying very high levels of self-esteem predicated on a keenly developed perception of their own emotional and stylistic refinement. They are feathered with sensitivity. Summon a crooner to your imagination and you are calling to mind a bird of paradise.

Standard wisdom has it that "crooning" begins in the late 1920s/ early 1930s, with the invention of electrical amplification to make the human voice audible in large spaces in front of mighty instrumental ensembles, and of course for broadcast. But really, what this means is that "crooners" began then: "crooner," the marketable heartthrob type of singer who makes love to the microphone and is self-conscious about his tailoring and smell. "Crooners" are always preoccupied with style, sometimes interestingly.

But I am not interested for the moment in "crooners," the type of singer. I am interested in crooning, the type of singing.

As an activity, crooning goes way back beyond the 1920s. Of course it does. It goes almost as far back as you can go. It is difficult to offer supporting evidence for this, but we can be confident that parents have pretty much always sung soothingly to their children, as a comfort and as a seduction into the warm embrace of sleep. (I cannot have been alone, I imagine, in spending hours of my life as a younger parent sighing "There's on-ly *one* Den-nis Bergkamp" to my eldest in a vanishingly soft voice, while the fiercely sleepless tot roiled in his cot and demanded "Now the Vieira one!") And centuries of culture, if not actual experience, tell us that would-be lovers have always sung softly to the objects of their admiration, as a stimulus and as a seduction into the warm embrace of themselves.

Crooning is ancient, universal, atavistic, and variable only in the variety of ways that expressions of intimacy can get a point across: points such as "go to sleep!" and "sleep with me!" One internet dictionary informs the curious that to croon is to "sing softly in a sentimentally contemplative manner," which is a pretty good definition. But it doesn't go far enough. It doesn't convey the key crooning dynamic of *persuasion*. (The same dictionary also implies that there may be an etymological linkage between the words "croon" and "crone"—but let's not get drawn into that.) Crooners are persuaders. And the unassailable truth of it is that crooning is everywhere to be found, in one form or another, even among those who yell. Iggy Pop has always been a good crooner.

For to croon is to manipulate. Much as it is manipulative to deliberately speak to others in a voice too quiet for its surroundings, crooning requires that the listener draw closer, alter his stance, bend his ear, hunch his back; *demands* that attentiveness be redoubled. Iggy croons when he wants either to engender a peculiarly alienated form of anxiety in the listener, or when he is looking to overlay his music with a sense of closeted oppressiveness or brooding irony. His *basso* incantations on 1977's *The Idiot* do not speak of emotional intimacy or physical proximity or authentic personal revelation—and they do not replicate the sound of any mother I have ever heard—but they do share the crooner's appetite for close manipulation: the manipulation of space, the manipulation of temperature, the manipulation of mood . . .

And so it would make sense that post-rock 'n' roll pop music has had crooning in it pretty much from the start. Which is to say that rock 'n' roll embraced crooning out of pure expediency once it had got over its initial impulse, which was to yell. Elvis Presley's early croon was merely the obverse of his yell: it was the sound of the would-be-genteel, mother-loving Presley seeking to persuade the listener of his sincerity and/or sensitivity and/or remorse. He meant it, too. No, really. Until Roy Orbison came along and changed the channel, rock 'n' roll crooning was the outcome of the absolute need in life for good manners: it was the sound of teenagers learning how to say "please."

But R 'n' R crooning could not remain an irony-free zone forever, as nothing can. Let us leap forward a couple of decades to consider briefly the utterances of such differently beloved postmodernist pop crooners as David Bowie and Bryan Ferry, and then Green Gartside (of Scritti Politti), Paddy McAloon (of Prefab Sprout), Chris Isaak, Marc Almond, David Sylvian, Stuart Staples (of Tindersticks), Richard Hawley, even the gory, melodramatic Nick Cave, whose crooning is always to be understood in its relationship to his screams. They are all men, yes (more on that later). They want your attention like they want their next breath. Furthermore, they most assuredly crave your identification—they want *you* the listener to consider, in the most heartfelt terms possible, what it must be like *to be them*. And so their crooning is complex, layered, knowing, playful; it flirts with your expectations of what crooning is and what it does and how you ought to respond to it. It invites you to join in with what appears to be going on, whatever it is (let's call it "the construct"); it proposes that somehow there already exists between you—between the crooner and the croonee—an intimacy, an understanding, a feeling of absolute mutuality that is predicated on a presumed shared sensibility. You cannot listen with enjoyment to any one of those voices—from Ferry to Cave—and not feel those shared sensibilities seething in your flesh and bones like mercury.

For the contemporary pop crooner's art is nearly always a referential one. It refers to many things, such as earlier crooning styles and earlier ideas of what crooning is for and how it works and for whom; it refers to the relative positions of crooner and croonee; it refers to the mirror upon which the crooner fixes his gaze to sing, as if his reflected selfhood were, in essence, the very deepest subject of his croon. The croon might sometimes sound like pastiche; it may make use of the instruments of parody; it is nearly always theatrical somewhere in its heart. But the idea persists with quite wonderful dedication that the appreciative listener must, at some level, play along: connect with the artifice, share that mirror-gazing trajectory, *identify*. The act of crooning in our postmodernist, individualist world is nearly always a dogged act of self-regard.

But it doesn't have to be, does it? Why should that necessarily be so? There is no rule written down anywhere that I'm aware of which stipulates that crooning has to be knowing, ironic, and narcissistic.

* * *

For men of my temper and vintage, born in and around 1960, an instinctual aversion to both crooning and crooners runs deep. In my case, it's akin to the aversion I have to the taste of pineapple: it's intractable, inexplicable, ineradicable. It's kind of eye-watering. I don't want to listen to the crooners of my childhood for ironic purposes, thank you, let alone to Bing Crosby, the forebear of all homely crooners, either for sentimental or for nostalgic purposes. There are no guilty pleasures to be had there. And I really don't want to hear today's crooners channeling yesterday's crooners for effect or for style or for a clever idea's sake, let alone to make me *identify*. I have no use for Michael Bublé—not when I already have Frank Sinatra. In fact I only want to hear crooning if there is no other way for a song to be sung. This is important to me.

We grew up, my generation, with crooning as a cultural norm. It was mainstream. It was on telly. It was everywhere, softening the landscape, hushing things down, plumping things up. It was on *The Val Doonican Show*, on comedy and variety shows, on anything that might involve the deployment of Perry Como or Matt Monro or Johnny Mathis in the context of "Light Entertainment." It was almost as everywhere then as Taylor Swift is now—although mediated by different means, obviously.

I suppose this aversion can be partially explained by noting the simple evolutions of musical fashion. By the 1960s, the decade of my childhood, the very idea of crooning had lost its prewar lustre, novelty, and sensualism, as well as the sense implied by the original crooners that intimacy ought to be, at the very least, rawly stimulating. Raw stimulation came by other means in the 1960s. Intimacy's terms had changed. Instead, the mainstream pop and "Easy Listening" crooner of the period proposed that intimacy is above all a matter of safety and circumscription, blandness and sanitization. His chief objective appeared to be to persuade listeners to leave things just as they are: your heels on the pouffe, the cosy on the teapot. Sixties crooning no longer toyed with the neural zizz of forbidden proximity, nor suggested the whispers into eternity of lost souls sitting alone at the existentialist bar. Your TV crooner's narcissism was neutered and trimmed with modest self-deprecation; he no longer hovered, preening, spotlit in front of a dinner-plate microphone, nor moved to slip a hesitant hand about your waist just long enough to justify bringing his lips a few centimeters closer to the trembling flesh of your earlobes. Where he smirked, your sixties crooner smirked contentedly.

As a televisual experience, crooning helped to blur the line between "chat" and "performance" (chat is, after all, conversation in its most passively contented form). The crooner sat in a comfy chair or on a sofa or a low dais, one leg jauntily out, the other tucked decorously under, or stood next to a Christmas tree or in front of a picture window disclosing either a beautiful landscape or the outskirts of Birmingham. Crooners held pencil-thin microphones lightly between fingertips. They almost certainly smelled of freshly laundered cashmere and aftershave, and rejoiced above all things in soft furnishings, and to hell with sharp tailoring. In its new dispensation to soothe, quell, and mollify, crooning seemed to be about keeping everything in its place and just *so*. And so I grew up contemptuous of anything that remotely resembled a croon. Even Sinatra's.

* * *

The unrelenting clangor of punk changed all that, and in 1977 I developed a ravenous taste for one of the greatest crooners ever to draw breath in tiny sips.

I did it, I suppose, because I needed respite from all the punky shouting; I needed to feel that a sense of intimacy still belonged in my relationship with music: I wanted to be seduced for a change, not upbraided. And of course, being seventeen at the time, it was a basic requirement that I get these things from an impeccably cool source, one totally free of sophistication and irony. The willing hipster could not, in all conscience, buy James Taylor records as a seventeen year old in 1977, so I got stuck into the Cool Ruler.

Gregory Isaacs may or may not have been a nice man. He may or may not have been piously observant of the Rastafarian faith that provided the esoteric cladding for many of the songs he sang; he may have paid only lip service to it. It mattered not. But when he sang, Gregory appeared to mean what he said, even if he said it quietly and with motives that, while plain, were not always easy to digest, even for a seventeen year old who had as yet not grappled properly with the cardinal tenets of feminism. Isaacs was endowed with a strange, slightly alien, wholly unique persuasiveness. For all his patriarchal hauteur ("If you wa-a-ant to be my number one . . ."—I *beg* your pardon?), Gregory was at least gentle in the way he addressed you and your girlfriend, if she existed. He was courtly. It did not sound as if unpleasantness would be the inevitable consequence of you (or your girlfriend) not responding positively to his suit.

There was plenty of contextual texture to this. Jamaican roots music had just entered its most stridently political phase in 1977, raised on a platform built by the international hit-making of Bob Marley, by increasing sensitivity regarding racism, and by hobbled financial conditions in the Western economies, and yet further buttressed in the UK at least by the onset of punk, which made common cause with reggae on the grounds that both punk and Rasta shared a common "Babylonian" enemy, in addition to some of those untoward social conditions. Patriarchal religious liberation cult met anarcho-nihilism and agreed to agree on the issues arising from the social conditions at least.

Roots-rockers were obliged to "chant down Babylon," just as punks were expected to bellow at it. But Gregory Isaacs did very little in the way of chanting and no bellowing whatsoever. He seldom troubled to raise his voice above a papery whisper. Indeed he murmured, and wailed when he wasn't murmuring, in a brittle, light, supplicant tenor like wind sighing through reeds. That was his "sufferah's" voice. Sometimes he found a middle way between the two, between the murmur and the supplicant wail. But that third voice—a more singerly, melodically strenuous kind of utterance—contained elements of both of the others, so there was never any doubt as to whose voice it was or that it was coming for one thing or the other: either for your sense of righteousness or for your girlfriend, and quite often both. It remained unmistakably a croon.

His spheres of persuasion were several and interlocked with one another most satisfactorily. But chiefly, Isaacs was a lover. That was the first thing he wanted you to know about him. It was his starting position. He was tender, he was achingly humble, he was impoverished, he was alone in the world, he had an abundance of love to give. These simple propositions—rooted authentically enough in the extremely severe experience of his childhood—supported an entire musical persona that was as thematically flexible as it was possible to be, given the strident inflexibility of so much Rasta business. He could go anywhere with it, so long as that place was "rootsical": into testy social observation via dry Rasta reasoning, apocalyptic biblical exegesis and corny aphorism, not to mention the mysterious discourses of Jamaican folklore. He was wont to personify Babylonian consciousness with names and titles—"Mr. Brown," "Mr. Cop," and all the rest. He could go anywhere, yes, but, like a bluesman he always came back to love—as if love were the universal elixir, the transcendent lotion. The final, settling issue. No voice has ever drifted in reverberant sonic space with quite so much leafy lightness and dryness, yet carried such earnest freight.

His masterpiece? Well, it depends of course upon your vulnerabilities, I suppose. But, if one were to overlook his great, echo-drenched epics of asperity and hope, "Mr. Know It All" (on the DEB label) and "The Border" (GG), you are left perhaps only with his version of Dobby Dobson's wistful 1960s rock steady lament, "Loving Pauper," which Isaacs cut in the mid-seventies. The song found multiple release over the decades in a variety of production guises, some dry as a bone, some with augmented instrumentation, one weirdly split into two completely separated stereo channels (voice one side, rhythm the other), and another, my favorite, a twelve-inch Gussie Clarke discomix, which arrived unheralded on this side of the Atlantic in 1977 with a muggy thud, jointed to an even muggier, heavier dub version. (For readers interested in tracking it down, it was finally digitized in the 1990s by the British label Greensleeves.)

It's a miraculous thing, a sort of quantum paradox among reggae records in that it contrives to be both heavy and light at the same time, as if challenging the human imagination to conceive of love as the ultimate reconciliation of incompatible conditions. To make it sing, Isaacs deploys his papery whisper, just about hitting the high notes of the melody, but *only just*—he's reaching that jar on the top shelf with the very tips of his fingers—and absolutely never sounding anything other than delicately hesitant; not exactly apologetic but certainly not pushy or, heaven forbid, overweening. Just persuasive. Meanwhile Clarke's almighty rhythm submits to the laws of gravity as readily as a sack of sand on a mattress, yet remains somehow mobile, moving slowly forward like a galleon through fog, pennanted with a simple counter-melody fingered on a cheap organ and by silk-soft falsetto vocal backups that sound like the Mighty Diamonds.

"Ca-a-an't take you out to fancy places / Like other fellas that I know can do . . ."

"Whoo-ooo oo-ooo!"

"Loving Pauper" is a strange, otherworldly but simultaneously earthy utterance and it takes the listener on a journey directly into the heart of Isaacs's psychic world of croon, his transactional world, his world of earnest persuasion, a world quite untouched by irony or secondary inflection and, least of all, by self-revelation: it's a mendicant world of misunderstood expediency and virtuous poverty, in which the put-upon Rasta projects his goodness on to his presumed lover through his very quietness, his delicacy, his impecuniousness, and the humbleness of his place in society: the world of the "poor and clean" and of the "lonely lover"; a world in which low social status allied to good intentions, torn raiment, and absolutely no purchasing power whatsoever amount to the perfect engine of sleepy desire.

* * *

Though sleep can be frightening too. We dream when we sleep and sometimes we have nightmares. Moreover, when we are asleep we are oblivious of the material, knowable world around us and are therefore vulnerable to it. We might be murdered in our sleep. We might, quite simply, never wake up from it. We might drown in sleep. When I was a small boy I used to wonder quite often about the possibility of not waking up from sleep and it caused me sometimes to lie awake for long stretches, stimulated.

What if . . . ? What if I went to sleep and everything just stopped? My heart. My brain. What if I just ceased to be? Or the world? What if *it* just ceased to be? What about my mum and dad, who must be nearly as susceptible to the perils of sleep as I am? After all, they are old. They might just cease to be and where would that leave me? Crumbs. Where do we go when we sleep? Sleep is so close to extinction, after all. It looks like extinction from the outside. It feels a little like extinction on the inside. Nothingness, dreams, more nothingness . . . Well, you're no longer you, are you? You're no longer leaving a mark on the world (unless you sleepwalk or snore or habitually fall out of bed, and what kind of marks are they?). I used to murmur to myself sometimes in the dark, just to hear the sound of my own voice, real in the world and alive—"Nick . . . Nick . . . *Nick!*"—a concrete, crooning affirmation of my actual presence here, now and in my bed, neither asleep, nor dead.

* * *

And here is Kate Bush, neither asleep nor dead, face up to the Moon, drifting alone and helpless in a horizonless sea at nightfall, murmuring; borne up in the water by the spread of her clothing and by the last flattened cubic inches of air remaining in her life jacket, alone and drifting.

And drifting . . .

* * *

In 1985, Bush released the *Hounds of Love* album, her fifth, to a chorus of rapturous sighs plus the occasional American raspberry. By most, though, the album was hailed as a work of originality and inspirational reach, a sort of fluted pop hypnodrome composed of carefully deployed artificial/organic instrumental textures and expressive voices, serving to extend both the scope and the profundity of Bush's storytelling gestalt and to soften her musical palette somewhat; possibly to bring her indoors, psychologically speaking, from the outhouse where she'd been tinkering the past few seasons, oblivious of the frost forming on the inside of the glass. Her previous album, the cold, clattery, uncozy *The Dreaming*, had not done well commercially.

I liked *Hounds* a lot at the time, which was unexpected. It was unexpected because in 1985 I was busy with a sulky middle-twenties renunciation of all that white commercial pop had to offer. Pop no longer spoke to me of things I cared to hear about. The vast majority of it, or so it seemed to me, was dull and formulaic, not even pretending to creativity for creativity's sake any more, too often mistaking artful retrospection for reach, new technology (and trousers) for new ideas. And a lot of it was just plain lumpen in its listless pseudo-danceability. So I was through with it. I was certainly unimpressed by the make-up, props, glamour, and "attitude" which together seemed to constitute the only calibration of value in an aspirational pop world that was every bit as bankrupt, to my scourging mind, as the morality of the banking world and its great sponsor, the current Tory government. Call me a prig if you like. I certainly was one. Actually, looking back, it's a miracle I even bothered to listen to *Hounds of Love*.

But somehow I managed it and was very smitten. I was smitten not with the music's textural novelties or its generous thematic surprises (Wilhelm Reich!), nor with the technological wonder of Bush's Fairlight CMI programming and its not-quite-frigid atmospheric temperature, nor even with *Hounds*'s conceptual structure—impressive though all of these things were. It was the singing that thrilled me. And it thrills me still. *Hounds of Love* has singing on it that fills the sky like weather.

What we might describe now with fingered quote marks as "side two" of the album is devoted to the exploration of a kind of thought-into-music experiment, which goes like this: What would it be like to be cast adrift and alone on open sea with only a life jacket to keep you afloat? What would pass through your mind? What would you hear in the dull slap of water against your cheeks and neck? Would you sink or soar? What feelings would visit you as you lay there, spread out like a picnic on the surface of the brine, wholly passive, awaiting rescue or death?

Or sleep.

Strangely enough, the very first song of "The Ninth Wave," the suite of songs that constitutes "side two" of *Hounds of Love*, is entitled "And Dream of Sheep." It is a slow piano song, a pillow-soft wallow in the exposed harmonies that slow piano songs do best, its melody cleaving to the underpinning instrumental frame like wet fabric to sodden limbs, ridged, bubbled, and clinging flush. As the song begins, Bush is already adrift, bobbing and pitching in the dark, quite alone, her boat (or plane) now lost, her mind already wishing to submit to the pull of sleep . . .

She begins to fantasize, first of rescue—the rescue which is inevitable, surely. No?

Yes!

Yes. They must come. They will come and see the tiny light on her life vest, bobbing in the dark. She will be stirred soon enough by the sound of engines. She will be safe . . .

She drifts some more.

Then slowly, irresistibly, her unmoored consciousness fills up with the downy sensations of her bed at home—her pillows, her sheets, her radio on low, her comforts. Her mind becomes an envelope containing only the soft stuff of incipient sleep.

"I'd tune into some friendly voices . . ."

And she begins to be drawn into it, unable to resist her drowsing as she sinks deeper and deeper, like a stone.

The final verse of "And Dream of Sheep" is in effect a coda and, as it settles quietly on the ear, the song's tempo appears to attenuate, thinning and lengthening like sleepy breathing, while Bush's voice, now accompanied by pipes in tiny harmonized bubbles, draws nearer still, impossibly soft, close, and warm, intimate to the point of touchability, to the point where nothing exists for the listener but its intoxicating beauty as it describes the jostling arrival in the drifter's mind of the sheep that will escort her to her repose. They too are soft and warm "and they smell like sheep." And they speak. They tell her what she wants to hear—that soon they'll be bringing her home . . . And with that intrusion into the song-text of the olfactory sense, the sense of *smell*, a new feeling suffuses the mind of the listener with a terrible perfume.

Terror.

"And Dream of Sheep" is oblivious of the terror it stimulates: it is a lullaby. It is sleepy. It is above all a croon. It is a quiet, contemplative description of a mind afloat, adrift and then letting go, finding beauty in that drift, as well as hope and comfort. It embraces disorientation and passivity as if they were friends—it is sung to them as a welcome song. The voice means what it says; it is persuasive of its own truth. There is no irony in it. The only irony to be found anywhere near it is Aristotle's dramatic irony, which is located in the mind of the listener who knows what is going to happen next while the sodden protagonist adrift in the song has not a clue.

It is the croon of a sacrificial lamb.

* * *

And what of Frank, the least innocent of all crooners? What of the great bronze bell of twentieth-century popular music?

To me, Frank Sinatra has always been something of a sacred cow as well as a bell; the totem of an alien faith—worthy of respect, no doubt, admirable in very many remarkable ways; fascinating to behold when encountered in the right context and under suitable lighting; always sharp, stylish, economical, usually swingin'; all of these things, yes, but somehow not connected to my own species, as if he were built on different principles and finessed by a different book of rules.

This non-connection is, in great part, a function of my musical age and upbringing. As a small child I was raised on the gentle percolations of A. A. Milne and church music and the less grandiose early, baroque, and classical forms, as if together they constituted the basis of all aesthetic value in music. And later on, rock music—the music that defined my adolescent arousal—had very little time for Frank. Well, the feeling was mutual; Frank didn't have much time for rock 'n' roll either. He and his courtiers stood well back and held their noses while they waited for rock's moment to pass, with the result that the shadow Sinatra cast over the new form was neither long nor inky. His direct influence was virtually nil, in fact, except in a few very exceptional cases. Indeed until the 1980s at least, rock and Frank agreed, like good fellows, to ignore one another on the street and just get on with their own business. Yes, you can hear slow Sinatra in the esoteric boom of Scott Walker, and you can see traces of him in the poise, tailoring, and cultivated references of the British glam icons, Messrs Ferry and Bowie, who were nothing if not fascinated by the way the future is readable in the residue of the recent past. But it did not go deep. Sinatra was never in rock's grain.

Indeed, it is only after rock had concluded its serious business and was feebly attempting to cauterize its own hemorrhaging vitality and relevance in the 1980s that you began to *hear* Frank again, in rock, pop, and R&B. Marvin Gaye had always aspired to the condition of the black Sinatra without actually being prepared to do the kind of work required to get him there—something for which, in many ways and for all kinds of reasons, we should be grateful. Instead it was one of Gaye's spiritual successors, the late, great, and often sadly misunderstood Luther Vandross, who actually came closest to fulfilling that aspiration: his melancholy professionalism and attention to detail certainly took him into Sinatra-like spaces atmospherically, even if his orchestrations and singing bore no resemblance musicologically. Like Frank, Luther combined bravura displays of technical excellence with lush intimacy, and he made songs really sing. He came very close indeed.

And then, in the late 1980s, a small regiment of grim-faced Scots in hats and suits identified Sinatra as the active ingredient at the core of their masculine display, as if Frank and not the Beatles/Stones/Kinks/Who were the most valuable relic of their juvenile years—the prevailing music of their 1960s childhoods repurposed for a whole new post-rock 'n' roll world. Who now remembers The Blue Nile, Danny Wilson, and Hue and Cry? Well, of course you do. There are plenty of good reasons to. And let us not forget the Associates. Billy Mackenzie was Frank Sinatra on steroids and laughing gas. And Edwyn Collins? What is "A Girl Like You" if not Sinatra's croon assimilated into Iggy Pop's, then welded with a blowtorch to a gigantic nineties retrobeat?

So Sinatra arched pretty much unheeded over more than thirty years of rocking rebellion, barely making contact at all apart from, briefly and toward the end, in Scotland. Rebellion was just not his style. And it remains the case that he has never persuaded me of anything at all other than his genius. Between Frank and me there lies only an expanse of dead water.

This is not a rational thing. Yes, I did manage to overcome some of my conditioned aversion to the great bronze bell in those selfsame 1980s, while embracing the then forty-years-old modern-jazz aesthetic as if it were the only musical game in town now worth playing. Sinatra was by no means a jazz singer but you could not, in conscience, devote yourself to the exploration of the modern-jazz canon without including him in your calculations, at least as part of the furniture in the modern-jazz room. He swung like the clappers, after all. He accorded Time the slide-rule treatment. And he wore a suit and hat. So I listened to both *Songs for Swingin' Lovers* and *In the Wee*

Small Hours with a serious face on, and I admired them. I felt as if I were learning something. And I admired myself for at least doing that. But Frank himself never moved me, in the sense that he never got inside me and held me from within, my heart pinioned, my mind pinging. And he does not, even now, thirty years on from that earnest moment, transfix the middle-aged, slightly melancholy, hat-wearing man that I have since become in order that we might share a moment's manly identification. Hell, no. It just doesn't happen. I am simply not one of the guys.

But why am I not one of the guys? What is my deficiency?

Indulge me briefly while I listen now to my favorite upbeat Sinatra tune, "I've Got You Under My Skin," one of the two great Cole Porter songs that adorn the justly famed *Songs for Swingin' Lovers* album of 1956. Let me embrace it like an old friend, without bothering to put my serious face on.

Yes, it's a joy. "Under My Skin" opens side two of *Songs* with a bump. Nelson Riddle's fabulous, dinging arrangement trips along in its early stages like a scene-setting dance number in an MGM musical, diligently prompting the voice and its comely burden, the tune, with bobbing confraternities of baritone sax and trombone, exhibiting cool restraint and snap as a matter of policy while offering to break out into full chorus at every turn—if only it were the done thing. But it isn't done. It just isn't. In the world of 1950s show business, abandonment to anything other than an acceptable norm is an abomination. Nevertheless, the riffage is intoxicating: it's the sound of guys bantering as they head for the bar, blood up, ties askew, all joy and clipped relaxation; and Sinatra's voice is in there somewhere. Yes, he's definitely a participant, if only serving to peg out the melody and hold his own space open—a sort of auditory gap, a Polo-Mint hole for the ears without flavor or texture or grip; a cipher, in fact, defying the logic which says that the voice is the sole reason for the existence of this magnificent affair . . .

Then, for a brief season, the orchestra breaks discipline and goes mad. The sung melody drops out to allow strings to surge and trombones to cockfight for a whole chorus while the rest of the orchestra gathers round to cheer, and pretty soon the soloing trombone is tearing itself into strips just to be heard . . . It's a vulgar moment, but it's a thrilling one, too. And afterward, the returning Frank is obliged to turn his own brightness up to the point where he is no longer crooning but ringing that great bronze bell, not quite for all he's worth but certainly with intense commitment to the upped ante—kind of going for it, though naturally never threatening to lose his cool. Heavens, no.

Pung! . . . Pung a-pung . . . a-punnng! ringing right up flush against the beat for a change.

And for a chorus repetition or so I find myself actually listening to him with attention, and not the arrangement, as if the voice and the song were the main thing; as if the hole in the middle of the mint has suddenly become the whole point of the mint and the orchestral arrangement is, just for a change, nothing but an encircling form . . .

Then there's slow Frank. The Frank who reveals not only his genius but himself, or so the theory goes.

The handful of albums Sinatra made in the fifties dedicated exclusively to the more introspective aspects of the American songbook—*In the Wee Small Hours, Only the Lonely, Where Are You?, No One Cares* are the ones I've heard—are gorgeous artifacts that ought to be high on the listening agenda of every soul that harbors a care for nuance and the diligent excavation of emotion with the tools of art. This is the motherlode, the seam that exposes Sinatra's ore to the light. Or so it is often said.

I am partial to "Angel Eyes" on *Only the Lonely*. It's a peculiar song, which never resolves itself into clear thinking or coherent imagery but, rather, describes in period language a fetid hell of sexual jealousy and self-loathing at a tempo so low, thick, and elastic it might be a sleepy anaconda. It makes its first representations sardonically enough, with the voice offering to stand everyone in the bar to a gargle: "The drink and the laugh's on me." But it then rolls slowly over and over down a slope spiked with Gothic pentatonic intervals into a swamp of resentful longing and graceless resignation, where it does not drown but keeps on rolling, gathering algae.

Melodically, it's a Bond song. Emotionally, it's had one bourbon too many. And Sinatra, with a touch of reverb, drives deep into his most resonant baritone range to make the great bell ring like a knell. *Punnnng!*

Pu-u-unnnnng! He cleaves the air. He peals with immaculate clarity. In fact, now that I am listening to it properly like this, he is more articulate than a wordless bell. "Angel Eyes" is a speech from late Shakespeare rung out by a talented old ham. You hear in it mortality and magic and bitterness and retrieval and the uncertain passage of Time, and the very air is shaken. For he—the singer—is poised on the edge of Prospero's cliffs, contemplating the surf and the jagged rocks below, oblivious of the wind that tugs at his loosened tie, enjoying the rain that stings his face. Glad to be unhappy.

So, no, he won't chuck himself off. He won't chuck himself off because he knows that it is a man's obligation to contain this sort of feeling safely: contain it with main strength and with the strength of philosophy and not let its unsightliness disfigure the landscape. Besides, he is circled all about with iron bands and firmly planted in concrete. The wind may blow and crack its cheeks. He can hold the posture. He is not in danger, and neither is the landscape; and nor are we. Sadness is great and beautiful and the bullshit that is neurosis has no business here.

And I feel nothing. Or at least I feel only awe and admiration. I can hear what he's getting at, but what he's getting *into me* is not the crisis of his existence but the sureness of his touch and the certainty of his eventual return from the edge, once the music stops. It's a beautiful act, to my ear—in itself a real and hugely impressive thing, but not for me an emotionally moving one. It brooks no frailty.

It speaks only of its own strength.

* * *

The cultured elegance and rigor of the Sinatra canon is not in question—I genuinely believe the fifties and sixties recordings for Capitol to be one of the century's great bodies of work—and yet I am quite unaffected by it, as I am unaffected, emotionally, by the changing price of oil. I can see that Frank Sinatra has mattered immensely and matters still, as a relic of his time as well as a voice so magnificent that it lingers alive into our own time; and

I can imagine only too well how he matters to others, too. So why can't I feel anything myself?

What is wrong with me?

* * *

Music is a pleasure. This we know. We wouldn't have music otherwise.

It is a stimulus to both the mind and the body. The feeling of exaltation brought on by a surge of the neurotransmitters dopamine and oxytocin is potent and is sufficient for some neurologists to explicate the connection between music and pleasure, as if the relationship were essentially a biochemical one. We get pleasure from music, the argument goes, because music stimulates our hormones. Ba-doom! There it is. That's *all* it is. Music, like sex (and eating pineapple), is just a biological action, which may or may not stimulate a reaction. It is mere fodder for the pattern-seeking propensities of the human brain, a stimulus requiring a binary response: off or on, pleasant or unpleasant, mmm or yuck. Like/don't like. The binary that makes life into a procedure.

But we all know it's more complicated than that, don't we? We know that music cannot be properly understood in isolation from the needs of the listening mind and body, and that it is the listening mind and body that *discover* meaning in music, irrespective of the intentions of the musician.

Music is music, of course. It is what it is: an arrangement of tuned sounds organized by one or more creative souls into a schematized pattern expressed in the dimension of Time, sometimes involving the deployment of verbal language, sometimes not. In itself, it is only itself; it is nothing else. In isolation from the listening ear, music does not mean anything. It's a pattern. But music, in its relationship with the mindfully listening organism, is rather more meaningful. We all know this and feel it, even if we don't trouble ourselves to explore that knowledge very often—if at all. It's not that we're lazy. It's just that music is a pleasure and we are not inclined, as a rule, to question our pleasures. We just enjoy them.

But pleasure in music is complicated. It is arguably the most compli-cated pleasure there is, depending as it does on the engagement of the full range of our most deeply felt emotions. There is nothing *responsible* about music—it will do what it's going to do, with or without your permission. Some music goes straight for the headline emotions; some skirts the head-lines and flirts with your emotional small print—the important stuff you hadn't bothered to read earlier and rather wish you had. Some music doesn't touch us at all. Its impact depends on who we are and what the music is, and even where it is. But all of it depends to some degree or another on what we, as selfhoods, bring to the engagement. And that is complicated. It's as complex in structure and hard to elucidate as a brain. We don't *want* plea-sure to be complicated, but sometimes it just is. And this is never made more evident than when you're addressed nose to nose by a crooner.

It's the intimacy that is troubling. The presumption. The sense that a not-so-subtle invasion is taking place, an invasion of your personal space by an insurgent armed with his (and sometimes her) own agenda, with a view to persuading you to see things his (or her) way, maybe for a moment, maybe for a stretch. Oh, and by the way, you'll both get on so much better together in the tiny space afforded by this nose-to-nose engagement if, beyond merely seeing eye to eye, you actually take the trouble to *identify* with your invader. *Be* him for a moment. *Be* her. Assume the mantle. Discover the truth of your own scrappy selfhood in his (or hers).

And this is why Frank Sinatra and I can never occupy the same space without diffidence and/or embarrassment and/or suspicion on my part. I can admire his technical assurance. I can be awed by his éclat. I can even put on a serious face and learn something from the experience of being eyeballed like that. But I can't identify. It just isn't in me to be that man, even for a moment. I could never be that kind of guy, even if I put on a suit and tie and yanked the tie down two notches and hooded my eyes and drank shots on a high stool at a dimpled bar with a hat on the back of my head. I just don't have the masculinity for it, the sort that gleams quietly like bronze and is concerned above all things with projecting the reserve and grandeur and sophistication of its own strength. No, really not. Not even if I wanted to. Not even if it were good for me to do so—as it might well be. By and large, I'd much rather be Judy Garland.

GRACE NOTES

GEORGE JONES: "THINGS HAVE GONE TO PIECES"
Musicor Records, 1965

Just as it is possible to croon without irony, you can also do it with soul—and still be quietly, intently persuasive. Of course you can. Here's George Jones contemplating a shopping list of besetting woes, from the tap dripping in the kitchen (the kitchen is an empty, reverberant shell since she left) to the imminent repossession of George's goods by "the man," not to mention the loss of his job, the arm falling off his favorite chair (again), and the light bulb going *phut* in the hall. Damn. Where to start with that lot? Things have certainly gone to pieces since the little lady hitched her skirts and ran.

Leon Payne's song is funny, pathetic, and heartbreaking in equal measure, although it would not be anything like as heartbreaking without Jones's particular treatment of it. On the evidence provided by other versions of the song, it would just be funny and pathetic.

But then that was Jones's métier, bringing the heft of real feeling to bear in the robust emotional environment of the honky-tonk, through a combination of horn-like vocal tone and phrasing, unstinting conviction and obvious personal vulnerability. It was as if his voice—a curiously heady *and* throaty instrument that was capable of controlling the tiniest variations in tone and timbre—had special tenderizing properties. Jones would stand rooted at the microphone and look out through widening, terrified eyes as he sifted the gamiest country lyric into a new state of refinement and flow. George really could have sung tragic life into a bag of flour.

"Things Have Gone to Pieces" is a slight song making fun of masculine self-pity and incompetence, ferruled with the pathetic conviction that things'll turn out fine if you just let them. That's "conviction" in its special drinker's meaning, signifying "vain hope." It's a gag over a beer in a bar, basically. But sung by George Jones, the gag is transformed into a touching hymn of self-reproach—and when, at the end, he clings on to "the pieces of my dreams," it is not in a spirit of ironic hope but with the grinding force of necessity. He really thinks that if he clutches at those pieces steadfastly enough then she'll come back and change the light bulb. That is self-persuasion of a very high order indeed.

THE CARPENTERS: "GOODBYE TO LOVE"
A&M Records, 1972

The Carpenters resided, like ABBA, in a strange bubble of pop serenity, possibly because life outside the bubble for constituent members of the group was far from serene. But let us not dwell on that. The facts are that these two close siblings, Richard and Karen Carpenter, were endowed with sumptuous talent which they chose to apply to the creation of what many of us are pleased, somewhat sniffily, to call Easy Listening—soft, unchallenging, appealingly melodic pop music that was wholly magnetic to anyone in the 1960s and '70s vulnerable to an old-fashioned croon.

And what a voice Karen had. It was as warm, open, and inclusive as a kindled hearth on a dank afternoon. It traveled effortlessly from deep contralto through mezzo to touch the soprano range, but settled most expressively in her area of greatest cogency: the middle-to-low regions. She had extraordinary natural control. She could spin out a melody with flowing legato phrasing and then leave it hanging, as if finished, for you to contemplate at leisure in memory. She was what you might call a lapidary singer: she engraved her phrases on your sensibilities for all time. She saw herself as a drummer, really.

There was very little audible affect in that voice. No Gladys Knight, she. The pain of a difficult life was not for externalizing but for containing within the bounds of all that loveliness, so as not to contaminate the perfect world of which Karen and her brother dreamed so tenaciously. Which meant that, also like ABBA, the Carpenters were utterly formalist in their approach. Leakage into the music of any kind of psychological waste matter would be taken as a failure of personal discipline but also as an exhibition of poor taste. "This isn't about *us*," was the tacit assertion, expressed as silently as sunshine. "It's about *the music*."

"Goodbye to Love" is one of the most heartbreaking pop singles ever made because of the earnest perfection of that formalism and because it contains not a moment, not a nanosecond, of emotional leakage throughout its four-minute length. The emotions implicit in the song pulsate beneath a perfect surface that has been polished to allow the reflection of the enquiring gaze but no penetration. Agony? Not in here, matey. You'll have to go elsewhere for that. Self-scrutiny? Well, it depends on what you mean . . .

In fact "Goodbye to Love" is self-scrutiny as executed by a broken woman who will not give in to the effects of the breakage, preferring to hold her own gaze, steady and stoical, as it reflects her own surface back from the surface of her bedroom mirror. She is saying goodbye to love, and here's why; oh, and here's why she won't be caving in to her feelings any time soon, either, no sir, no matter how great the pressure from within . . . This is all about inner fortitude and outer control, as is life, when you boil it down. It is another song of self-persuasion.

Richard Carpenter's long melody is beautiful almost beyond words, and Karen phrases it as if breathing were not actually necessary. The combination of melodic and harmonic flow plus implied spiritual resolution brings to mind the feel and tone of a resolute Bach cantata—an impression not diminished by the contribution of Tony Peluso, whose famous guitar solo dares to express all the histrionic feeling eschewed by the voice and then takes off at the end, over chorale-ing Karens and Richards, for a descant that runs the harmonic substitutions down as if this were a Lutheran church in eighteenth-century Leipzig and not Radio 1 in 1972. It is that rarest of phenomena, a breathtaking Easy Listening pop record. And it stands, four decades on, as nobly as a neoclassical statue embodying an allegory of self-effacement through self-affirmation, shining and impermeable as polished marble.

PRINCE: "IF I WAS YOUR GIRLFRIEND"
Paisley Park Records, 1987

Prince died the day before yesterday. It appears that he died of an overdose of prescription drugs at his Minneapolitan HQ, Paisley Park. He was fifty-seven. He breathed his last breath in a lift, all on his own—a tiny man in a sealed mechanical box, falling silent too soon. A musical box suffering a terminal breakdown.

But then it was apt for him to depart in such a location. How inappropriate would it have been for Prince to die in a ploughed field or on a rocky outcrop, or in a meadow by a stream while enjoying a picnic? Prince belonged in small, confined, virtually airless spaces, as Aaron Copland belonged in wide-open, rangy ones. And he lived and died by his taste for intimacy: all he ever wanted, or so it seemed, was to be shut in somewhere private, unobserved and with no possibility of outside intrusion—and no prospect of escape into the world either. Confinement, closeness, exclusion, control: that was Prince.

Compare and contrast with his opposite number in the four-cornered fight for the high, central ground of 1980s American pop: Bruce Springsteen (and let's leave the other two corners, Madonna and Michael Jackson, right out of this). Springsteen was—is—unambiguous, open, unconfined, muscular, masculine, political, epic, bossy: he has the American landscape at his command and its people in his backyard. His backyard is America. Prince's backyard was where the bins were kept and he never went anywhere near it. Springsteen would be only too happy to die in a ploughed field or on a rocky outcrop. He would feel nothing but horror at the prospect of expiring in a lift.

But only one of them could really croon.

Prince's croon was the most salacious ever heard. It was a croon for the ages, in the sense that every age has had inexpressible things to say about sex—but for our age for the obvious reason that we are not, in our age, half so shackled by tasteful and/or uptight restraint as our forebears. Prince's croon had nothing in common with Perry Como's. It was suggestive, close, silken, indecent, persuasive. It knew coziness only as a fix for post-coital tristesse. It was a continuation in sound of the trajectory of his blinking, calf-like gaze, coyly looped to ensnare listeners in the coils of his narcissism. Prince always kept his listeners close, even when dancing.

"If I Was Your Girlfriend" is a semi-croon off the *Sign O' the Times* album, delivered in large part in a constricted, genderless whisper-squeal. It is by no means his greatest song, nor does it contain his most affecting singing, but it is a song only he could have written and sung like that, so indecently closely. Its protagonist—let's call him Prince—is addressing an ex-girlfriend and enjoining her to think of him now not as an ex, but as a current friend who happens to be a girl, free in his girlishness to be intimate, attentive, and insightful as only a best friend can. It is many things, but it is persuasive above all. It says, look how close we can be: we can be so close that it would be difficult to tell us apart. Let us at least try this on for size—and I have a feeling the rewards for both of us will be even greater than before.

The programmed rhythm that supports it is completely airless.

8

So, What?

So what about instruments?

People playing instruments. Tooting, parping, farting. Tweeting like birds. Roaring like lions. Making the saxophone sound like an old bear or like Billie Holiday singing. Do the instruments count as voices too? Or do we have to think of them differently, as another kind of agency for a different kind of message?

So yes, what about jazz?

Tricky. It's not that I don't like jazz singing—I do: I have boundless admiration for the voices of a few jazz singers. Admiration and feeling, too. But there are only a few to whom I connect properly, and I do wonder about this habit of non-connection, as if there is a blockage in me, a snag. Yes, Billie Holiday, Louis Armstrong, Sarah Vaughan, Eddie Jefferson, Ella Fitzgerald, Betty Carter . . . These are all great voices, one way or another, and they have all said great things in great ways. But I don't often want to listen to them and, indeed, don't find that the voices linger within me for long afterward when I do. They don't stick. It's as if they are coated in some oily physic that makes them slip out the same way they came in, even though, as voices, they are as musical and distinctive as any great voice in any field of vocal enterprise in all music history. I like jazz singing well enough, but it doesn't seem to have the capacity to stick with me. Or rather, I don't possess the will to stick with it.

Yes, Ella Fitzgerald can make a song sound as if it has never been sung so transparently before—when Fitzgerald sings Cole Porter, you really hear Cole Porter. And no one will ever cut into the tissue of existential pain with as keen a blade as Billie Holiday. For that matter, no one has ever swung so deftly and so expansively as Louis Armstrong, even if there is something ingratiating about him. Armstrong is arguably as great a singer as he is a trumpeter, which is to say really great. But even so. Even so. It is a fact that whenever I hear a fine jazz voice, I always find myself wondering how much deeper I might be taken into the moment and its emotion without the encumbrance of *language*, without having to decipher the experience the words describe and the ideas it depends upon. It's as if the words actually get in the way of what really needs to be said. However much I might enjoy that moment, I can't help but want the voice to pipe down so that I can hear what the horns have to say . . .

* * *

I make no bones about the fact that I made myself listen to jazz when I was a teenager in the 1970s because I wanted to be hip. At least, I wanted to be the kind of person who listens to jazz. I was not at that stage, in the excitable early days of the punk moment, an aspiring jazz hat: I preferred torn drainpipes and brothel-creepers. (The beret arrived a little later on, in the early stages of the following decade, along with a real 1940s demob "zoot" suit and a trench coat.) Nor was I particularly keen to mark myself in such self-consciously incendiary times as a pipe-and-slippers man, a contender for the Big Armchair. But in 1976/7, at the age of sixteen, on the uneventful edge of my dreary East Anglian fen, I did think that I ought to be at least *au fait* with the brothers and what they'd been saying all these decades on the swingin' side of the pond, with their heroin and their funny glasses and their suits and hats and the grainy low-lit monochrome austerity which held their look together in a wash of steely tone and texture.

The photography counted for quite a lot. I dug the modern-jazz look, as I observed it in books and magazines and record racks. Indeed it was much easier then to see the pictures than it was to hear the music. So, long before I had a clear idea of what modern jazz had to say, I had a pretty clear idea of how Miles Davis and Thelonious Monk looked. Dizzy Gillespie too—even if I hadn't been very touched by his recent appearances on British TV, bull-frogging his busted cheek muscles for the benefit of Michael Parkinson. But still, in 1976 the old stuff, the 1940s and '50s stuff, *looked* good to me.

So I bought a secondhand copy of Miles Davis's *Porgy and Bess*.

I was slightly familiar with the opera already, from my exposure to the classical canon and its attachments. *Porgy and Bess* was a properly composed work by a proper composer, George Gershwin, who was American, admittedly, but could still be relied upon for seriousness with a blue twist.

The blue twist was important. It seemed inevitable and wholly necessary to me that formal composition in America should sound as if it had America in it. And so jazzy-bluesy-gospelly classical opera by a proper composer in a suit added up. In fact it sounded to me like the future of accessible, not-quite-so-modernist classical composition. Apart from anything else, I liked the idea of jazz leaving marks on the hulking body of the classical leviathan as it continued its slow dive to oblivion. So I plonked this wordless, jazz-orchestrated, concerto-like *Porgy and Bess* on to the turntable of my two-bit stereo and waited for a new kind of seriousness to enslave me.

This it did, but not in the way I expected.

One of the primary features of the Western classical tradition is the way it doesn't tolerate mistakes. Or at least what it calls mistakes. Mistakes in classical music are just wrong, and you may not play classical music wrong and expect to be taken seriously, whether the errors arise from technical deficiency or from bad judgment or lapses in taste. Mistakes are an insult not only to the music but to the composer himself (it's usually a he), because the composer is the *primum mobile* in the classical way of thinking. The godhead. The author. You might as soon rewrite Shakespeare for easy comprehension as not follow a scored instrumental part in precise, devoted detail, paying full attention to the composer's marks and responding to them with musicianly taste. As for technical errors . . . Fluffs, tonal inconsistencies, phraseological hiccups, goofed articulation, audible indecision, wrong notes—the list of solecisms can be as long and as rude as you like.

Yet the first thing that struck me, when I listened to Miles Davis's *Porgy and Bess* in my bedroom, was the incidence of technical imperfections in it. Fluffs. Hesitancies. Inaccuracies. Mis-valvings. Split notes, smeared notes, late notes, notes which seemed to issue sidelong from some place other than the Bank of Absolute Musical Rectitude. And that was just Davis. Sometimes I thought I could even hear what sounded like mistakes in the orchestral accompaniment too, for heaven's sake—mistakes made by the professional guys sitting down in the studio with the music in front of them on music stands. These did not occur often or obviously, but they were there all right, I was sure, contributing to the general atmosphere of instability. In fact it sometimes seemed that whole passages were being skated through as if the composition were river ice: there was an inherent dicey-ness in the music, a sort of built-in wobble and slither, as if perfect balance were not a given and at any moment the whole shooting match might go down in a heap. The ice might even crack. It was really quite startling for a sixteen-year-old music prig to encounter such *inefficiency* in an admired orchestral work and I struggled at first to see what they'd been driving at, those writers I'd read who'd asserted that *Porgy and Bess* was a timeless classic of the jazz-concerto art—a match in every conceivable artistic way for the edgy small-group recordings for which Miles Davis was apparently most famous.

But then *P&B* was also beautiful. Stunningly beautiful. Beautiful in its instability as well as in its carefully sifted layers of stridency and delicacy. I loved Gil Evans's stringless orchestral arrangements for their stately heft and for their paradoxical drift, like formations of heavy, cold cloud—so different from most things I'd heard before; as abstract as any *fin-de-siècle* tone poem but somehow less a product of purely aesthetic thinking. Less arty; more soulful—whatever that might mean . . .

Hmm.

The slippiness perceptible in the music might, I supposed, be ascribed to a jazzy desire to sound spontaneous, as if the music were being made up on the spot, when in fact it couldn't possibly be and quite clearly wasn't. Furthermore, the fluffs, splits, and smears might not be mistakes at all but, rather, the marks of a deep, searching authenticity. They might actually be an intrinsic part of the music—there to be taken as seriously as the notes that don't split or smear. This *Porgy* was not, after all, the buffed product of a conservatoire, but of a tough urban milieu in which funny hats and narcotics are currency and communication is judged not by its refinement but by its realness. These blemishes were not mistakes, then, but the necessary by-product of real communication, as poetic in their accidental nature as the meant stuff. "This is how people talk in the real world," I thought, still priggish but a little humbled. "With gaps and collisions, ums and ahs. Even the noises of breathing."

I played one track in particular, "It Ain't Necessarily So," over and over again. It seemed so like life itself and not like an aesthetic description of it. I loved the elasticity of the walking bass and the discreet little ensemble juttings and chorusings, which supported Davis's flugelhorn as it floated in its own space. Loved the delicate rimshots dropped by the drummer like tiny pebbles into deep water. *Plip!* Simply adored the way Davis seemed, quite audibly, to pass something of his being through the conical bore of his flugelhorn: soft, thoughtful, vital, elusive, even feminine. Not modest— by no means modest—but entirely without showiness or imperiousness. It seemed to me that I was listening not to a musician demonstrating his fidelity to a composer's intent or exhibiting the fineness of his technical ability—not actually *exhibiting* anything at all, in fact—but one exploring the sound of his own voice in its relationship with a predetermined pattern of notes in the context of a larger chorus of voices. His voice, their voices: the call-and-response ritual that the average social anthropologist would be only too happy to finger backward in historical time for you, as if it were a thread. Voices calling, voices answering.

"It Ain't Necessarily So" begins with high-wheeling birds but ends in the perfunctory sound of breath pushed through an instrument without forming a note, just a top-of-the-lung gust of air amplified and hardened by its passage through a couple of feet of brass tubing into the transducers of a studio microphone. A bubble bursting. A *pfff* with an undertone of dribble—Davis insouciantly clearing his spit-valve, perhaps, before the piece has reached its final cadence. Or perhaps he's punctuating his final sentence: full stops sound no note, after all. Or perhaps he's fluffing again. You can hear in the *pfff* the barest traces of two harmonics, one high and one low—perhaps he just missed the note altogether . . .

But the truth is, it doesn't really matter what was meant. What matters is what you hear, and what you hear is the sound of a voice reduced to its raw componentry: thought, feeling, muscular action, exhalation. Breath, but no utterance. The sound of air.

* * *

A few years later, in 1983, I had assumed the full jazz-hipster condition, as it was then configured.

At the subcultural level at least, real interest was beginning to be shown once more in the subject of modern jazz, following the fragmentation and then displacement of the punk and post-punk accounts of British life. And although much of that interest concerned sartorial issues and the way both jazz and its look expressed political attitudes and a certain kind of social sophistication—a fantasy of antediluvian purity in style—that was quite all right with me. Anything was better than identifying oneself with the pretensions and superficialities of mainstream pop.

I had officially—almost ceremonially—renounced all interest in pop and rock the previous year and was now working in a hip record shop in Portobello Road in London called Honest Jon's, and DJ-ing for the local pirate radio station, Dread Broadcasting Corporation. I considered myself to be *au fait* at last. Well, getting there. I wore a beret and a dangly earring.

I read Nat Hentoff and Norman Mailer. I cultivated an amiable jazz-hipster vibe and hoped that my middle-class provincial origins weren't too screamingly conspicuous.

Most importantly, I had done my homework and I now knew one end of the modern jazz spectrum from the other, roughly speaking. I knew that "West Coast" was no mere geographical designation. I dug hats. I understood that the socioeconomic climate that gave rise to hard-bop might belong to a postwar, pre-civil rights context, but that modern jazz also spoke deep and universal truths to my own time, provided you made the effort to acclimatize yourself to the language—which was not easy, but was as rewarding when it clicked as any cultural commitment I'd ever undertaken. I certainly enjoyed a deeper connection with *The Black Saint and the Sinner Lady* than I ever had with *Peter and the Wolf*, or indeed with Echo and the Bunnymen. I also had the beginnings of a new sense of taste. Real taste. Not any old casual infatuation for the sake of one's self-image—the sort you go in for because of its potential to reflect yourself back to yourself in ways that seem attractive. No way. My new taste arose from a deep-churning sense of identification with certain voices, their choices, their context, and what they had to say about everything to do with being alive. This seemed like the very least one could do, were one a university-educated English white boy in his early twenties living under Margaret Thatcher's monetarist Tories in the decay of post-imperial London.

I liked Jackie McLean, Dexter Gordon, Booker Ervin, Clifford Brown, Art Pepper, Harold Land, Horace Silver, Booker Little, Eric Dolphy, Elvin Jones, Herbie Hancock, Joe Henderson, Sonny Clark, Ornette Coleman, Charlie Parker, Thelonious Monk, Bud Powell, Charles Mingus, Wayne Shorter, Donald Byrd, Tony Williams, Lee Morgan, Jimmy Smith, Stanley Turrentine, Jimmy Knepper, Bill Evans, Tina Brooks, Hampton Hawes, McCoy Tyner, Cannonball Adderley, even Hank Mobley, who didn't always connect with me because of his inbuilt conservatism and held-back tone. But I could tell he was an all-right guy.

No, actually, I didn't just like them.

I heard what they were saying.

The list of people I wasn't so keen on was much shorter: Sonny Rollins, Freddie Hubbard, Stan Getz, Sonny Stitt, Oscar Peterson, Keith Jarrett, Jan Garbarek, Art Taylor, Dave Brubeck . . . Greats, all of them, in their respective ways. But I had my reasons to doubt and I wasn't afraid to articulate them. This showed, at least, my capacity for discernment. All in all, I was quite the Young Jazz Turk.

And it was great fun working in the record shop, dispensing wisdom and hipness like Bopping Billy Bountiful in a black beret, occasionally rubbing my sensibilities up against those of actual jazz musicians, actual drug dealers and actual nutters, and otherwise listening, listening, listening to tricky music all day long. It was, to use an expression beloved of old-school hipsters everywhere, an education.

Then a young guy walked into the shop—a younger guy than even I—and presented himself at the counter much as fighters present themselves in the ring, not flexing his muscles so much as making a muscular gesture out of his entire being.

"All right," he said, pressing his sense of self over the counter like a bag of spanners. "All right. I got a question for you."

His voice was surprisingly light, given the depth of his chest. He must have been eighteen or nineteen but was built like a box. He obviously worked out. He wore a flecked American jacket and pegs and had his hair styled in the then-fashionable American flattop, beloved of those who wished they lived in the 1950s.

"I want a record," he said, "by the best saxophonist ever. Not the second best. Not the third best. But the best. It has to be the best. You get me?"

"Yes, I think I get you," I replied. "But there's a problem . . ."

"A problem?" he asked reasonably coolly. "Is this a record shop? Do you sell jazz records?"

Yip. Nod.

"Do you sell jazz records by saxophone players?" (Nod.) "In that case, I want the best one. Don't care what it costs . . ."

"Well, it all depends on what kind of jazz you like, and what kind of saxophone player. It might even depend on what kind of saxophone . . ."

"Look," he said, "I'll make it easy for you. Just sell me the record that has the best saxophone playing on it that *you* like. There must be something that *you* think is the best saxophone record you can buy . . . Well, that's the one I want. I can see you know what is and isn't good in saxophone playing, so just sell me the faaaarckin' record, all right?" This appeared to be an attempt at good humor.

Crikey.

"Tell you what," I said, pretending that it wasn't anxiety I was now feeling. "Tell you what. The record I like best at the moment is by a guy called John Coltrane. Lots of people think he's the greatest tenor saxophone player ever, and I don't think I disagree with them. He's amazing. Really exciting. Got this rock-hard tone. Goes through harmonic changes like an adding machine. Absolutely pulverizes everything and anything that stands in his way—he's a sort of dreadnought among saxophonists. The heavyweight champion."

The fighting talk was obviously hitting the mark. My customer appeared to be impressed.

"Now, the album that is usually cited as *the* one, the one where he reaches a kind of peak of heightened expressiveness and where everything else in jazz history suddenly seems to change up a gear, is called *A Love Supreme*, from 1964. It's an amazing record. A really challenging record. It's . . . it's . . ."—second thoughts were now piling in—". . . Perhaps not the best place to start. No. Um. Tell you what, if it were me . . ."

"Just tell me what your favorite one is *now*, right now . . ."

" . . . Er, probably the one I'm listening to most at the moment is called *Impressions*. It's a live album, just been reissued, and Trane plays a lot of soprano on it and it's quite . . . impressionistic. It's not as pulverizing as *A Love Supreme*. Tell you what: why don't I play it for you?"

"No, mate, no need for that. I'm in a hurry. If you think that's the one, then that's good enough for me. It's the one. Now shove it in a bag and I'll leave you in peace."

So I shoved it in a bag, and he left me in peace.

And then about an hour and a half later he reappeared in the shop, sheened with sweat.

"I trusted you," he said, brokenly, and then hardened himself. "And you've just taken the piss. I said I wanted the best sax there is and you sold me this . . . this . . . *shit*."

"Look, I'm really sorry—I wasn't doing anything of the . . ."

"Save it, mate, save it. I know when I've been a mug. I should've let you play it for me. It's partly my own fault. But it's also partly your fault—you sold me shit pretending that you thought it was great. And this . . . this is *faaaarckin'* shit."

He sort of half laughed and rolled his shoulders in his boxy jacket.

"Are you going to give me my money back?"

I didn't hesitate. I gave him his money back and was glad to do so. Apart from anything else, I couldn't have stood another minute of him talking to me in his dad's voice.

But then, surprise of all surprises, a couple of days later he reappeared in the shop, looking rather less belligerent but still pretty muscle-bound. This time he was wearing a porkpie hat.

"Listen, mate," he said, extending a hefty fist across the counter. "I think I owe you an apology. That record you sold me . . . you know, the shit one. Well, it was shit, but it was my mistake. I shouldn't have asked you for it like that. Perhaps you just *like* shit." This was another of his jokes. "Can't be helped. But when I came in the shop I'd just been to see the Chevalier Brothers the night before and they were great—you know what I mean? Faaarckin' *great*—and I should've asked you for "the best saxophone player who's like the one in the Chevalier Brothers" or something like that. That would have been a lot better. I just didn't realize there was so many different kinds of jazz, ranging from shit to the Chevalier Brothers. It was really my fault. So sorry, mate."

He stuck out his hand again. Fixed me in the eye.

"Are we square?"

"We are. We are totally square. Now, perhaps I can interest you in Earl Bostic . . . ?"

* * *

It's always hard to know what is "meant" by instrumental jazz. I certainly struggled with the issue in 1976, and still do, if literal meanings are what's required. How does it generate meaning, a voice, when it makes no use of the language you speak yourself? What is being *said*?

Where do you start?

Well, learn the language, is one answer. It's a time-consuming activity, but worth the effort. But if you really can't be bothered with that, you can always start with what's *not* being said. The standard observation to make about Miles Davis's trumpet voice is that, whatever it is he's saying, he's saying it laconically, as if the absence of utterance is as important as the utterance: the gaps, the space not played in—this has become the platform on which everything else to be said about him stands. Miles Davis is the lyric poet of Laconic.

But of course he was by no means always laconic; you only have to listen to his mid-sixties recordings to know that: his playing then was full of roiling, yelling, sometimes confrontational articulacy, as full of language as the average argument. So the first thing we have to consider when wondering what is being conveyed, precisely, by all that language is that the uttering of it is always a choice, someone's choice: to speak or not to speak—and then *how much* to speak. No one makes a jazz instrumentalist say whatever it is he or she has to say, whatever the volume, amplitude, frequency, and tone. They say what they say because that's *all* that they can say in that particular seized moment of time; it is the sum, in that seizure, of what may be said by that individual and it is not predicated on anything other than that individual's capacity to make an utterance in the moment (that's the reason jazzers practice their chops so much: so they can never be caught out with nothing to say). Perhaps the most important point to be made about any jazz articulation, whether experienced live or via some recorded medium, is that the utterance is indivisible from the moment.

So that is what you listen to.

The moment.

But sometimes the moment is all too much. I still have vivid recall of trying to make sense of Coltrane's *A Love Supreme*, when I dutifully bought it a year or so after my first tentative engagement with Miles Davis in the seventies.

A Love Supreme has, since the 1960s, been considered one of the cornerstone works of the modern-jazz canon, along with Davis's much easier-on-the-ear *Kind of Blue*, with the result that anyone with any desire to acquire hip credentials over the past fifty or so years has been obliged to get their head round it, as well as inside it.

Just listen to the thing now, fifty years on from its first release. It still comes at you. It is still a truly extraordinary outburst: a four-part suite but a single gout of energy—hortatory, profuse, intimidating; one of those occasions when "the moment" is just so full of stuff that there seems barely any room in it for melody or breathing, let alone the tender sensibilities of the listener.

It's always risky using such language, but I can think of no better comparative noun for *A Love Supreme* than "torrent." The notes come at you unstoppably, like a fast-moving wall of liquid, a flood of rhythm, tone, and syntax smashing down the course of a long valley, as if suddenly released by the catastrophic failure of a dam upstream. It is torrential both in sound and in feeling. And at first, all it seems to consist of is that fierce press of rhythm, syntax, and iron tone. Nothing else. No content. Not as such. When it first crashed through my teenage bedroom, I thought, "What *is* this shit?" and I shut my mouth and covered my ears.

It seemed to me that, compared to the disciplined laconicism of 1950s Miles Davis, *A Love Supreme* represented a failure of muscular control. Much as my burly friend in the record shop did, I at first thought in excremental terms. Here was an expulsion of something noxious and hot, something rushing—something incompatible with a sense of well-being. Certainly something affronting one's sense of good emotional hygiene.

And so I backed off and *A Love Supreme* remained an outlier in my listening landscape throughout the punk years and the first couple of years after that, like a building on the edge of my psychic estate I was too frightened to visit for reasons that were compelling but obscure. The building was dark, it was mysterious, it was full of hazard—that was all I knew. To me, the album somehow integrated Pandora's box with the chapel perilous. It was as if *A Love Supreme* were a container enclosing dangerous secrets and it was imperative that the lid should stay firmly on it, for fear that the contents might escape and contaminate not only me but the world.

They are dramatic years, your late teens and early twenties.

But in due course the lid came off, inch by inch, nudge by shove, helped no doubt by an intensifying desire on my part to consider myself hip and by increasing courage with regard to religion, which I had been despising stroppily since my defection from the church choir in 1973 following the breaking of my singing voice.

The point being that *A Love Supreme* is quite overtly a religious work. It says so on the cover. It is the saxophonist's thank-you note to God, for . . . well, for everything. Coltrane "believed in all religions" and, increasingly, as the 1960s gathered momentum, he worshipped as he played—which is perhaps another reason why he felt obliged to go to such inordinate lengths to "get it all in," as he famously explained to Davis when admonished by his leader for going on for too long. That was Trane's inner compulsion and drive: the act of getting it all in, or at least getting as much in as he could. He needed to exhaust the possibilities of the available harmonic and modal language before he could countenance the possibility that he had said enough: and you can never say enough when the point of language is to be ecumenical. Not really. There is always one more prayer to be said in a different, perhaps more prayerful way, for different ears . . . (Which is perhaps why Coltrane's is such infernally difficult music to describe. Miles Davis, with his keen determination never to say more than is necessary, has boundaries which can be limned: you can see to the edge of Miles; whereas Coltrane implies that there are no boundaries capable of containing the truly seeking voice. He sees infinite possibilities and unending permutations, so no matter how keen your description, it always falls short of using the right terms. Infinity knows no limits, by definition.)

So what does it consist of, the album, formally speaking? Well, the four thematic elements that constitute *A Love Supreme* add up to a little more than half an hour's music and are unambiguously entitled "Acknowledgement," "Resolution," "Pursuance," and "Psalm." It is not a worldly work. It is solemn, ritualistic, profuse, and, finally, throughout the length of "Psalm"—and somewhat counter to first impressions—peaceful. It is deep and motionless as a lake, once you penetrate its busy surface. And what you discover in due course, as you find the confidence to immerse yourself fully, is that the music is actually incredibly communicative. It does have tunes in it: seething, scouring, rawly hewn tunes for sure, but tunes nonetheless, for all that they appear on first contact to be nothing more than pointillist (and pointless) acreages of notes. They are there all right. You just have to ride them as they come, like waves.

But it is as exhausting and exhaustive a work as exists in the Western music canon, by which I mean that it is not only an exhausting experience for the listener, but also exhaustive of possibility. By the end of its half-hour-plus duration, you are only too ready for the worship to stop, not just because you're pooped but also because you feel the language used is pooped. Wrung out.

Coltrane died less than three years after recording *A Love Supreme*. And after it, jazz has never sounded quite the same to me, despite its continued and sometimes really quite vigorous evolution into a variety of forms, some of them noble, some less so, from 1965 right up to the present day. I still love jazz. I still follow its developments, up to a point. But I have never been able to escape the conviction that everything jazzy that follows *A Love Supreme* only counts really as an afterthought or further meditation; is akin to gloss or exploration for the sake of exploration or, in period jazz parlance, the rigging of "new conceptions" for the sake of modernist and postmodernist strategy. It seldom sounds to me like a voice saying what it has to say, and then shutting up.

Which is not to say that I am now in a position to offer precise translations of what the voices of Miles Davis and John Coltrane were saying when they said what they said so definitively. Nothing like. Who would be so foolishly presumptuous? But I am more grateful than I can say that they said it, whatever it was, and I surely experienced some of the truth of what they were saying in those moments, in my heart and in my mind and in my bones, fat, and muscle.

I cannot answer the question "How does it feel to be alive?," so forgive me if I dodge the much harder one: "Yes, but what does John Coltrane *mean*?"

* * *

What of Hank Mobley, though? What of the moderate, reasoning, warmly articulate, relatively conservative tenor-saxophone voice that never suffered from logorrhoea and was seldom laconic in temper, but usually something in between—always available, ready to play and equipped with something attractive to say but never particularly fussed about the grander implications of the moment, or what the moment might mean for the gleam of his reputation, or indeed for the gleam of history. What of Hank, the man with no big picture?

Mobley absolutely belonged to Davis and Coltrane's era, dying nineteen years after one and half a decade before the other, in 1986. Indeed he played with both men, most notably in 1961 when Davis was searching for Coltrane's replacement in the Miles Davis Quintet—perhaps the most prestigious and pressurized jazz job of its day. What an audition that was.

By way of a tryout, Mobley was invited to contribute to one studio album, *Someday My Prince Will Come* (Columbia), and then had the privilege of being cut to pieces on it by the man he was supposed to be replacing in the group. Coltrane was meant to have gone on to higher things by then—higher and further things—and one can only presume that he didn't just happen by the studio that day on the off-chance that Miles would give him his old job back. But he was there on one day at least and he was utterly, cruelly magnificent on that record: "Teo" in particular but also "Someday My Prince" itself are both overwhelming examples of big-picture playing: fast and fluent yet colossal, as if the saxophonist is engaged in an altogether different scale of enterprise to everyone else. Giant steps indeed. And poor old Mobley sounds intimidated; barely gets going at all when it's his turn. It is almost as if he cowers in his predecessor's shadow, even though they only play together on one piece, the title track. Who among us wouldn't have cowered?

He sounds rather less choked on the live album with Davis, *In Person . . . at the Blackhawk*, recorded at a club residency following Trane's final *final* departure that same year. But it is plainly not a great fit. The inference is clear: old Hank was not the questing, dramatic, inspirational, ground-churning sideman of Davis's dreams, neither authorial nor sonically imposing enough to cut out a big space for himself in the creative swarm of this most self-searching of modern-jazz groups, and evidently not bothered one way or another about the status that might accrue from committing his all to the advancement of the Miles Davis *oeuvre*. Davis and Coltrane were interested in their places in history. Mobley knew his place on the stand.

Instead, we have to go elsewhere to find *le vrai* Mobley, perhaps to any one of a number of records he made as leader and sideman for the Blue Note label between 1957 and the mid-sixties, but most compellingly to his own album *Soul Station*, in 1960 (a year after *Kind of Blue*, four before *A Love Supreme*), a quartet session featuring Mobley as the sole horn voice.

Here is the Mobley of his own dreams: a warm, ample, melodic, subtle, supple, swinging, lucid, articulate, even playful voice. Here, away from the competitive cut and thrust of the Davis Quintet and no longer obliged to fight for ear-time in the zoo format of a standard bop quin-, sex- or septet, he is neither magisterial nor imperious, and he is very far from majestic. But he is himself, and with great authority. This is the sound of a man making his utterances without inhibition while digging his toes contentedly into ground he knows.

On *Soul Station* there is no strain. Mobley's tone is grainy, reedy, occasionally nasal, sometimes even plummy like a clarinet, his articulation feather-light when required, masculinely assertive on other occasions, pushing his way through his choruses with an even, imperturbable certainty, as if reading out loud to beloved children. So perhaps it is right to say that he is magisterial, in a warmly intimate way: teacherly without being authoritarian. In detail, Mobley's tenor is a lovely, diversely expressive sound, never robust but always convinced and clear and generous. There is suction in his phrasing as well as blowing, for it is as necessary in life to draw breath as it is to exhale, and Mobley phrases as he breathes. Sometimes it is possible to hear a little shake in the notes at the end of those phrases, as if he is referencing the way the grand old swingers of earlier decades liked to punctuate; and then he'll sink into the ursine woofliness of Ben Webster—because, in that moment, woofliness is what makes the bear.

Soul Station is what we mean when we talk about a voice "having authenticity." It is full of a real truthfulness that belongs in that moment to that speaker and to no other—and could never belong to another in any other moment. And it is very easy to see why, when you listen to music like this, Hank Mobley has such a devoted following among a small cross section of humankind. He may not have a big picture, but Mobley has his own cult.

* * *

There was a taxi driver who used to come into Honest Jon's back in the early 1980s. And who knows, he might still go in there, although he'd be an ancient taxi driver now. He used to come in several times a week, wearing his shirt open to his middle to reveal the string vest he wore beneath, and he always wore a string vest, winter, spring, and summer. We used to call him Ank Mobley because that was all he ever wanted: Hank Mobley.

"Got any more 'Ank Mobley?" he'd say on Thursday afternoons, having already asked the question on Monday morning. "Anything new in by 'Ank?" And we'd always say, "Don't think so, mate. But have a look in the Hank Mobley section," because it would be as pointless as it would be rude to say to him, "Hank Mobley is old and infirm and off the radar and hasn't made a record in donkey's decades and is probably not going to make another one anytime soon—and everything that's currently available is in stock in the racks anyway, plus a handful of secondhand albums which you've already got—just as this was also the case three days ago on Monday morning." How impolite would that be?

Ank needed to ask the question though, so that he would have the warrant he needed to go through the Mobley section on the off chance that we'd overlooked something and might be shown—ha!—to have been derelict in our duty. He wanted to catch us out. He was not actually hostile, but he certainly suspected us of not loving Hank Mobley enough. And it was always a viable possibility in Ank's mind that either Mobley *had* made a new record that we hadn't noticed, or there was a new reissue we'd overlooked, or, most desirably, a rare secondhand mono copy of something from the outer reaches of the Hank *oeuvre* had somehow sneaked into the racks unobserved by us. Ank was, you see, a one-saxophonist man, a man of loyalty and devotion, and he needed always to be one step ahead in the Mobley game.

Another thing he liked to do was buy repeat copies of Mobley records he already owned for presentation to fellow cabbies in the taxi drivers' café down the road in W11: cabbies he considered ripe for conversion. He was a Mobley evangelist. He wanted everyone to benefit from the good news. Behind Honest Jon's counter during idle hours, we used to speculate about the taxi drivers of west London living in fear of Ank and his record bag.

"No, mate, no," the cabbies would bluster over their breakfasts as he approached. "Stay back. Stay back or the bacon sandwich gets it! How many times do I have to tell you, mate: Mobley's not my thing. I like Connie Francis and Hawkwind."

And then a very strange day dawned. I cannot give the day a date, though it feels as if I ought to be able to. It was the day, a couple of years into my time at Honest Jon's, when Ank came into the shop, shambled up to the counter with his shirt open and said, "Got any Stan Getz?"

We didn't know where to put ourselves. We were struck dumb. We looked at one another, my colleague and I, and we both gestured in the direction of the Stan Getz section and smiled feebly, as children do when told by their father that all is not as it seems in the family.

"I like Stan Getz," said Ank amiably. "Do you like him? He's good, isn't he? Do you like him?"

We both nodded but remained stupefied. What could this possibly mean for us all?

I quit the shop a year or so later, to do other things (though I was never as happy in work again). During that year, Ank dutifully came into the shop twice a week, sometimes three times, and on every occasion he would approach the counter cagily, like an overweight, world-weary, bungling assassin, and would ask the question: "Got any Getz in?"

And Hank Mobley was never mentioned again.

GRACE NOTES

JACKIE McLEAN: "BLUESNIK"
Blue Note Records, 1961

It goes "Nyyyah-na-nah na-*nah* / nyyyah-na-nah na-*naaah*." Which is then repeated several times over for thirty seconds, with a four-bar bridge passage dropped in halfway through, as if to buy time. And that's it: a smear, a splotch of notes. Perfunctory. Undecorated. A tossed-off melodic figure rather than a tune, metered like a playground taunt, curt enough to be humiliating. More than once I have heard the melody of Jackie McLean's "Bluesnik" not as a descending sequence of unison notes on trumpet and alto sax, blatted out over a pulsating bop rhythm, but as "Get lost / go on / fuck *off.*"

But I don't usually get lost, because I know what's coming next.

What comes next is McLean's solo, which starts parenthetically, as if returning to the middle of a sentence left some moments before—"as I was saying"—and then squirts on for four whole minutes in a style which expresses everything you might ever want to know about hard-bop, plus a whole lot of stuff you possibly didn't. The solo is one long wrangle, a sort of stick-fight between the clichés of Jackie's own personal post-Charlie Parker blues-bop idiom—McLean goes in for percussive, short, angular, flaring phrases executed with eye-wateringly sharp intonation—and the saxophonist's abiding modern-jazzy determination to make everything sound like it has never been expressed quite as spontaneously as this before. Or as candidly. Or as modernly. It's a fight between idiom and spontaneity. Lots of people can't stand the way McLean plays.

I love it, though. This is partly down to my wiring. I can't help but hear in that lemony intonation a sort of agitated, even neurotic, straining beauty, ugly though it appears to some. And something in my body revels in McLean's percussiveness—it feels deeply human to me to hammer like that against the passage of time. Listening to McLean always results in the switching on of my entire nervous system.

And for that same reason I also like his haltedness—his intrinsic lack of fluency. His hobble. Pegleg McLean is an unfluent mover, reluctant to resort to ready-made turns of phrase but occasionally prepared to use them to paint his way out of a corner. The solo on "Bluesnik" is full of such ready-mades but they are deployed with such cranky conviction that you can only listen and digest, as if, really, no one has ever said this before in quite those terms.

In fact, taken as whole, the solo is like a rebuttal of an unheard accusation, in which the speaker (the saxophonist) has a multitude of things to say in his defense, and is quite prepared to be aggressive about it, but isn't always possessed of the command and the fluency to get those things out smoothly, elegantly, or even necessarily in the order that reflects most felicitously on his communication skills. Yet he is always idiomatic. He is always deeply in the pocket: *his* pocket. Jackie is profoundly authentic, psychologically speaking. He may well resort to his own clichés occasionally (and they are his clichés)—but the case he makes with them wins you over with the sheer force of his will and the atmospheric credibility of what is being said. He sounds wonky but he is nearly always *true*. Here's the point: even when Jackie McLean isn't playing like a god, he's communicating like a human.

This, I suspect, was an issue he wrestled with himself, as a card-carrying student of the Charlie Parker bop school. As the 1950s turn into the 1960s and his contracts with the Prestige record label give way to better ones with Blue Note, you can hear it bothering him more and more: How do I move on? How do I make new? How do I get free—but stay true?

A year after the rigorously bluesy *Bluesnik*, he recorded *Let Freedom Ring*, also on Blue Note, a quartet set without a second horn on it—just Jackie, piano, bass, and drums—affording the saxophonist much more room in which to express his brand-new vision without having to make accommodations.

Let Freedom Ring represents, as it ought to with a title like that, the clangor of a voice released from the shackles of standard harmony into the freer space of quasi-modalism. It includes tunes that would strike the ear as discordant were there any real chordal underpinnings to support them. But there are none. Well, there are and there aren't. That's the thing about quasi-modalism: It has one foot in conventional harmony and one foot out. It's ambiguous. It is, by definition, unsettled.

None of which stops *Let Freedom Ring* from being a peal of a record. The musical scheme provides a festival setting for McLean's tone and angularity, its open, propulsive, unclogged rhythms allowing him to lay out his oblique strategies with greater latitude than ever before. Zig, zag, and zog.

But it doesn't change what he has to say, not one iota. Whatever that is. He never stops saying it, and I always find it beautiful. But as I say, lots of people just hear a grumpy guy playing a saxophone out of tune.

BOOKER ERVIN: "YOU DON'T KNOW WHAT LOVE IS"
Prestige Records, 1966

A convinced Freudian and jazz expert once told me that the tenor saxophonist Booker Ervin "makes the sound of a man who can't make up his mind whether he wants to kill his mother or fuck her."

Well, it's a hypothesis. But this declaration did seed an idea which took hold in my mind and has not yet relinquished its grasp: the idea that an accomplished instrumentalist cannot help but show himself up in the involuntary detail of his musical articulations. The more accomplished a musician he is, the more he can't help himself.

Poor old Booker.

But then good old Booker. Here was a man who, whatever the truth about his deepest, most hurt feelings, was certainly incapable of putting a saxophone to his mouth without revealing that he at least *had* wounds. In the particular case of this mournful ballad, I would suspect that it isn't the "you" of the song's title who doesn't know what love is, but Booker himself.

For this is the human voice expressing itself as bleakly as it ever did through the medium of brass and reed—a harrowing, hopeless despairing yowl of an utterance, in which tenderness is assayed and somehow, you feel, rejected as a bad lot, given what Booker knows of reality.

It is all too possible to hear in Ervin's endless, needling pain the crying of a tiny unwanted baby. It is certainly hard to listen to with your heart.

JOHN SURMAN: "SALTASH BELLS"
ECM Records, 2012

Saltash is a modest town on the westerly bank of the Tamar River that divides Cornwall from Devon. The town faces Plymouth. The river is spanned by both a suspension bridge, which carries road traffic, and Brunel's Royal Albert railway bridge, which was constructed in 1859. The town's name means "The ash tree by the salt mill." I have never been there. I certainly wouldn't know what to say about it.

But John Surman has plenty to say, and he takes nearly eleven minutes to do it on the album of the same title, by deploying what sounds like a contrabass clarinet in a dew of twinkly electronic condensation. It's a piece of gaping contrasts. Throughout its long, uneventful length, the voice of the Really Big Boy of the clarinet world is modified with brief interventions of multitracking, repeat-echo, and conventional reverb, as a dub record might be modified at the mixing desk. The digital dew persists throughout but, if anything, gets wetter as it goes on and the whole thing comes off as a sort of sleepscape of gurgles, grunts, snorts, and rumbling sighs, as if a giant is dreaming pleasantly in a morning belfry. It is not clear whether the giant is woken when the real bells of Saltash ring at the end, but the clarinets dissipate like birds into cloud. The scene is entirely tranquil.

The music could not be anything other than English. Surman is a marvelous technician and all that, but it is his search for an idiom hived off within an idiom that makes him. He does not sound to me like a man who wishes he was in Chicago or down at Minton's on West 118th Street in New York City—this is a voice that has lost whatever traces it once possessed of a relationship with America. In fact, it seems beholden to nothing much at all apart from its environment, its locale. It has no swing, that's for sure. Tone, texture, shape, intensity, yes—but nothing of America. It exists in its own Devonian space.

But then English music has always turned to its environment in the end, as if that were the only way to confirm to itself, finally, that it *is* English music. It is as if England can only be reached through its landscapes and its social arrangements rather than through the articulation of the experience of selfhood; as if our sense of self were something perhaps to be embarrassed about in our kind of society. Vaughan Williams, Finzi, Elgar—they might have something to say about this, were they still around. But whether this is a good thing or not, I cannot begin to judge.

However, I like to think I now know a little of how Saltash feels.

9

The Spectacle of Anguish

H ey, what's this? What's going on, man?"

Even though the punk moment is still warm in the memory, I continue to use "man" to my closest friends, the ones who antedate punk and go all the way back to childhood. It's a sign of affection—and of a shared past in provincial freak juvenilia.

Danny is saying nothing. He is hunched against the toilet door, half turned away, his face thrust into the door frame at an unnatural angle. He is beating without rhythm against the wood with the heel of his hefty left fist, and without apparent sense. The door is shut, and he is on the outside but he is perfectly capable of opening it—it is not locked. There is no one on the inside. Danny is not actually trying to smash the door down. He is trying to speak. But he appears to be unable to utter a word, so he hammers on the door instead.

"C'mon, Danzig, speak to me. Say something. Anything. What's upsetting you, man? This is crazy ..."

Danny turns back to face me, puts his right hand up to his mouth and makes spastic yanking motions with it away from his face, as if trying to pull words out. But they won't come. They may be in there, but they will not come. He is dumb. All that is escaping from his mouth are noises shaped around the palate and in his nasal cavities, sounds without vowels that do not require a column of air for support. *Nnnnnn-nnn* sounds. He is neither inhaling nor exhaling. His tongue is also not functioning, and Danny is beating his fist in frustration.

"Danny," I say, now starting to panic. "You need to start breathing properly. You're not breathing. Come on now—breathe!" His face is flushed. "Come on, man. You can do it. Stop trying to talk and just *breathe ...*"

And then all of a sudden, presumably because he is now freed from the obligation to explain himself, Danny starts to respire again in a great explosion of breath. *HWWWAAARFF!* His shoulders go right up to his ears and then down again. He sucks in air like a man who has just come up from the bottom of a canal, his feet still tangled in shopping trolleys and bike wheels; he's still in the canal, and held there fast, but his head is clear of the water at least. He breathes. He breathes again. His chest rises and falls in great juddering spasms. His fist has stopped beating now, too. But his face is wet, as any man's face would be if he'd spent minutes alone trying to disentangle himself from rubbish at the bottom of a filthy canal. His face is wet and dissolving with distress. He cannot meet my eyes.

"Hey," I say. "That's better. That's much better." Danny is back in the room, but he is in pieces. And as the word "better" crumbles in my mouth I realize that I am weeping, too. I am weeping because I am not sure what has just happened and because I am frightened.

* * *

It is just after Christmas 1980, and I have come home to East Anglia from Manchester, where I have been studying at the university. I suppose you could call it studying. I am certainly a very contented fellow. Things are going well. The course is enjoyable. Extracurricular activities are even more enjoyable. I am in love. And I am in love with Manchester, which in 1980 is a decaying ex-industrial incubator of strenuous post-punk creativity. Rubble-strewn waste ground and long gray macs are everywhere, especially if you view Manchester through the prism of the *NME*, as I do.

I have arranged to meet a couple of friends for a drink in a pub to use up some of the long gray time after Christmas. Derek and Danny work in different parts of a local chain of record shops; I worked there, too, during my "year off" before heading north. Derek and I became friends then, but I have known Danny since I was twelve and have sometimes wondered how it must feel for him to watch old associates leave town to pursue new interests.

We have had a few drinks, but nothing excessive, and we have repaired to the tiny house Derek rents in a back street. It has been raining, and when it rains, this part of town has a hunched, resistant feel to it, as if shouldering off the weather: small terraced houses in blackened yellow-gray brick built for brick-workers, railwaymen, and laboring folk a hundred years ago, crammed together in narrow streets on the edge of the town center. I like it a lot.

We have settled in Derek's front room to warm up in front of his gas fire, and he has shoved the recent Joy Division album *Closer* on the stereo, probably because I have declared an ambivalent attitude toward it in the pub. Everyone hip I know thinks it's great. I think it's interesting but intractable. Perhaps Derek is going to make me explain myself, with examples.

I don't remember now, thirty-six years on, how much of it we'd got through that evening, or which side of the album we'd started with—the torturous, over-mixed, alloy-twisting first side or the rather more sepulchral second. But I do remember that we sat in front of it not saying a word; and I have vivid recall of the moment it dawned that Danny was no longer with us in the room and had in fact been gone for some time—and then being visited by the sensation that something was wrong.

"Where's Danny, Derek?" I said, as Joy Division slammed across another deserted monochrome cityscape. The first words uttered by any of us for some time. "He's been gone for *ages*."

I also have close to perfect recall of the spectacle that presented itself a few seconds later of my friend suffering some sort of psychological meltdown against the toilet door down the passage, and of calling Derek, who came and then said hurriedly but purposefully, as if this were only the first step in a procedure, but a crucial step: "It's the music, it's the music—I'll turn it off . . ."

* * *

In all my twenty years I had never experienced anything like that before. The phrases "panic attack" and "extreme anxiety" were new to me then, conceptually. In fact I am certain that they were not part of my functioning vocabulary. Middle-class children raised in rural security in the 1960s and '70s had no use for such language. "Depression" was an acknowledged part of everyday life, and the reality of it sometimes had terrible real-life consequences—a fellow sixth-form student had taken her own life only a couple of years before, and that had been "depression"—but the word was only ever deployed as a hushed account of other people's behavior, a way of explaining stuff away efficiently, not as the beginning of a serious conversation about an observable psychiatric phenomenon that had parts and dimensions and variety. I had certainly never found the need at home to engage with the concept of depression, preferring to avoid the subject where my parents were concerned and ascribing my own experiences of low mood to "the blues" or physical malaise or external agency, such as the fact that my school was run by bastards for bastards. I knew what sad was. I even knew anguish. But mental disturbance was another game altogether, and it was someone else's.

I was certainly aware that Danny was vulnerable to the blues, too, rather more so than me. But it was never discussed, never even alluded to. There was no need. We had music for that.

* * *

If you were our sort of age, born in the late 1950s or early 1960s, there was a fixed menu of places to go to acknowledge bad feeling. Places to go, things to see, books to read. Sounds to hear.

I am pretty sure that my first encounter with extreme feeling in pop music came a couple of years before I was capable of registering any kind of extreme feeling myself. Janis Joplin was the sound of approaching anguish for my generation of eleven year olds. Her sandpaper howls were for us, I suppose, what we thought of when we thought of the existential scream of nature (as we often did)—an auditory update of Edvard Munch for the post-hippie generation—and when she let rip, the world not only formed its mouth into an O and put its hands up to the sides of its face but also said "blimey!"

The Joplin song you heard emanating most often from the bedroom doors of your friends' elder siblings, and very occasionally from the radio, was her version of Erma Franklin's defiant minor soul hit "Piece of My Heart," a not wholly unsubtle genre piece penned by jobbing writer/producer Jerry Ragovoy, who was also responsible for such diva-friendly heartscalders as Lorraine Ellison's "Stay With Me." Franklin's original 1967 "Piece of My Heart" is a hymn to strong-willed, if slightly irritable, stoic self-possession in love; Joplin's version, from the following year, takes another road. While her gang of accomplices, Big Brother and the Holding Company, slash psychedelic weeds out of her path in a far-from-deft rock pastiche of soul instrumental style, Joplin drives a bulldozer through the sentiments expressed by the song. She literally screams it into subordination, beginning the confrontation with the sergeant-majorish bawl to attention, "*Co-o-ome* on, come on, COME ON, *co-o-o-ome on*!" as if ordering reluctant listeners to assume the brace position.

What follows is a sort of musical description of bipolarity expressed in the form of extreme dynamic peaking and troughing: LOUD-soft-LOUD, it goes. LOUD-soft-LOUD-LOUDER-*LOUDER STILL*-soft again . . . SCREAM-whimper-SCREAM-whimper-SCREAM-SCREAM LOUDER-whimper . . . It was one of the features of the relatively uncompressed rock music of the late sixties that you could do this and get away with it provided you set about your work "with soul." And as a demonstration of unbridled Texan lung power, "Piece of My Heart" could hardly be bettered. But to pull it off—and I use the expression advisedly: Joplin is circus-theatrical in her display, as if attempting some daredevil stunt—such a performance entails the pulverization of any kind of nuance in the song. It is as if, in Janis's take on it, the song has no expressive value of its own and its sole function as a structure is to serve as a vehicle for the overpowering private anguish—and oomph—of the singer singing it. It's a trapeze. A highwire. Joplin does not sing the song; the song sings Joplin, as if what's inside the singer is all that counts, and never mind what's inside the song.

* * *

But then rock always did anguish well because anguish is dramatic and so is rock. The precipitate plunge into low mood or worse is well served by the dynamic potentialities of the form, from Black Sabbath's flat, surging minor-key dirges to the up-and-down histrionics of Nirvana. Rock tends to express itself in caps and italics. LOUD to *soft* and back again (ending in terminal silence) are the signature dynamics of one kind of extreme emotionalism and, just as a healthy spike on a heart monitor is the sign of a working ticker and a flat line means you're dead, rock is all spike and to flatline is not a viable option. Viewed purely from the formal and textural perspectives, rock is better equipped than any other form to go to harsh extremes.

And extremes can go in a variety of directions, as well as up and down. For every protracted feel-bad ecstasy by The Doors (such as "The End") there was, in the late sixties and early seventies, a Sunday-morning comedown courtesy of the Velvet Undergound. For every ivy-decked mausoleum visited in the company of Nico, there was an airless tunnel of language shaped by Leonard Cohen—or, much more obscurely, Nick Drake's butterfly tunnel, in which uneasy feelings flittered delicately and the listener felt as if he were always one careless step away from treading on something fragile and beautiful. Rock and its associated forms, both loud and soft, have always offered a multiplicity of routes into the dark.

In fact it was assumed from rock's earliest days in the middle sixties that if you didn't account for bad feeling somewhere in your *oeuvre*, then your *oeuvre* was not of the requisite weight and density. You were not to be taken seriously, and you were a lightweight. Bad feeling was what made rock more serious than pop, and therefore it was good practice to feel bad in due proportion. After all, depression, anxiety, and low mood are as much a part of life as excitement, hedonism, high spirits, and shagging. They ought not to be excluded from the party.

But back then bad feeling was always only ever a part of what rock had to express and not the whole. Even the dank and dolorous Pink Floyd lightened their fenny gloom with arcing guitar solos and an easygoing pastoralist concession that sometimes it's nice to just chill out, kick back, and feel the grass tickling the backs of your ears. While the Stooges explored self-loathing and self-abasement only partially, being otherwise quite happy to rock brutishly in celebration of the spirit of Puck—and nobody took much notice of them at the time anyway, until punk made it compulsory to do so. In the 1960s and throughout the first part of the following decade, rock was depressed only in parts.

It was punk that engendered the notion that, really, it was rock's social duty to feel bad all of the time; and it was a punk idea that a proper band ought to have a fixed emotional temperature—angry, bitter, contemptuous, mordant, waggish: take your pick from an extensive menu of energetically dismal feelings—and that to deviate from that temperature was to compromise in the worst possible way. It was to give yourself over to hippie self-indulgence. Following Year Zero there was to be no room for shades of feeling. Hence the short life and narrow gauge of most punk bands: you formed the band, you decided what the band stood for temperamentally, you expressed that emotion . . . and then what? Better break up before you blanded out completely.

It was a good system to employ if the point was to stimulate instant activity and reaction, and it made for great excitement. It just had its limits creatively. There are only so many times you can express anger, bitterness, contempt, mordancy, or waggishness before the experience palls for all concerned. It did, however, clear a lot of space, emotionally speaking, for what followed: the glamorous artifice of pop postmodernism and its war with the eternal glumness of the indie mind.

* * *

What punk understood only too well is that extreme feeling makes for a compelling spectacle. It is very difficult for the onlooker to look away, once his attention has been drawn by exhibitions of heightened emotion. They lock you in, those exhibitions. In fact, faced with them, it seems less than human to avert one's gaze, as it is almost impossible to drive past a car crash on the motorway and not have a quick empathetic dekko, to see what may be seen. It is profoundly human to do so.

And car crashes were one of the standard by-products of the musical culture of the twentieth century, long before rock stuck its nose in.

I know from my own frustrated experience that in the 1980s lots of people bought late-period Billie Holiday records in preference to her earlier work with Teddy Wilson and Count Basie, precisely because she sounded so utterly ravaged on them. Holiday's crash was a slow, sad, sordid affair involving heavy drugs, heavy alcohol, and exploitative men, and toward the end you could hear it in her voice, a voice that was no longer the thinly searing instrument of the 1930s and '40s but a Hogarthian caricature of dissipation and unhappiness. I spent many hours behind the counter of the record shop I worked in explaining with exemplary condescension to earnest would-be Billie-buyers that sounding sad, intoxicated, and fagged-out were not the same thing as "radical phraseology"—*buy the earlier stuff!* But they had to have the grim ones.

Likewise, it was always easier to sell Charlie Parker's fucked-up "Lover Man" than the quicksilver Savoy recordings of his pomp. But then, to some ears, music is not truly gripping unless it involves spectacle—an accompanying mental image of the musician playing the music while either tripping or dying or pissed or going under psychiatrically. Indeed, an entire generation of post-MTV American rock fans in the 1980s and early '90s took the view that music *is* a spectacle, primarily, and that it has nothing to say worth hearing unless it entails the auditory display of extreme and sometimes pathological feeling. Degradation and death were thought somehow to authenticate music as a consumer product.

* * *

Back in Edward Street in 1980, with the drizzle slicking steamed-up windows and my friend Danny hunched on the sofa trying to drink tea out of a mug held unreliably in trembling hands, the silence contained very little drama. The silence was a guarantee against drama. I looked at him in his bewilderment and wondered whether this was as new a thing for him as it was for me, or whether Danny's twenty-one years had been strewn with such incidents and that he was used to it, as we all get used in time to our own little peculiarities. But that did not appear to be the case. At least he looked calm now: calm and shattered. Nevertheless the atmosphere still clung to him of a man taken totally by surprise and left shocked beyond words. He was still saying nothing, apart from the occasional mumbled "sorry, guys" in between gulps of tea.

And I thought about *Closer*.

Joy Division's lead singer Ian Curtis had killed himself in May of that year, shortly before the summer release of the album, and already by Christmas you could tell that here was a cult in the making. And if not a cult, then at least the provision of an imaginative spectacle in the minds of the music's most ardent devotees, to accompany the sound of the music: a moving psychic picture in grainy monochrome of Joy Division's ice-eyed singer, fresh from his contemplations of Iggy Pop's *The Idiot*, going into the kitchen of his small house in Macclesfield to find the indoor washing line, the vault of his mind emptied of everything apart from the box of his intentions, which lay open at the center of his consciousness, the contents of which were now entirely practical and matter-of-fact.

And I thought: no, you can't have that.

You can have the music and you can have the feelings the music gives you. You can even have the imaginative spectacle, if that's what you need. If you must. But you don't get access. Access is not available to you. Don't kid yourself. Access is really not the point of all this—and if you think that it is, then you are *wrong*.

You may not be able to choose how you feel in life, but you can always choose not to listen.

I looked at Danny and Danny looked at the floor. I felt pretty sure that *Closer* was leaving his system now, at least for the time being. He could no longer hear in his head the clattering noise it made, nor touch with his mind the surface of Ian Curtis's uninhabited voice, as it moved from word to word, note to note, syllable to breath to syllable, methodically, unemphatically, impermeable as a stone, like a man who knows where he is going and knows that he is taking not a soul with him.

GRACE NOTES

CHRIS BELL: "I AM THE COSMOS"/"YOU AND YOUR SISTER"
Car Records/Rykodisc, 1978

A lot of time was expended during my teenage years trying to locate the sound of my anguish.

My existential pain was neither great nor noble and it did not use up a lot of juice when resting in standby mode. I was not oppressed by it. I felt that it was contained safely enough within my person and did not constitute a risk to the wider public. Yes, of course my anguish retained the potential to be infinitely expandable depending on events, but it manifested itself only modestly in my day-to-day psyche, if left to mind its own business. It was companionable and ever-present, and not oppressive.

Nevertheless, I yearned to hear it described in sound and always felt that it must be a *lost* thing, rather than an undiscovered one; something I'd always known but had misplaced or forgotten, rather like Arthur Sullivan's Lost Chord. And over the years I encountered lots of contenders for the role of The Sound of My Anguish, songs that I thought might have a claim on my darkest, most troubled emotions—including, briefly, one by Deep Purple, of all groups. But none of them ever quite fit the bill. "Close, but no banana," I got used to thinking, as I reluctantly discarded another contender like a bad hand at whist.

Then, rather late in life, during my nineteenth year, I heard Chris Bell's "I Am the Cosmos," and for a while it fit the anguish-shaped recess in my heart and soul very suitably. Better at least than any of its predecessors. It was the right shape and weight and intensity, and the words of the song were about stuff I identified with keenly.

In early 1979 Bell was newly deceased, having driven his car into a telegraph pole in late December of the preceding year, and that probably added something, too. He had been, naturally enough, twenty-seven years old—another ripe sacrifice. He had also been for some years a persistent victim of depression and a practicing Christian, either of which may or may not have been the consequence of an acute shortage of luck in his music career. As co-founder and co-leader of the critically esteemed, zealously hyped but sales-free Memphis rock band Big Star, he had been far and away the biggest talent in the group, if not the most admired figure (that distinction went to the rather more charismatic Alex Chilton). But nothing seemed to stick. Big Star never caught on.

The truth of it was simple. At the time of their creative flowering in the early 1970s, the group's bright amalgam of jangling Beatlesy Anglo-pop and faintly psychedelic R&B was wholly out of fashion, and would not come into fashion again for more than half a decade, and then only as a retrospective pleasure. Big Star were not just unlucky, but also had bad timing.

Yet Bell's own troubles seemed to cut deeper and more abstractly than that, and he left the band following the release of their brilliant first album to launch himself into the world as a solo artist. Except that he didn't actually launch himself. Not really. He pottered about and did odd jobs and dwelt inside himself and worked in the studio and then dwelt inside himself some more. He was a guy beset with seriousness. Nothing was heard from him, and no one noticed.

And then in 1978 he put out a double-A-side single, "I Am The Cosmos"/"You and Your Sister" on the obscure Car label. It would prove to be the only solo work released during his lifetime. I bought it as an expensive import following a formal introduction by my new friend Derek, who had a look in his eye that said, "This is the real stuff." He was bang on the money.

"You and Your Sister" is a gorgeous acoustic ballad of perceived failure in love, sung directly at (rather than to) the object of that love. It has a melody and arrangement worthy of McCartney at his most austere and Bell sings it with a crushed passion which suggests that too many hours have been spent alone in a room listening to his own voice circulating in his head.

It is an account of a certain kind of addiction: the addiction to longing. You can hear Bell's lowered gaze. His shame. It is anguish as self-effacement.

"I Am the Cosmos" is less self-effacing but even more troubled. Here the longing is not deprecated but squeezed up into a mountain range of agonized lamentation, buttressed by cliffs of slowly arpeggiating electric guitars which somehow between them maintain enough harmonic flow to support a sense of forward momentum at a nearly dead tempo. It is a brilliant example of how subtlety can still play a hand even when volume levels are high.

And in the middle of this cascade of noise Bell's lightly distorted, feverish voice drills into the words protecting the sealed-up chambers of his emotions. He finds only contradiction: "My feelings always have been something I couldn't hide / I can't confide. Don't know what's going on inside," he sings, palpably aware that something isn't right when you can't hide your feelings yet you have no idea what they are.

It is a literal description of the condition of unhappiness.

And then he cuts to the chase. "I *really* wanna see you again," he pleads repeatedly, over and over again, as the guitars avalanche around him and he departs into silence pursued by the ghosts of his own delusion. Yes, he does tell himself every night that he is the cosmos and that he is the wind. But not only does it not bring her back again, it also reminds him that he is nothing. That everything is nothing.

But mostly it's him.

AMY WINEHOUSE: "LOVE IS A LOSING GAME"
Island Records, 2006

The anguish that ruined Amy Winehouse was possibly as unknowable to her, at bottom, as it was to the rest of us. Depression is a dark cellar in which the victim has been restrained and blinded, and the worst of it is that you cannot choose to find a way out, not by making a decision or by exercising mere strength of will. That option is not available to you. The blinding and the restraint see to that.

But Winehouse managed to shine a torch, even as she languished. She switched the torch on and off again with no great reliability but, in those moments when it was on, you were gifted with fleeting suggestions of what her cellar might contain. Shadows, ambivalences, compulsions, more shadow . . . Her anguish may have been impermeable and complexly subdivided, and it may not have been subject to cure but, in her music at least, it was illuminated by brilliant flashes.

Of all her accounts of her own bad feeling, surely the most desperately moving is among the most cursory of a brief bunch on the *Back to Black* album. It is also among the least dramatic—in fact its dynamic contours are close to flat. The torch is switched on just long enough for the listener to take in the scene in all its detail—for roughly two and a half minutes—sufficient to register that it is a littered scene and its darkest corners are alive with subtle movement. "Love Is a Losing Game" is as vivid a description of irredeemable, ambivalent regret as can have ever been recorded, and its blacks are deep.

Mark Ronson's production installs the Winehouse pipes in an uptown bower of the sort once inhabited from time to time by all early-sixties Motown artists, but most comfortably by Smokey Robinson, whose carnationed milieu this truly was. There's a smoking jacket hanging alongside the designer dresses in the closet, and there are flowers everywhere. French windows give on to a balcony overlooking the downtown lights.

But all that ideated luxury is an obvious lie. Or at least it is treacherous, because there is no comfort in it to Amy's heart. It has no value. The only feeling in this superficially elegant room is the filthy gut feeling she has that arises from the knowledge that what is most compelling to her is also the thing that is most toxic. This knowledge is chipped out in half-formed gaming metaphors which then twist in the light of her supra-detailed phrasing just sufficiently to reveal the delusory side of longing—"self-professed, profo-o-ound" is the beginning of a golden reflection snuffed out as soon as it has been sung—not to mention the terrible, bone-eating pain that is always the result of too much compulsion. Her impulse control may have been lousy, but her ability to represent its emotional consequences was peerlessly subtle and dignified. I think it is important to say that.

The awful truthfulness of "Love Is a Losing Game" is located in its austere refusal to make a spectacle of itself.

10

Psalms and Raptures

According to the Venerable Bede, who was an authority on these matters, the seventh-century Anglo-Saxon poet Caedmon was a natural—one of those innocent artists upon whom God's instrument, Nature, bestows mysterious gifts without the artist even knowing it.

Bede tells us that Caedmon, a low-status herdsman at Whitby Abbey, was invited one evening into the refectory to share in the bounty of the abbess's table. And Anglo-Saxon monasteries being what they were, the communal harp was soon being passed around the hall so that guests might entertain their hosts with a song or recitation—the Dark Ages origins of singing for your supper. But Caedmon didn't fancy it. Singing was not his thing, especially in front of other people. Not his thing at all. And so, long before the harp reached his downwind station at the trestle, he had melted away to sleep in the byre among the animals in whose company he felt most at ease.

But as he slept, he was visited in a dream by a strange figure who instructed him that he ought at least to have a go at singing, even if his only audience was a bunch of cows; after all, how difficult can it be, singing to cows? Cows don't snigger.

"But what should I sing?" said Caedmon in his dream. "Not only have I a horrible voice but I don't know any good songs."

"Oh, I wouldn't worry about that," said the figure. "Just go with the moment. What I'd like you to sing is the song of creation, about the beginning of all things and the appointment of the lands of the earth to the children of men. Come on. How bad can it be? What's the worst that can happen? Just give it your best shot, eh?"

And so, on waking from the dream, Caedmon gave it his best shot. And lo, he found that he could sing beautifully. Not only that: he had a song to sing, too, about the beginning of all things, and he could sing it from start to finish with fluency. It was as if he had known the song all his life and it was part of him, like his flesh and breath, and all that was needful in the moment was the power to release it into the world. To test his composition out, he sang it over and over again to the cows and they seemed to enjoy it, even if their expressions of appreciation were understated.

And in due course Caedmon took his new "hymn" to Hilda, the Abbess of Whitby, who marveled, naturally, but still had him checked out by experts. And the experts decreed that, yes, Caedmon was indeed a herder of cattle and it defied all reason to believe that an illiterate cowherd could have actually made up a Hymn of Creation from scratch, so confirming that what they were looking at here was to all intents and purposes a miracle, if not one technically. Whereupon the abbess turned Caedmon into a monk and commissioned him to set to work immediately, converting as much divine doctrine into song as he could. And this he did very successfully. In fact it became his life's work.

It is worth noting here, incidentally, that Bede is careful to point out that what motivated Caedmon was not the prospect of celebrity, nor the opportunity to gain promotion from his station in the cowshed, but the desire to turn mankind away from the love of sin to a love of doing good.

* * *

I often think of Caedmon when I hear Van Morrison.

This is not because I regard Morrison's rise from shipyard electrician's son in 1940s working-class Belfast to international musical eminence as in any way equivalent to Caedmon's more modest elevation from the byre. Nor because it is miraculous that one so recessive in disposition can sing affecting songs. Nor even because one imagines that Van is any more interested in turning mankind away from sin than he is in turning himself into a celebrity. But I do suspect that Morrison is of Caedmon's party in the sense that he is happy to accept divine intervention in the creative act. Whenever he opens his mouth to sing, it is as if he has had no prior knowledge of his gift, except perhaps in dreams. The sound just comes out of its own volition, as if someone else had put it there some time ago and it has been waiting impatiently ever since for the opportunity to burst forth. Morrison's singing is less an act of will than an act of release.

And what a voice it is, and what confidence its owner must possess to allow it out in the way that he does: often in an abrupt, gruff, hard-edged blurt, which attacks the moment as the edge of a spade chops into a sticky clod, all short-armed functionality and no flourish. But also sometimes a high fluting croon or a distracted stutter or a low burr or a carnal roar . . . You could spend all day describing in fancy terms the way he sings with his dauby voice and you'd get no nearer to understanding what's going on inside you, the listener, as you receive it; and you certainly won't have a clue as to what generated the sound in the first place. It is what it is; it is what it is given to be; and no amount of intellectualization of it will get you any farther up the tree, as the voice's owner himself has been only too keen to stress. Van Morrison's singing is by Van Morrison's own contention not a process of the intellect.

Moreover, just as Aretha Franklin's voice arched over a couple of decades'-worth of the hope expressed in African American music that better must come, so does Van Morrison's, over a couple of decades'-worth of the hope for an authentic transatlantic soul music: the effort to find out what communicable feeling feels like when your roots are sunk deep in the blowy outposts of Northern Europe but your face is turned to the imagined warmth of the west. If the singer hadn't coined the phrase "Caledonia Soul" himself, someone else would have surely done it for him. It is the perfect description of what he does.

Yet despite the persistence of his gruffness and his nonintellectualism, he never trots it out. He has never sung by numbers. Hardly ever, anyway. Morrison's voice, while identifiable as his, has always been a chambered vessel, a voice with compartments. He always seems to have somewhere to go with it.

With Them, his Belfast R&B group of the middle 1960s, he scratched out an edgy simulacrum of high-energy electric American blues, all bite and bark and sense of impending doom, thinly amplified, coarsely rendered. It is the sound produced by a callow young man taking a position on a subject that is close to his heart, but as yet unavailable to yours. Look at the footage on YouTube: Van is a bewildered bystander at the marvel of his own out-pourings. He hopes, narrow-eyed, that you won't be embarrassed by it, as he stubbornly refuses to be. If you are—well, tough.

Then there were his first soundings in America with "Brown Eyed Girl" and the ill-favored deal he struck with Bert Berns's Bang! label, which soured Morrison's attitude toward the business of making records for decades to come. The music was joyous, scrappy, underpowered, flagrant pop, and it had no bottom to it whatsoever.

His first major-label album in 1968, *Astral Weeks*, changed everything, though. If it didn't make him a rich man overnight, it certainly furnished him with a sort of creative matrix, in which all future inspirations might find their seed and nurture, and against which they might be evaluated.

Astral Weeks was a sort of jazz-folk meditation on perception as it is experienced both in memory and in the instant of the here-and-now, and it caught the hippie tide at its high point. Although the album did not sell well to begin with, it did develop such reliable momentum over the first ten years of its existence that it came to be lionized as something of a sacred text, possibly even a sacred cow; indeed it became—and remains in some quarters—the pious hipster's late-night precoital soundtrack and morning-after mood-enhancer of choice: music to intensify the experience of going with the flow.

But only the flow: the jazzy harmonies and riverine rhythmic undertow of the music (it had swelling, flexuous double bass on it, played by Richard

Davis, a significant avant-jazzer of the era), allied to its composer's incanta-
tory phrasing of impressionistic lyrics, lent the album an atmosphere that
bordered sometimes on the merely fluent, as if the point of the music were
to render life as a pattern in water—a rapturous, recollective river—and not
as a feeling in the body. In the world of *Astral Weeks*, it is as if bodies barely
exist.

So we should regard the arrival of *Moondance* a couple of years later as a
proper evolutionary step, in which bodies emerge from the flux and rapture
comes at you not as a recollective experience but as an actuality belonging
to the lived present, manifesting itself dynamically from every conceivable
angle in robust three dimensions, one song after the other. *Moondance* contains some of the most naggingly, earthily rapturous music ever committed
to two-inch tape.

It has been observed more than once that every song on the first side
of the album is sung differently, from the boxed-in gravelly wonderment of
"And It Stoned Me" (a song about a juvenile fishing trip that culminates
in a quasi-biblical vision worthy of William Blake, or Stanley Spencer, or
perhaps Huckleberry Finn) via the suave swing of the title track to "Crazy
Love"'s delicate, stroking falsetto intimacy, then the extrovert joy of "Cara-
van" recessing only a little in the end into the facial foghorn sound of "Into
the Mystic." It's as if the singer is receiving instructions from somewhere:
"now I want to hear you try it *this* way . . ."

He is not being instructed, of course, nor dreaming bashfully in a cowshed of the imagination. He's in a New York studio working his mojo. But
you can hear him responding to a call: *Moondance* is the sound of a man
caught in the very act of being stirred to the bottom of his soul, by life, by
work, by leisure, by sex, by everything. There is fantastic certainty evident
from the outset about what kind of work he is doing here and what its purpose is, and there is a palpable conviction in the music itself that if he, the
singer—the object and vessel of that call—listens hard enough to it, the
right thing will present itself to the world at the end of his effort, somehow.

Morrison produced *Moondance* himself using wholesome American
players during the period of his brief sojourn in Woodstock in upstate New

York with his wife Janet "Planet" Rigsbee, when things were, ostensibly at least, going well for him—temporarily settled as far from the troubled streets of Belfast as can be conceived of, psycho-geographically speaking, and at some remove from the champing maw of the music industry. Nobody is telling him what to do. No one is shaping his world for him or ripping him off or threatening him. Trees are abundant, as is Janet. And the album in its entirety feels like an attempt to capture and then inhabit for a stretch those states of happiness that might be available to anyone in the course of an attentively lived life, yet are all the more bountiful because of their unexpectedness. The horns are tight, the rhythm section trips like deer. Morrison's writing is profoundly economical. *Moondance* is a description of an encounter with unlooked-for glory, naked in its surprise and suffused with warm feeling, like treetops bathed in the last sunlight of the afternoon. It is secular gospel music.

That last song on side one of *Moondance*, "Into the Mystic," has everything to say about all of this. It rocks gently on its tub of a hull, and it regrets nothing. In fact the song is an explicit denial of regret with every note and beat of its brief yet compellingly numinous length. The line "It's too late to stop now" is thrown out at the end as a cadential thought but also as a defiant declaration of faith in whatever happens next. You can only feel naked optimism. The foghorn shivers the air in part to hail the return of the redeemed voyager and in part to signal his feelings of transcendence and joy in having made the journey in the first place.

* * *

The popular music of the second half of the twentieth century begins and ends in the profane. There is no shortage of profanity occupying the space in between, too. If you were to generalize about it in the loosest possible terms, you might say that the pop of the late 1950s and '60s, whatever its generic stripe, was governed by a desire to celebrate release from commandment and regulation, to announce freedom from conformity and to issue an all-out endorsement of the individual spirit as it bursts the bonds tied by the collective, the traditional and the circumspect. Pop was a rage against time; it embraced the secular and the material. It was nonreflective. It was the art of the now.

Yet gradually, over the course of the 1960s, it became apparent to more and more bright souls that taking the work seriously—and producing serious work—need not feel like a betrayal of pop's irreverent founding spirit. It could actually be part of it; in fact it could be the better, most impactful part of it. The Beatles and Bob Dylan fully embraced seriousness in their work, even as they adopted all-out facetiousness as a social armature. The Velvet Underground were an earnest outgrowth of the Pop Art movement, even as they sulked and sneered and held whatever personal warmth they might possess in reserve. Jimi Hendrix plunged into the hot cauldron of the working moment with a commitment that bordered on the unworldly at times, while cultivating an atmosphere of either cool diffidence or indolent charm for deployment against life's trivialities. Aretha Franklin brought church tone into the R&B recording studio. Marvin Gaye brought social issues to bear in the Motown canon. Van Morrison made himself into a vessel of rapture . . .

It was as if beneath pop's brightly colored, ever-busy materialist surface something slower and graver was taking hold, something to do with self-conscious maturation and the desire to bite deeper into life's groove— and the desire to explore how it might feel to make a *better* fist of the hand you've been dealt, both in pop and in life.

The tools were there, ready and waiting. After all, seriousness of one very particular kind was built into rock 'n' roll and R&B and all their associated forms from the very beginning. It was present in their regular structures, their chord sequences and their extemporary flights, their melodies and their rhythms; in the hard-edged attack that prevents the music from washing into blandness. Seriousness was indivisible, in fact, from pop's most frivolous impulses. It was indivisible because the profane world of rock 'n' roll and R&B shared musicological roots with gospel and the sacred music of white American nonconformity. It was inextricable: the same music, in essence, with different words and dynamics and performance styles applied to it. But the same music. In fact, three of rock 'n' roll's four great originals,

Elvis, Jerry Lee, and Little Richard, never entirely shed the practice of prais-
ing God—or, in Lewis's case, of worrying about the Devil. (It is impossible
to listen to Elvis's better religious songs and not concede that here is a man
trying hard to be serious about life—and succeeding sometimes.)

So we should not be at all surprised that the distance traveled in time
between the first Beatles album and *Astral Weeks* was as short as it was: a
little over five years. To use a modern cliché, that distance certainly represented a steep learning curve; one that could only have been plotted at that
time and in that particular historical context—and with that measure of
entropic excitement. For the middle 1960s was a period of extreme cultural
acceleration, one creative advance knocking into another as it tripped over
a third. It was a chaotic spree involving real-world forces which catalyzed
one another dramatically: forces such as heightening political and social
awareness and the accompanying imperative to break new artistic ground,
and quickly; the newly expanded range and scope of electronic media; the
appearance of realizable social mobility within an enlarging consumer economy; indeed the sheer pell-mell independent-mindedness of 1960s creativity
in general—they were all expressed in popular music's desire to grow up fast
and become more than just popular.

And you could hear it in voices everywhere. Consider the sound of Lennon's "Twist and Shout" in the light of Morrison's "Madame George" or
"Into the Mystic": you might as easily discern the cries of an angry baby
in the incantations of a psalmist. They are so different and yet so close to
one another. For to recognize true psychological authenticity in both those
voices is to be at ease with the relationship between the twinned raptures of
desire and the spirit, the profane and the sacred, and the way those two raptures have always been distinct yet proximate: correlative, even. They constitute the double helix twisted tight at the core of everything worthwhile.

* * *

The Book of Psalms is a constituent of both the Hebrew Bible and the Christian Old Testament and was composed, it is now thought, over the span

of five centuries. The numbered Psalms the book contains were conceived as texts for singing—strictly regulated utterances of praise, lamentation, thanksgiving, and consolation. And there are 150 of them, roughly half of which are attributed to (or associated with) King David, although modern scholars do not go along with that attribution any more—which is hardly surprising, given the slender likelihood of David living to the age of five hundred. Instead, in conventional parlance, "The Psalmist" is the identity given to a nominal author of the Psalms for general ease of reference—for the book could hardly have been the product of one pen, nor even of one institution, tradition, or geographical location. The Psalms are eclectic in origin. And in the Christian liturgy, you'll find them deployed as texts to be sung or intoned in the Roman Catholic, Orthodox, Presbyterian, Lutheran, and Anglican churches alike. I sang them as an Anglican choirboy, and they are still sung by choirboys, most of whom regard the Psalms as a parcel of dirges.

Nevertheless, as dirges go, they can be pretty involving, if you are lucky enough to be singing the right one in the right place and in the right mood. A good psalm of lamentation will be voiced in the first person and require the psalming mind to venture into the wilderness, to hang its harp upon the willows and be purged with hyssop, thereafter to lift up its soul once again to places divine or go down into the pit. Not forgetting of course the imperative to, wherever possible, lie down in green pastures as a desirable alternative to walking through the valley of the shadow of death. These activities may not seem all that wildly attractive to modern sensibilities, accustomed as we are to the availability of Center Parcs, but they do take you places, show you sights.

Still, you have to be careful when picking your psalm of the day. Broadly speaking, the Psalms can be broken down into five main types, and then again into subdivisions: principally, hymns of praise (a bit one-note, these), communal laments (less dull but lacking psychological focus), royal Psalms (really dull, being mostly about the issues arising from the nature and practice of kingship), individual thanksgiving (lots of good vibes on offer here), and individual laments (very far from dull). It's the individual laments that have always interested me.

That's because you encounter in them a solitary, suffering voice that is keenly engaged in what appears to be a life-and-death struggle to be heard. You hear a lot of humanity in the laments. You hear the bite of perceived injustice and the desire for restitution. You hear selfhood in a state of riot, and you visit a psychological wilderness as well as a geographical one. You hear the solitary soul addressing God with a sense of longing and with an intimacy that is by no means sacramental: the language used sometimes presumes a personal relationship between Psalmist and Deity (and often there is no other addressee). It is as if the voice of the Psalmist is licensed differently, to go to places and make representations that the rest of us can only identify with when we go to our own most broken places. You hear in Psalms the deep reaching of the blues.

Here is Psalm 141:

Lord, I cry unto thee: make haste unto me; give ear unto my voice, when I cry unto thee.

Let my prayer be set before thee as incense; and the lifting up of my hands as the evening sacrifice.

Set a watch, O Lord, before my mouth; keep the door of my lips.

Incline not my heart to any evil thing, to practice wicked works with men that work iniquity: and let me not eat of their dainties.

Let the righteous smite me; it shall be a kindness: and let him reprove me; it shall be an excellent oil which shall not break my head: for yet my prayer also shall be in their calamities.

When their judges are overthrown in stony places, they shall hear my words; for they are sweet.

And so on.

I don't know about you, but I can hear Howlin' Wolf barking these words at a nicotine moon; or perhaps Robert Johnson, in some godforsaken flyblown flophouse, feeling those syllables buzz in his sinuses as he wonders whether words can ever be more than flies. Most of all I hear Winston Rodney (a.k.a. Burning Spear), alone in a barren place, lifting his eyes up to the heavens and chopping out a single, repeated, skanky, slightly out-of-tune acoustic-guitar chord to accompany his supplications, like some wild and lost thing.

* * *

The voice in the wilderness is a basic building block of culture. It is to be found in religious texts, in secular literature, in films, in post-punk records. You find it sometimes in TV soap opera. It is everywhere people are. It makes stories live and breathe and express emotion directly, as if the stories are nothing but emotion organized in a narrative style. It transforms the here and now. Think of Lear in the wilderness of his own failing mind. Think of Hamlet in the wilderness of his indecision: without "To be or not to be," the play is a dead narrative. It loses its heart and mind and becomes, instead, a dull list of killings.

The language of the wilderness voice may be intimate and madly over-ripe, but then it has the entire sky to address and a terrible weight to bear in the knowledge that if the voice is to be answered at all, then it won't be with direct speech or immediate action or even with the identifying empathy of onlookers. The wilderness voice is not narcissistic; it does not perceive its own beauty and cannot be distracted by it. It can never be crooned. If you are a voice in the wilderness, then you are quite alone. Although, yes, there may be occurrences . . . If you're extremely lucky, a bush may burst into flame and start talking back. But God himself will certainly not then appear from behind the next boulder with a jug of oil to anoint your brow and the affirmation, expressed in his own massive, dense voice, that he is armed and ready to smite the hosts of thine enemies. The voice in the wilderness does not utter its pleas in the expectation that it will be answered, only the failing hope.

The point is that the voice is marooned and it knows that it is, even as it hopes against hope that this may not be the case. And as such it can make no assumptions—it perceives that it has very little prospect of gain and possesses nothing of its own that it can't do without. The wilderness voice is by definition a humble voice, one that is only too aware of its own smallness. It is a voice of rapture in suffering and grief.

Psalm 143:

> For the enemy hath persecuted my soul; he hath smitten my life down to the ground; he hath made me to dwell in darkness, as those that have been long dead.
>
> Therefore is my spirit overwhelmed within me; my heart within me is desolate.

And so on.

The voice in the wilderness is in the wilderness because it does not know where to turn. And because it knows that the wilderness may be the place where God is hiding.

* * *

Winston Rodney was born in St Ann's Bay in the parish of St Ann, Jamaica, in 1945, a month or so after that other well-known native of St Ann, Bob Marley. Like Marley, he grew up listening to black American R&B on those southern US radio stations endowed with a signal powerful enough to finger the Jamaican coast. Also like Marley, he became a practicing Rastafarian during Jamaica's first decade of colonial independence and a convinced Garveyite Pan-Africanist. And it was with the endorsement of Marley that Rodney first approached Clement "Sir Coxsone" Dodd's Studio One in the late 1960s with a view to launching a singing career at that most idiosyncratic of record labels. Over a handful of years of fitful labor, he made a handful of singles and a brace of albums that remain, to this day, unmatched among the self-transporting raptures of the wilderness.

Those early Studio One records have a sound all their own. Because of the limitations imposed by Coxsone's basic studio hardware and the room in which the singers and players were recorded, Burning Spear's first music is tiny in dynamic range and lo-fi almost to the point of no-fi. No matter how loudly you play the recordings back and no matter how probing the intent of your listening, the music remains resolutely dense and impenetrable, as if it were carved from a single block of compacted organic material—condensed still further perhaps by exposure to the elements. Add to this production sound the sparseness of the musical arrangements (sometimes little more than repetitious bass, drum, guitar, and two-finger keyboard rumbling and snicking on a single chord or sometimes two), not forgetting Studio One's traditional liberality in its attitude toward strict concert tuning, and what you are up against is a sound that is, to put it mildly, *raw*. It is a feral, wilderness sound.

And then there are the voices in the wilderness . . .

Jamaican vocal style of the "roots reggae" era drew some influence from African American R&B but an awful lot more from local tradition. And local tradition meant folk chant, the incantations of magic ritual ("obeah") and bare-bones Nonconformist Christian worship with a strong basis in biblical quotation. The roots vocal style is usually open-throated but not often propelled from the diaphragm. It is coughed-up singing, raw as tree bark and chatty in that its trajectory is conversational rather than operatic: the short, straight way in preference to the elevated baroque way. Roots vocalists never miss an opportunity to declaim in hieratic style, righteousness being very close to their hearts. You may not be merely decorative and expect to be taken seriously as a roots-reggae artist: you have to be saying something. You have to be "dry and heavy."

The *sine qua non* is Burning Spear, which is the name Winston Rodney assumed for all professional singing duties, whether accompanied or not by a pair of open-throated backup vocalists. His is the wilderness vocal sound at its most remotely compelling, a small, intimate, bubble of a God-bothering head-voice rising to a desperate keening when the pressure of historical suffering really comes on. He is a psalmist.

Take the early Studio One hit "Foggy Road," which is composed of just one chord, stabbed out step by step like the shuffle of feet. The road it treads is long and foggy and certainly unmetalled—the singer is turning his entire being to the effort of marking his own route through history's wilderness. Organ notes jag across his path, thorns gather and thicken. "No more stumbling block," he intones, eyes narrowed to avoid distraction. "Forward, my brother, forward—no more turning back." This is not just simplicity of design but simplicity of *being*—the Spear is attempting to distill into the tread of his footsteps an entire feeling for life and restitution. More than one chord would have represented an unacceptable deviation from the path and a fall into complexity.

Then there is "Call on You." It luxuriates in three chords because the song requires a built-in harmonic uplift to regulate the jitter in its step. It gurgles, it vaults. It summons. "When the sun goes down and we move along / I will call on you." There is no time to lose, he calls, we *must* go through. It is a voice reaching out from the wilderness to the world of men, calling them to join with the march to deeper understanding of what it means to be descended brokenly from slaves and, before that, from free Africans.

We find out even more of what it means to Rodney a couple of years later, on what would be Burning Spear's international debut for Island Records, *Marcus Garvey*, recorded for Jack Ruby in 1975 (and often accompanied these days by its own marvelous dub version from the following year, *Garvey's Ghost*). It's a harshly beautiful suite of songs that compresses slavery narratives, the burble of mystical religion, black history, and Pan-Africanist militancy into a transporting ten-song rapture for the ages. Rumble, snick. Chant. Mutter. Moan. Songs as exegesis. Songs as lists of things to do to quantify and resolve unrighted wrongs. Songs as psalms. It is not a parcel of dirges—far from it—but neither is it hospitable music. It is as resistant to easy assimilation as high moorland is to a casual stroll, a landscape pocked with dips and outcrops and hidden falls that demands absolute commitment from a willing traveler. But if you are prepared to go along with it, and watch your footing as you go, it reaches as deeply as any music created in the late twentieth century into the idea that music is itself, at its most serious, a ritual enactment as well as an auditory transaction.

Marcus Garvey is a true rapture because it is not an appeal to anyone to listen for his or her own enjoyment. It is more or less self-sufficing. It does not require your assent or participation or even your attention. You can do something else if you like. It will still exist and do its work, whether you listen or not. Whatever else might be found in *Marcus Garvey*'s starkly intimate snatches of rhythm, chant, and distracted mumble, it is not a cry for human connection—for this is the intimacy of the Psalmist in his relationship with God, the sky, the hillside, the briar—and with the awful knowledge of his own history.

* * *

I persuaded my sister to buy me "Anarchy in the UK" by the Sex Pistols for Christmas in 1976, when I was sixteen and it had just come out on the EMI label (immediately prior to the group's contract being terminated by that company in a fit of corporate censoriousness). I wanted to hear "Anarchy" desperately because punk had not really revealed itself yet, not properly—not to provincials—and I liked the idea of punk. There had been the Ramones in America, whom I loved instantly when their first works landed in Britain earlier in the year. And there had been "New Rose" by The Damned, which had made me smile because of its clumsy energy, analogous to four blokes chasing each other through an empty house with no carpets on the floors. But that had been about it, apart from the first punky scratchings of one local band in my province. Like the phoney war of late 1939, the back end of 1976 was all rumors of cataclysm and not much concrete evidence of it.

But not for much longer. For there it was under the Christmas tree, wrapped up in colorful paper and standing out among the other presents only for its thinness, flatness, and squareness. In due course this mysterious package was handed to me and unwrapped and thanks were proffered—I am pretty sure my sister and I enacted a sardonic ritual of feigned surprise and pleasure at the giving of a brand new thing requiring brand new language: "It's a punk record? How lovely! Thanks, sis." I am certain that no further discussion ensued involving my parents and the words "sex" and "pistols."

Nor did I play "Anarchy" on Christmas Day in front of the family on the 1950s radiogram that stood in the corner of the living room. That way madness would surely have lain. I loved my family, but not that much. I was not made of punky enough stuff for that; and I would not be now, were the scene to be reconstructed forty years on, even without the presence of my gran in a paper crown, disapproving of everything. Instead, I waited until Boxing Day when the coast was pretty much clear and everyone had left the house to do better and more constructive things. Quietly, furtively, I stuck the seven-inch vinyl 45 on the turntable, lowered the needle and . . . recoiled in shock.

The music clubbed its way out of the radiogram's bassy underbelly speaker like conventional hard rock. Hard rock with none of hard rock's pretensions to technical accomplishment. In fact it came out like a claw hammer, heavy, obtuse, dully brutal, horned.

Quoi?

So what's so "punk" about this? Where's the pace? The anarchic brio? The skiddiness? Both The Damned and the Ramones were fleet and relatively light on their tootsies, inspirited with levity, running with what they had—which wasn't all that much, let's face it—and traveling as fast as they could go, even if that meant tripping over their own feet sometimes. But this was oppressive and slowish: an auditory mugging in dragged-out, juddering march time. Drawled. Slugged. Beaten out. Stomped. Stomped with heavy boots. Not that different to Led Zeppelin, actually, whom one was supposed now to despise. The avalanching intro was even reminiscent of an intro on *Physical Graffiti*. "Anarchy" was well-recorded hard rock.

But it contained something else, too—something so strange that its very presence in the music stymied all my best efforts at branding the song a disappointment: a derivative disappointment.

I had never heard loathing in a pop record before. Not *loathing*.

Distaste I was familiar with, of course—it was standard popular-culture practice to dislike stuff. Theatrical horror and malevolence had their place too, as did indignation and contempt—especially the contempt of the hipster, who thinks he knows more about life than you do. But loathing and disgust? Gut loathing? Neurotic disgust? Repulsion? The shiver of irrational hatred? The out-of-phase laughter of the joker who despises you because you haven't seen what he has seen? Loathing not worked up for effect, but present as an ingrained psychological condition of the music? These feelings did not belong in rock; they belonged in the dark and filthy place where you get beaten up, beyond the reach of those who might save you; beaten up for being fortunate, for being oblivious, for harboring the sense of entitlement that you ought to be safe, and for being *there*, which was not your place. "Anarchy in the UK" was a pop record that hated you, whether you liked it or not.

Never mind the lovingly sculpted hard-rock form and the clear desire on the part of the production team behind it to make the record sound "good" as technical product, the voice of "Anarchy" was all loathing, disgust, repulsion, hatred . . . and loneliness.

* * *

In its time, John Lydon's voice has been likened to many unpleasant things, and we won't list them here. But I have always thought it rather beautiful, in its way, in the same way in fact that I once found the Sensational Alex Harvey's voice rather beautiful.

Both voices were thin, hard, and tensile, like wire. Both were sprung with neurotic energy, stretched by some inner attenuating force, intuitively theatrical and not at all bothered by the regulating conventions of "singerliness," not if those conventions stood in the way of getting the individual's true voice out. Singerliness was only ever to be tried on for mockery's sake and then dispensed with. And as with Van Morrison and Winston Rodney, neither Harvey nor Lydon made decisions when they sang; they just let their voices out, as the voices seemed to want to come out, melodramatic, wheedling, whiney, hogwhimpering, or whatever. Both Harvey and Lydon were interested in disgust. Only one of them was inclined to rapture.

Harvey's disgust found its most seething outlet in his 1973 version of Jacques Brel's song of existential horror, "Next." "Next," in the Sensational Alex Harvey Band's grip, was a clever, dainty polka but it was also a clenched discourse about what it is to find yourself the next in line for the "wet head" of your first taste of gonorrhoea; next for the ruin of your innocence; next for the unsolvable calculus of biologic disgust. Next, next, next. Harvey took you into the apprehension and the fear; he showed you how sharp its teeth were and how deep its throat. He dwelt fearfully in his foreknowledge of what was about to occur . . . But then he drew back from the vileness itself—and from his own unholy repulsion—and he stepped away, as if to drag the curtain decorously back over *what will surely transpire but hasn't yet.*

The difference in Lydon's disgust was that it had clearly *already* transpired, whatever it was. You could tell from every utterance he made that, for him, in his impoverished, neglected, Irish-immigrant, working-class Holloway childhood—which had not yet ended, incidentally—the worst had already come to pass. His disgust was not anticipative, but reflective. There was shame in his voice, the heat of shame and the cooling, squelching shit of self-disgust. When you listened to it, you heard not only the possibility of what is yet to come, but also the horror of what it feels like to have already been there, alone and unsafe.

Three years on from "Anarchy," in 1979, the Sex Pistols had already dissolved in a splatter of shame and disgust and Lydon had formed Public Image Ltd. (a.k.a. PiL), as much a conceptual brief as a rock band (the endless ill-tempered interviews and think-pieces in the music press about how that concept might be embodied musically had been as stimulating as the prospect of the music yet to exist). PiL's second album, released that year in the form of three twelve-inch 45s encased in a tin film canister, was entitled *Metal Box.* It was a cold, awkward-to-handle object, and the music it contained was awkward, too. Eventually, the film tin oxidized.

PiL were, however, utterly potent on that album. They were conceived as "what comes next" following the punk-inflicted death of rock and they, as a group of musicians, amounted to the abstruse sum of barely cohering parts, musically as well as conceptually: Keith Levene's trebly, coarsely distorted, arpeggiating, non-propulsive, "splinter" guitar; Jah Wobble's highly propulsive reggae-derived rumble-bass; assorted drummers playing in a variety of styles (from more or less straightforward thumping rock via reggae economy to the front-foot machine-drive of Can's Jaki Liebezeit); all of them leaving a void in the middle of the frequency range for the trickling snarl that was Lydon's voice—a metal box with no contents: top, yes; bottom, plenty; but no middle. Or at least, where there should have been a middle there was only the sound of a dull room occupied by the introvert blithering of the group's figurehead and chief ideologue, tuneless, distracted, and barely phrased, as if involved in some form of self-hypnosis in the corner.

Enraptured.

The opening track on *Metal Box* is eleven minutes long. Its title is "Albatross," and it remains, to my mind at least, the acutest description of the experience of depressive self-loathing that exists in popular music: a tiny wail of disgust and repulsion, corroding the world like a sort of dribbling acid. A rejection of the self as well as a rejection of the rest of us; a resentful single, skinless occupancy of an empty room, surrounded by everything else that exists but not receptive to it—everything else being salt to its raw body.

"I know you very well

You are unbearable

I've seen you up far too close . . .

Getting rid of the albatross."

There are holy raptures and there are unholy ones, and "Albatross" is one of the latter. The piece concludes with Lydon sarcastically quoting Roy Orbison as the rhythm breaks down. "Only the lonely," he sneers, first in his caustic Sex Pistols voice and then in a tremulous childish falsetto squeal.

"On-ly the lo-o-o-o-onely."

* * *

It was Mott the Hoople's cheerful 1973 hit "All the Way from Memphis" that included the clunky but oddly memorable line, "It's been a mighty long way down rock 'n' roll," as if the passage of significantly less than twenty years stood for the span of an entire lifetime or more—a golden age, perhaps. But then in 1973 rock 'n' roll must have seemed as if it were going to last forever. I know it appeared that way to me, and I certainly wanted it to be the case, because rock 'n' roll as it was then constituted was a rapture to me, and a psalm. It spoke all languages and it entailed all voices, all of them speaking freshly and unarguably of the world in which I seemed to live. Rock, soul, reggae, pop, funk ("rock 'n' roll" was a broad church): all of those musical styles retained the capacity to contain everything that it's possible to feel and to express absolutely anything at all. They spoke of the world with a rightness that nothing else in my thirteen years of experience came close to doing.

So in that sense, even in 1973, it *was* a mighty long way: it was a lifetime for a boy born in 1960. And six years on from Mott the Hoople in 1979, the year of *Metal Box*, it had come to seem like an even longer lifetime.

But of course *Metal Box* did not actually mark the end of anything in particular, not formally, tempting though it is with all the advantages of hindsight to think that it did. Culture is not neat like that. It has its way stations and its signposts; it is curved and junctioned and laced with byways; it has its births and deaths; and of course it has its dead ends. But it does not have *an* end. It goes on and on, being what it is, doing what it does, multiplying and proliferating and leaving unsightly messes. And we humans form our attachments to it according to our needs.

I have never ceased to be compelled by music, especially by the sort that reinvents the Psalms and expresses human rapture and the desire to transcend pain. I never will. Music and I are indissolubly attached; we shall go on together. But something in *me* stopped in 1979, at the time of *Metal Box*. Something ran out. Gurgled away. Evaporated. I don't know what it was exactly, this thing. But I suspect it may have been an emotional capacity; something to do with a certain kind of innocence or aptitude for belief, or maybe even a simple willingness to go along with things, with or without question. Let's not give it a name. Perhaps what stopped in me was the preparedness to take things at face value . . .

But there is one thing of which I am still pretty sure, despite all that, and it's this.

In the mid-1950s, rock 'n' roll had sprung out of postwar America with a sound that announced, in nonsense language, a new way for young people to perceive themselves: as potent, energetic, assertive, rebellious, creative, independent, stylish, uninhibited, and as mindful as they were sometimes mindless. And because of its close association with the regenerative benefits of a new consumer economy, rock 'n' roll actually made for societal change in ways that had never been seen before, and it encouraged some young people to dance and fuck while developing the capacity to think politically and to perceive in the wilderness all manner of extraordinary things, including the hiding place of God. It encouraged young people to be less like children and more like themselves—which in turn legitimized the way they *felt*, as if independent, deregulated feelings were permissible. And really quite quickly the contagion that such excitement engendered spread across the Atlantic to the monochrome, hunched, and shivering UK where a generation of austerity-bound class rebels with a cause of sorts seized on the idea of rock 'n' roll and ran with it, bringing new imaginations to bear and discovering in the process that bushes did under certain conditions catch fire and that rapture as an experience was not the sole preserve of those who knelt in church.

And rock 'n' roll rang those changes, as a musician might put it, for two whole decades, with varying degrees of aesthetic success but a whole lot of commercial and social welly until, around the end of the 1970s, something else happened in the world and the changes ran down and down and finally arrived at a strange unsatisfactory pause—what musos like to call an "interrupted cadence"—during which the people involved enough to care looked at one another and kind of frowned and scowled and felt uneasy and said to one another, "Well, I'm a little tired of that. Furthermore, I have grown suspicious of it—isn't there something rather phony about this stuff we buy into so readily? *Now what?*"

And suddenly it seemed very much harder to believe in anything you were told, whether the people telling you appeared to be like you or not.

But that's the risk you take if you allow young people to be less like children and more like themselves. Their raptures take them into new spaces. And after twenty or so years of confident self-assertion and mutual stimulation, they began to discover that there were rents in the fabric of their own illusions. They found that they were not invincible and they were not as beautiful as they once thought, nor as clever. In fact, for crying out loud, they had doubts, and worse than doubts. They began to experience the critical shiver of self-loathing.

And that is one big bird to have hanging from your neck.

GRACE NOTES

BOB DYLAN: "NO MORE AUCTION BLOCK"
Columbia Records, 1962

In 1983 Bob Dylan released an album called *Infidels*. It was notable for a couple of reasons, chiefly for being a first return to secular material after some years of releasing only gospel-influenced religious music; also for the deployment of a slick new rhythm section in the form of Jamaican superstars Sly Dunbar and Robbie Shakespeare under the direction of producer Mark Knopfler. It was a good album.

But it didn't have the song "Blind Willie McTell" on it, and that was perhaps the most notable thing of all.

"Blind Willie McTell"—an outtake from the *Infidels* sessions—is a lengthy, almost meditative reflection upon America's historical oppressions, using the dolorous old blues melody "St James Infirmary" as a vessel to slog through a swamp of incalculable pain. It is one of the great long-view songs, expressing the ruination that was slavery not as a troubling aspect of the nation's backstory, but as its spine. The seizure of American land from its indigenous peoples appears to be alluded to as well. It's an extraordinary song whose chief thematic material might be summarized in the lines, "But power and greed and corruptible seed / Seem to be all that there is." It would be a lament worthy of the Psalmist were there any hint in it of a willed connection to God.

Instead there is only Dylan and his fists at the piano, with Knopfler sitting close by with a twelve-string acoustic guitar across his knees. The song is austere enough in its non-arrangement to be a rehearsal or a demo, though far too intent in tone to be a simple run-through. It is a performance, in every sense of the word.

"Blind Willie McTell" finally emerged eight years later on the first of Dylan's *Bootleg Series* sequence of retrospective outtake albums in 1991 and is fit to be considered among the greatest recordings he ever made. Yet it would appear that Dylan regarded it as unfinished work—which would at least explain why the song never appeared on *Infidels* in the first instance. His singing goes deep, though. It is profoundly rapturous. It is as if he found in this old melody and in his own careful words about the suffering of others a way to reach into the remotest and most resonant chambers of himself. And once there you sense a desire in him to stay in this place of rapture, as if it's a better place to be.

It is striking how unlazy his phrasing is; how snappy and precise and hard-edged, pressing right up on the bar-lines, never hanging off the back of the beat, channelling the sung language as if hooked up to some other current. It is possible of course that the effort required of his body to bang out the chords in timely fashion on the piano keyboard meant that his voice was dragged into metrical line as a result, in a sort of neural whiplash. But that in no sense devalues the impact of the performance, which is towering.

There's another recording on *Bootleg Series Vols. 1–3* that I can't help but treat as a companion piece, even though it was recorded twenty-one years prior to "Blind Willie McTell" when the singer was himself only twenty-one years old and was scuffling a living at the Gaslight Café, among the other bohemian haunts that constituted the urban infrastructure of New York's early-1960s folk scene.

"No More Auction Block" was an African American spiritual of the eighteenth century. On the page, it reads as a gentle, rueful, bordering-on-mannerly lamentation of the obscenity that was slavery. But also as a sort of *requiescat in pace*. "No more auction block for me," it goes. "No more, no more. No more auction block for me. Many thousands gone."

It is not clear in the song, as it was sung by Dylan and recorded just this once at the Gaslight in 1962, whether there is to be no more auction block because the slave singing the song has escaped, been freed, or is on the point of death. But to hear it, you'd think it would have to be the last. And the twenty-one-year-old Dylan reaches into a sump of feeling that makes the act of listening to it a form of penitence. There is no way out. You *must* accept that your—the listener's—life is in part a consequence of the rewards of this historical iniquity.

The melody is a simple up-and-down swell, like a tide that creeps up and down a pebbled beach, and the voice goes with it in the simplest terms possible, just rising and falling like a boat. And as it goes, the singer seems to rock himself into a rapture of concentration; concentration on what he is doing here, in this moment, singing this inappropriate song for a white man to sing to other white people, all of them comfortable in their enlightenment in a coffee shop in the hub of world capitalism, as a consumer boom gathers unstoppable momentum in streets all around, the pebbles at the back of his throat stirring slowly to articulate the long vowels in "thousands" more with weariness than in anger or indignation, as if for a moment involved in something beyond thought and rationalization—just there, inside himself and looking out in sorrow. At the age of twenty-one, alone on the edge of the wilderness. It's a moment of uneasy rapture, and it is quite right that the exercise was never repeated, for all its beauty. For that beauty would have been lost in any repetition. The wilderness may only really be brought indoors just the once.

Epilogue

Harvest

I am deaf.

I am not completely deaf, but I am very deaf. One ear has no functional hearing in it at all—it is what's known in the professional slang as a "dead ear." The other one has some hearing in it still but is afflicted with what clinicians define as "severe hearing loss." It hears life as through a wall in a terraced house. Not much treble, no bass, and extremely muffled in the middle. I can hear full-on shouting and banging but that's about it, although the closer I get to the source of any auditory signal, the better I hear it. So I press my ear against the wall that divides me from audible life whenever I can, and I listen hard. I have been equipped with an excellent NHS hearing aid, and it does a lot of that pressing for me. If we were in a room together, you and I, and there were no other noise going on nearby, I'd hear you fine. Not so much without the hearing aid.

The killing of my dead ear took place overnight in the summer of 2007. I woke up one morning feeling rough and the hearing in my right ear went *pffffffff*, just like that—leaving behind a jungle of tinnital noise and auditory hallucinations in the dead ear and gross malfunction in the widowed ear on the other side, at least while my brain went through the long process of adjusting to its new auditory reality; and then at a reduced level and without the hallucinations once the adjustment had been completed.

This experience introduced me to the notion that we hear not with our ears, but with our brains. The outer ear and its inner workings are of course just a portal; a highly complex, sensitive, and damageable portal, which converts sound waves into the electrical lingo of the brain via the vestibular system of the inner ear and the subtle agency therein of microscopic hair cells or cilia. But hearing, in the cognitive sense, takes place in the auditory cortices of the brain. What you "hear" is only an interpretation of what's out there, and what's out there is subject to all kinds of modulation by both what you "know" already and the sensory mechanics of how you begin the process of hearing. It's complicated. And it is not a plug-in-and-go system, where you can simply replace damaged parts. When parts of the system break down, the whole system goes—if the broken parts are the wrong parts. The parts that broke in me were the wrong parts. What killed my ear in 2007 was a strange nameless phenomenon that goes under the descriptive title Sudden Sensorineural Hearing Loss, and there's no coming back from it.

Unfortunately, if you lose one ear completely, then the other one goes into a tailspin for a while. It took more than three years for hearing in the "good ear" to be restored to something like functional normality. By late 2010 I could hear music fairly truly again, albeit in mono through the portal of my one useful ear, and without distortion or too much damaging interference from the wild tinnitus that continued to crowd the dead ear. But it wasn't as good as hearing with two ears. Nothing like. You need two good ears to perceive dimensionality and direction in sound, and having two helps with timbre and tone and a sense of "presence." When you have only one, music is both flat as a dinner plate and seems to come from everywhere and nowhere, which is weird; also, once permanent auditory damage like this is done, the hearing that remains to you is wildly oversensitive and prone to distorting hyperacusis. Sustained exposure to music or noise of any kind at any volume at all brings on neuro-pain and the desperate desire for silence and solitude. Sound can be an enemy, even sound you thought you liked, or loved.

But still, after three years I had made what seemed like huge strides, given where I'd started. I wrote about the struggle to get back to music in a book called *The Train in the Night*, which documented the hearing loss in a sort of case study of how it is to lose access to a psychological mainstay in life—in my case, music. It also looked back on *why* music might be so important to one of my age, background, and disposition, and why we might have the tastes we do. The book concluded with an authentic happy ending grounded in the anticipation of further progress.

Then, late in 2012, some months after the book was published, I shared a six-hour train journey from Dumfries to London with the fans of not one but two football clubs. The first lot got on in the far northwest of England, at Carlisle, and they were joined by another bunch in Lancashire. Together, they enjoyed themselves all the way back to Euston. Good south London and Cambridge lads.

It was bedlam. There wasn't a single second-class carriage on the train that was not given over to a continuous uproar of singing and shouting and lunging and falling over and banter and clattering and banging and more singing and shouting. There was no escape. After a couple of hours I was wound up like a top. After three, my hearing had begun to melt down. By the time I'd clawed my way back from the station to the house in northeast London where I live, I was almost completely deaf in my remaining good ear. What little I could hear was distorted out of all recognition. Nothing sounded like anything at all, except for my wife who sounded like a run-down Dalek buried in the middle of a room packed to the ceiling with cotton wool.

And it stayed that way for nearly nine months.

I was bundled off to a neurology hospital. I had MRI scans. I had hearing therapy. I gave up alcohol. I tried meditation. I drank pints of water more or less continuously. I steamed my face off with bowls of boiling hot water laced with eucalyptus oil. I enjoyed twice-daily salt douches of my sinuses (you honk brine up your nose). I spent most of my time sealed off in our bedroom alone, with the door shut and the windows closed to keep noise out and my emotions in. I thought I might run mad. Every now and then my hearing would threaten to come back and I would enjoy two or three optimistic days where semi-normal hearing would approach, sidle up, sniff at me . . . and then bolt again, like a nervous heifer. At times I could not tell the difference between the sound a fist makes when it hammers on a door and the sound a voice makes when it speaks. Both sounds were also equal in their capacity to cause electrical storms to race across my brain.

And then with the onset of summer 2013, for no apparent reason, the hearing in that good ear came back. It might have been the water, it might have been the abstinence from alcohol, it might have been because I had given up hope altogether; I doubt it was the salt douches. I never found out the reason. But one morning I woke up and it was just there, as if it had never been away: half my hearing. The consultant at the hospital reckoned I'd fallen victim to an auditory migraine that had lasted two-thirds of a year.

I don't think music had ever been more important to me than it was that summer and autumn after half my hearing came back. I gulped it down like a man dying of thirst; stuffed it in my head like a starving man. Couldn't get it in fast enough. I listened and listened and felt things that I had never felt before. (I was, after all, a man reborn.) The fact that I experienced the music monaurally with an accompanying barrage of hisses and whistles and hums in the dead ear on the other side did not bother me in the slightest: I could hear music again—that was all that mattered. I sucked it all in and held it there. It sometimes felt as if I was holding my breath.

Perhaps not all that oddly, most of the music I listened to that year was music I knew already. It was overwhelmingly good to be back in the embrace of my family, so to speak, so why shouldn't I embrace them in return? Why shouldn't I focus all my energies on them, for a while at least? A pox on the neophiliac obsession we have with newness and novelty and the next thing. What on earth could be wrong with a deepening re-exploration of those things to which I had already formed a serious attachment? It would be weird not to, surely . . .

But then I noticed a pattern. I'd find myself bingeing. Not only that, I'd find that I was bingeing with a half-conscious sense of purpose, as if there was a job to be done. I'd listen to Aretha Franklin over and over again, not as I'd always done before as a source of pleasure and edification and for momentary life-giving contact with the ecstatic spirit, but like homework.

I'd keep at it, too, almost systematically, listening to her records in the right order, not skipping, not dodging, not stopping until—as it seemed to me—the tank was full and it was no longer possible to cram any more in. Only when I felt a sense of surfeit and Aretha was overflowing and pouring down the sides would I find it possible to move on to another voice.

Very strange. This was not how I was accustomed to listening to music at all. I have always dodged around according to mood and the expediencies of the moment—felt scornful of the "completist" mentality and its neuroticisms. Yet here was I behaving like the daftest kind of neurotic completist. Moreover, for the first time in my life I was not bothering to listen to much new music (with one or two notable exceptions), nor troubling to explore *everything* that I knew I liked; only certain things, certain voices—and very specific voices at that: voices that had throughout the course of my life affected the way I think and feel and get the world, and that I cannot imagine doing without. My listening was all appetite, governed only by desire: what do I *want* to hear, and how can I get more of that? I indulged in narrow greed. I did not, for instance, bother with those voices I know to be splendid and/or important which have never moved me (sorry Neil, sorry Adele, sorry Ozzy, sorry Kraftwerk, etc.) Nor did I particularly want to trouble myself with those voices that I quite like in some circumstances but can generally do without quite happily (sorry Todd, sorry Roger, sorry Dionne, etc.). I wanted only the essential voices: the ones which nourish and sustain, the ones of which I never tire; the ones that had succeeded in clambering inside me and pinioning my heart. It gradually dawned on me that I was engaged in the sort of obsessive-compulsive activity that dignifies squirrels.

Storage.

I was storing this stuff up for the next time; stuff that would help me to endure any new season of deafness, whether that silent winter was to be a lifelong one or only temporary (and of course you can never really define a winter until the snow stops falling and the trees start to drip). Voices, voices, voices. I had to get 'em in and safely stashed, like a harvest. I wanted voices that might be easily summoned to mind. Voices that haunt me to such a degree that when I do summon them to mind, I get more than just the sound of the voice: I get its *meaning* too. It seemed to me, over that intense summer and autumn, that this was a massive job but that it had to be done and that if I didn't do it properly then there could be real hell to pay further down the line.

Annoyingly, though, we lack the capacity as humans to store music with any great accuracy, permanency, or fidelity. We are not tape recorders; we fall short in our ability to encode music for reproduction in the way that digital files do. We can only store music insofar as we can remember it, and then not for straightforward playback at the touch of a metaphorical button. Music is stored in us not as sound but as a complex of thoughts, allusions, feelings, abstractions, and sonic images that enable all of the above to be processed into something that approximates in our minds to the sound of the music we're thinking about but is not the thing itself: which is to say that we store music only inasmuch and insofar as the music *does something for us*.

I should speak only for myself, I suppose . . .

I am happy to come clean. I internalize music with an appetite that is not matched by any other appetite in life, except my appetite for love. Not food. Not football. Not verbal information. Not numbers. Not health and safety procedures. Certainly not names. None of these things stick with anything like the same adhesiveness as music, and the reason for that is simple. None of those things—not even the health and safety protocols—have the same power to penetrate and stir my sense of who I am. They go in, those protocols, but they do not go deep. I allow them access but only so far, according to how stimulated I am by them, and then I stop them dead in their tracks. That's it. Stop now! That's quite enough information about how to douse a flaming child. But music always goes deep, if it's music I like. And as it goes it leaves traces of itself all over my consciousness; traces of itself that make my consciousness more palatable to me, more bearable. As I suggested in the introduction to this book, I like myself more when I am listening to music.

This is the sign of a slightly troubled soul, perhaps. But it is something that I have nevertheless observed to be true.

And so there I was in 2013 and '14, frantically stashing nourishment away on a daily basis in preparation for the proverbial rainy day and the long winter that would inevitably follow, the day when the auditory shutters would slam down for good and I would be left to myself in noisy silence ... And it was not a good prospect, not least because I was wholly aware that as audio-playback systems go, my brain is not the greatest.

Still, I was not *expecting* the worst to happen; indeed, I had been assured by one consultant that the chances of the shutters coming down for good were remote. Yet had I not just experienced, out of nothing, nine months' noisy isolation from the world of people and music? Yes, I had, incontrovertibly. And the part of me that is susceptible to terror and depression had since made me cram music into my head in the irrational conviction that, once there, the music would serve as both a haven and a bulwark against the ultimate horror. A lofty, ramparted seat. My own internal hill fort. It didn't make scientific sense but it certainly made a lot of sense to the part of me that was frightened.

And then it happened again.

Last Christmas, December 2015, just as I was writing in this book about Kate Bush tuning into friendly voices on a silent ocean, I copped a viral infection of the sinuses that spread first to one ear (the dead one) and then to the other, where it locked itself in. The virus set up shop in the pinched alleyways either side of the main thoroughfares of my face and refused to budge, then turned bacterial, filling up both middle ears with gunk, perforating at least one of my eardrums, possibly both, and bunging up my residual hearing almost completely.

It took a number of hospital visits and an awful lot of antibiotics to quell the infection, but nothing shifted the gunk. Neither drugs nor fumes did a thing. Not even thrice-daily salt douches. I was close to stone deaf. Nevertheless, I took some comfort in the knowledge this was *only* gunk and therefore a "conductive" issue for my ear rather than a "sensorineural" one for my brain. The eardrums would surely heal, in time. The prognosis was that I ought to get some hearing back as the gunk drained. But deadlines for that joyous drainage were passed repeatedly as the year wore on. As a result I sank lower and lower and silence became accustomed to me. At one point, before the arrival of the hearing aid in late March, I gave up speaking altogether, except when necessary, confining myself to the basics: "please," "thank you," and "sorry, I didn't quite catch that." I began to think that winter had come at last.

And then there was a shift. A sudden decisive shift.

It is now late July in the high summer of 2016, and I have recently had it confirmed that there is evidence of an improvement in my hearing—between ten and twenty percent across the frequency range, sufficient to make music flatly, thinly, tinnily, gratifyingly available to me again through the hearing aid—and that there is every chance that more may yet follow in due course. It certainly feels that way: I can now hear my feet if I stamp them. I am turning wary cartwheels.

And I now understand fully the nature of my desperate urge three years ago to get the harvest in early, when I still had the chance. It meant that this book could be written and it meant that I might get to grips with what those voices mean to me, before it is too late. It also means that if and when the shutters do eventually come down for good, I will have given myself the best possible chance of having something to attend to on the inside of the shuttered building.

I say "attend to" because that's what I mean. I wouldn't call it listening, because it isn't listening—how can one listen to something that does not exist as a sound? But it is something. There is *some thing* in it. It has a kind of form. I suppose it's a form of knowledge: it is the knowledge, as I have known it, of music as my best connection with the world, after love. Aretha Franklin is very far from perfect in my head as a sound, but she's better in the form of knowledge than in no form at all, believe me.

She is always good and true, especially when she has her doubts.

Acknowledgments

I have been immensely grateful over the past three years for the kindness and judgment shown by various readers of different parts of the *Voices* manuscript, all of whom have offered encouragement and sound advice.

Chief among them was Cam Provis, who seemed to grasp the idea of the book from first contact with it and made it a condition of our continuing friendship that I finish it. I would get commanding emails: "More! I want to read more. Hurry up and send me the next chapter. Quickly." This is exactly what an anxious and/or self-pitying author needs to hear, and it kept me going when stuck fast in more than one muddy gulch. If I hadn't already dedicated the book to my children, then Cam's would be the name gracing a pristine white page at the front.

But others were kind, too, responding with generosity and smarts to my twitchy requests for "a quick read of this bit." My thanks go principally to Jane Acton and Ian Blackaby, but also to Phil Johnson, the sadly missed Rebecca Swift, Miranda Kemp, Laurie Staff, Steve Shepherd, Xanthe Sylvester, Derek Chapman, Emma Perry, and Mark Pringle.

I also owe a debt of gratitude to Deb Coleman and Ben Hall for their musical wisdom and to Alice Goodman for her Bible expertise. You'd never think an afternoon spent under a pile of dogs discussing the history of the psalms could be so much fun. Any errors are mine and are the result of not listening hard enough.

Appreciation also goes to Moira Bellas at MBC PR, and to Guy Hayden and Toby Jeffrey at Universal Music for kindly fixing stuff. Likewise to Neil Storey and Jayne Gould of HiddenMasters.

And of course thanks go, in abundance, to my editor at Cape, Dan Franklin, for his abiding support and enthusiasm. Dan has great ears and a mind that complements them perfectly (as if mind and ears could ever be separated—of *course* they can't). Also, grateful noises must go to Clare Bullock, the copy editor Beth Humphries, and the designer Stephen Parker.

Finally, this is the best place I can think of in which to formally acknowledge the friendship and encouragement over the years of three men, whose wisdom about life and its relationship with music has been valuable to me beyond measure: Angus MacKinnon, John Clare, and the late R. D. Cook.

Index

Author photograph by Linda Nylind

Following a brief spell as a stringer at *NME* in the mid-1980s, NICK COLEMAN was music editor of *Time Out* for seven years, then arts and features editor at the *Independent* and the *Independent on Sunday*. He has also written on music for *The Times*, *The Guardian*, *The Telegraph*, *New Statesman*, *Intelligent Life*, *GQ*, and *The Wire*. He is the author of *The Train in the Night*, which was shortlisted for the 2012 Wellcome Book Prize.